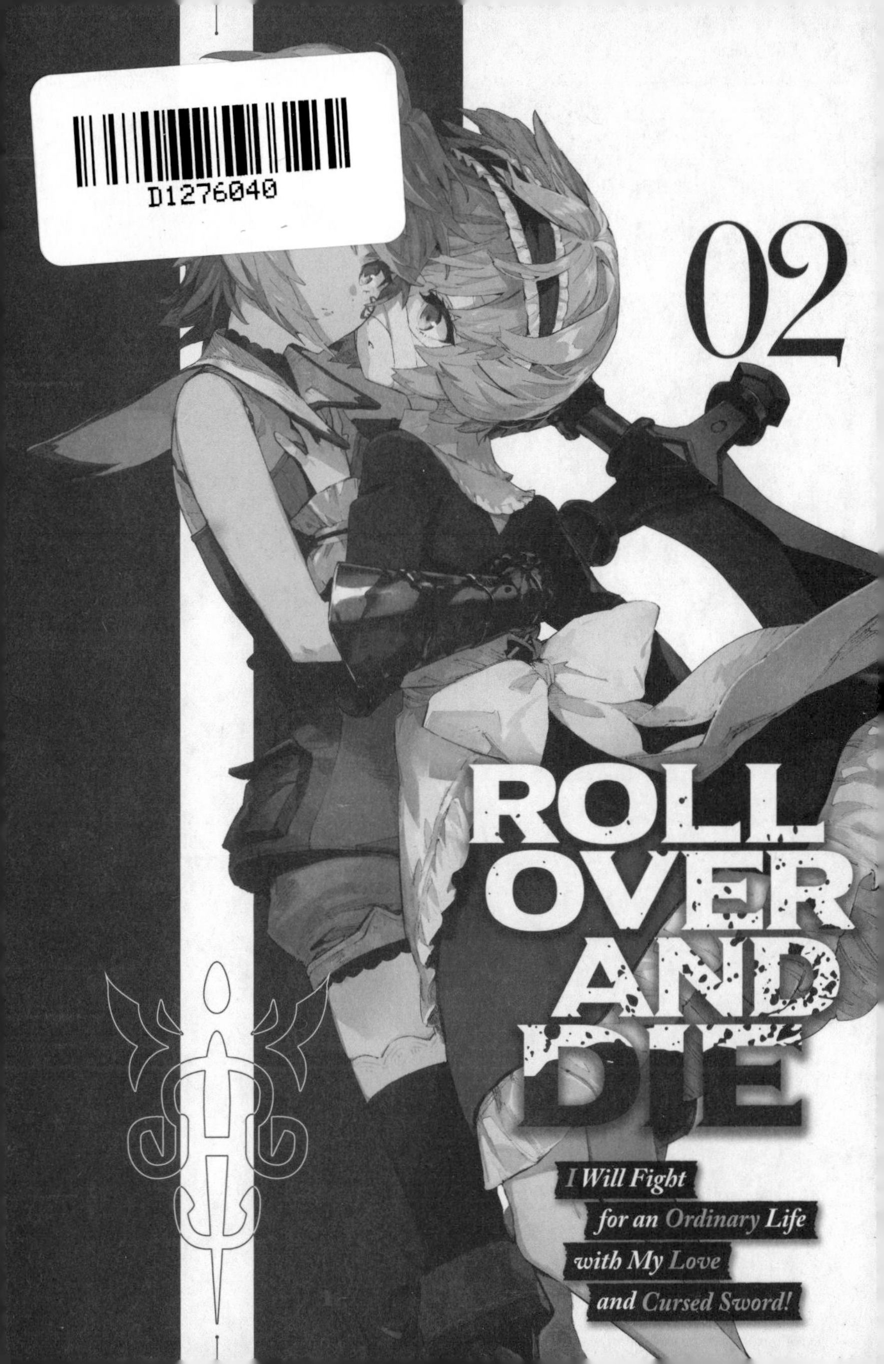

02

ROLL OVER AND DIE

I Will Fight for an Ordinary Life with My Love and Cursed Sword!

CONTENTS

Chapter 5:
Their Respective Paths —————— 3

Chapter 6:
The Starting Signal —————— 035

Chapter 7:
The Entrance to Despair —————— 065

Chapter 8:
Cursed Hope —————— 099

Chapter 9:
The Demon and the Saint —————— 133

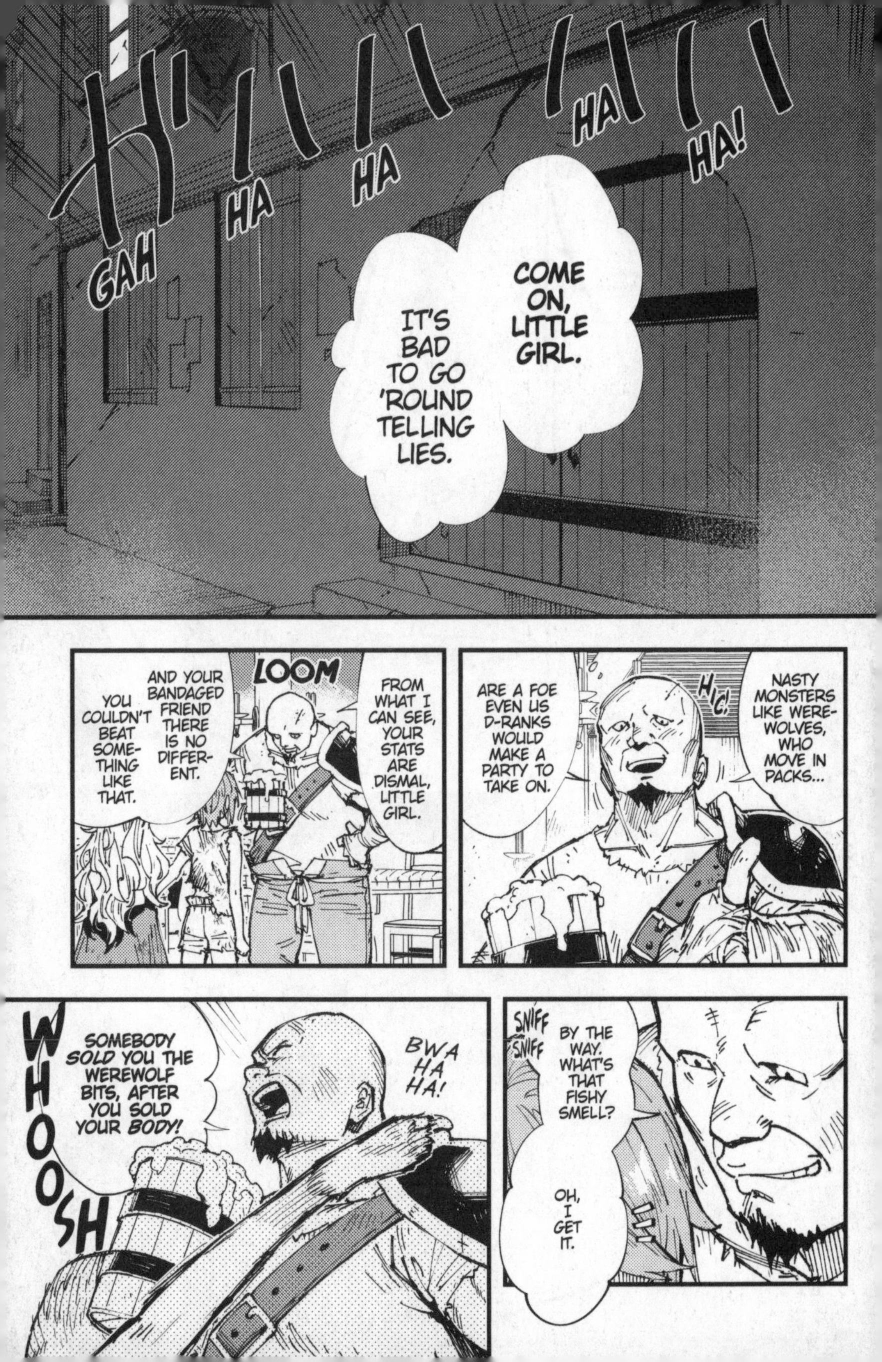
GAH HA HA HA HA HA!
COME ON, LITTLE GIRL.
IT'S BAD TO GO 'ROUND TELLING LIES.
NASTY MONSTERS LIKE WERE-WOLVES, WHO MOVE IN PACKS...
HIC!
ARE A FOE EVEN US D-RANKS WOULD MAKE A PARTY TO TAKE ON.
FROM WHAT I CAN SEE, YOUR STATS ARE DISMAL, LITTLE GIRL.
LOOM
AND YOUR BANDAGED FRIEND THERE IS NO DIFFER-ENT.
YOU COULDN'T BEAT SOME-THING LIKE THAT.
SNIFF SNIFF
BY THE WAY. WHAT'S THAT FISHY SMELL?
OH, I GET IT.
BWA HA HA!
SOMEBODY SOLD YOU THE WEREWOLF BITS, AFTER YOU SOLD YOUR BODY!
WHOOSH

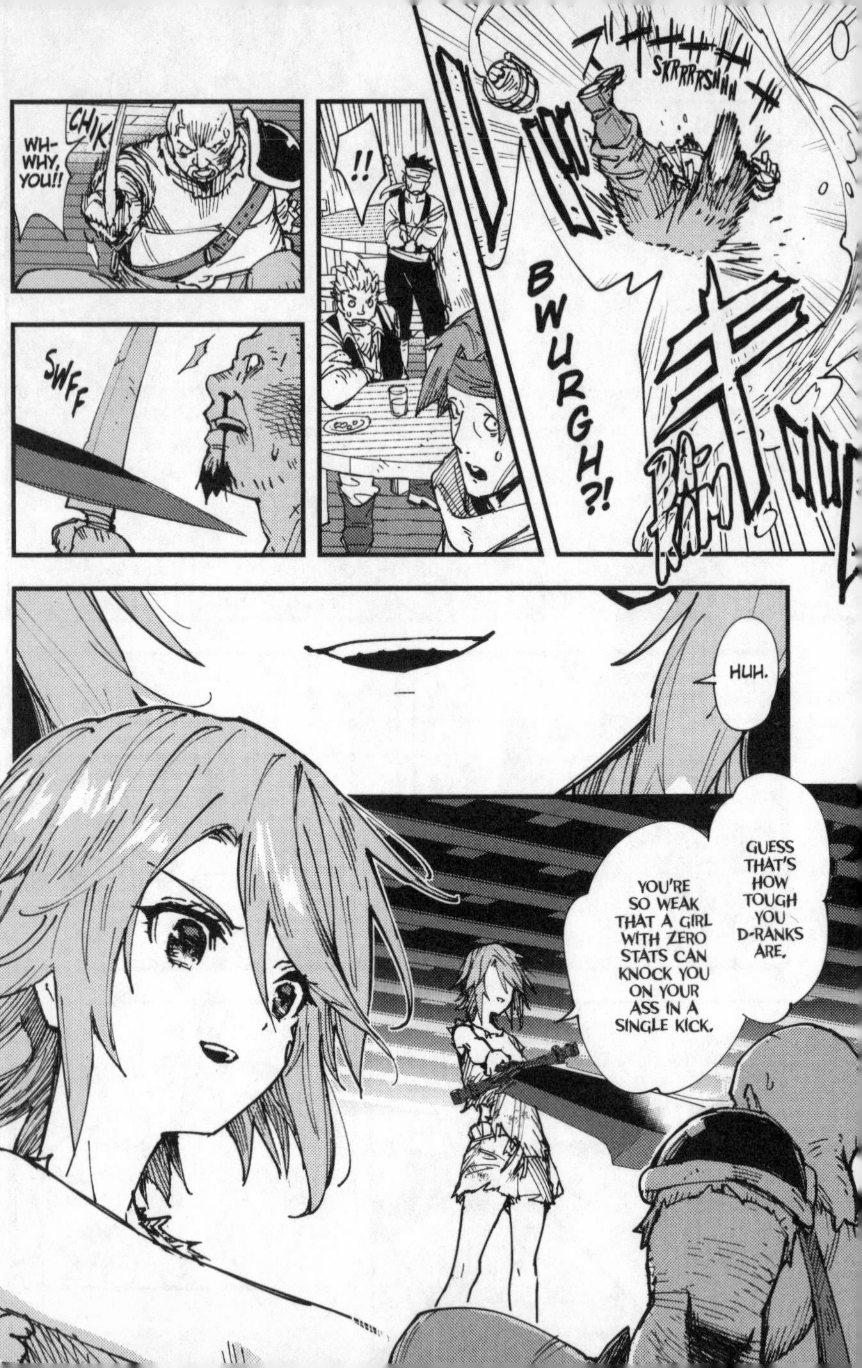
SKRRRRSHHH
BWURGH?!
!!
CHIK
WH-WHY, YOU!!
SWFF
HUH.
GUESS THAT'S HOW TOUGH YOU D-RANKS ARE.
YOU'RE SO WEAK THAT A GIRL WITH ZERO STATS CAN KNOCK YOU ON YOUR ASS IN A SINGLE KICK.

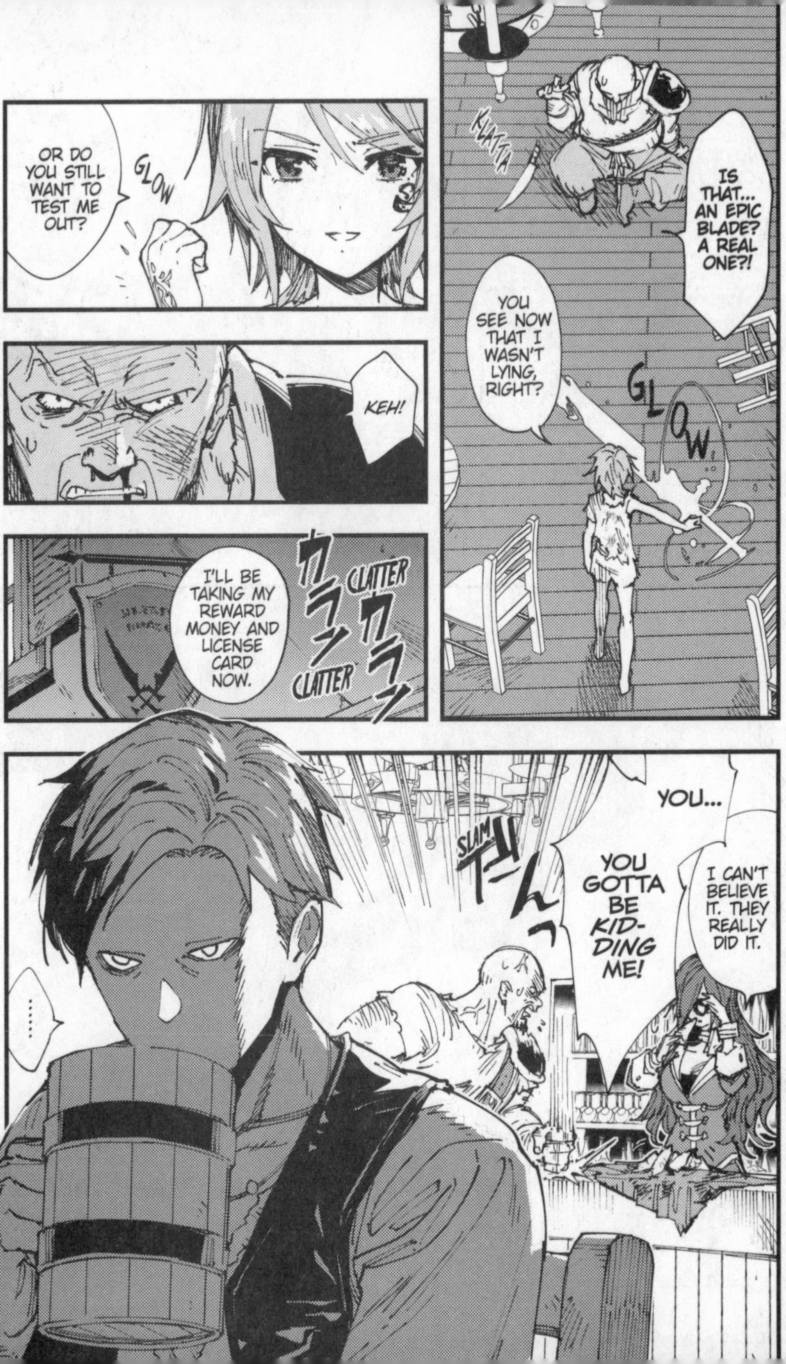
KLATTA
IS THAT... AN EPIC BLADE? A REAL ONE?!
YOU SEE NOW THAT I WASN'T LYING, RIGHT?
GLOW
OR DO YOU STILL WANT TO TEST ME OUT?
GLOW
KEH!
I'LL BE TAKING MY REWARD MONEY AND LICENSE CARD NOW.
CLATTER
CLATTER
YOU...
I CAN'T BELIEVE IT. THEY REALLY DID IT.
YOU GOTTA BE KID-DING ME!
SLAM
......

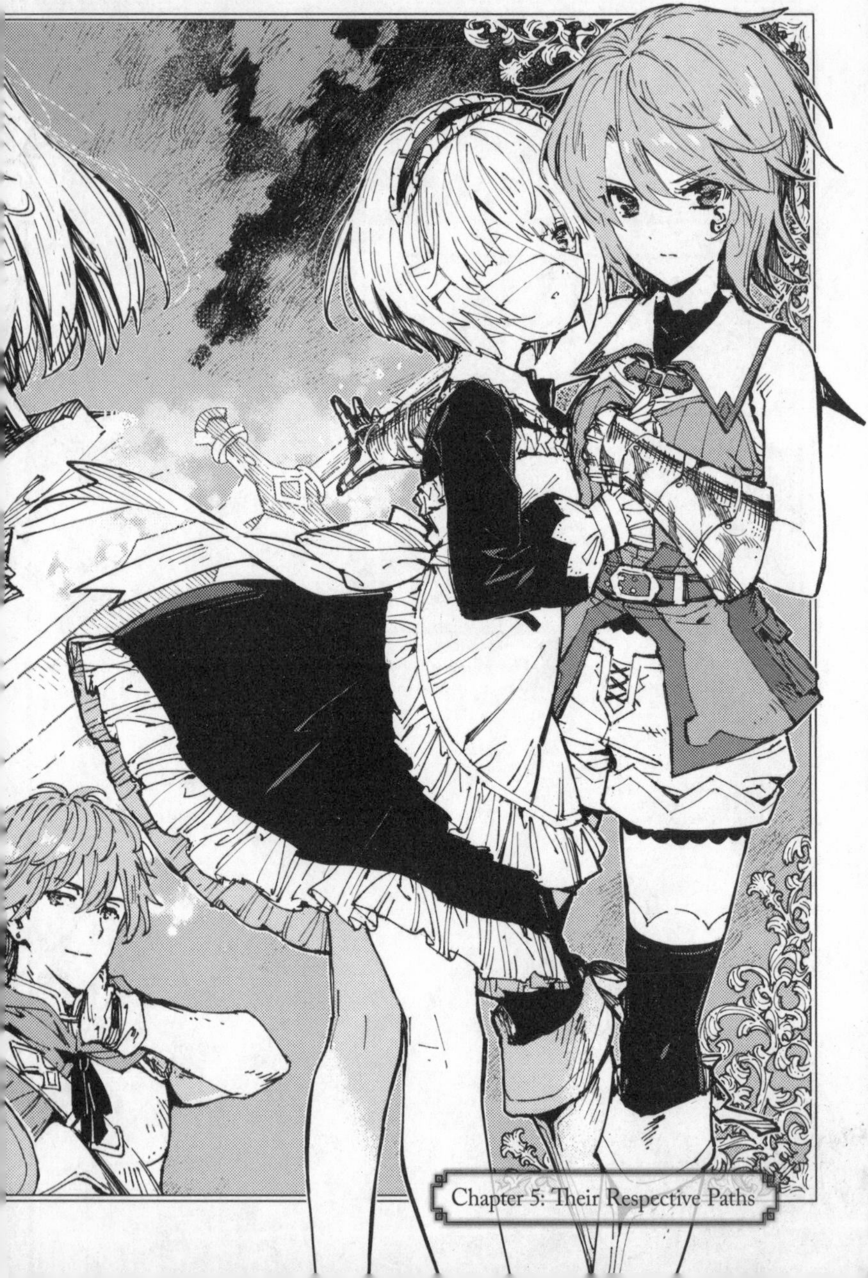

Chapter 5: Their Respective Paths

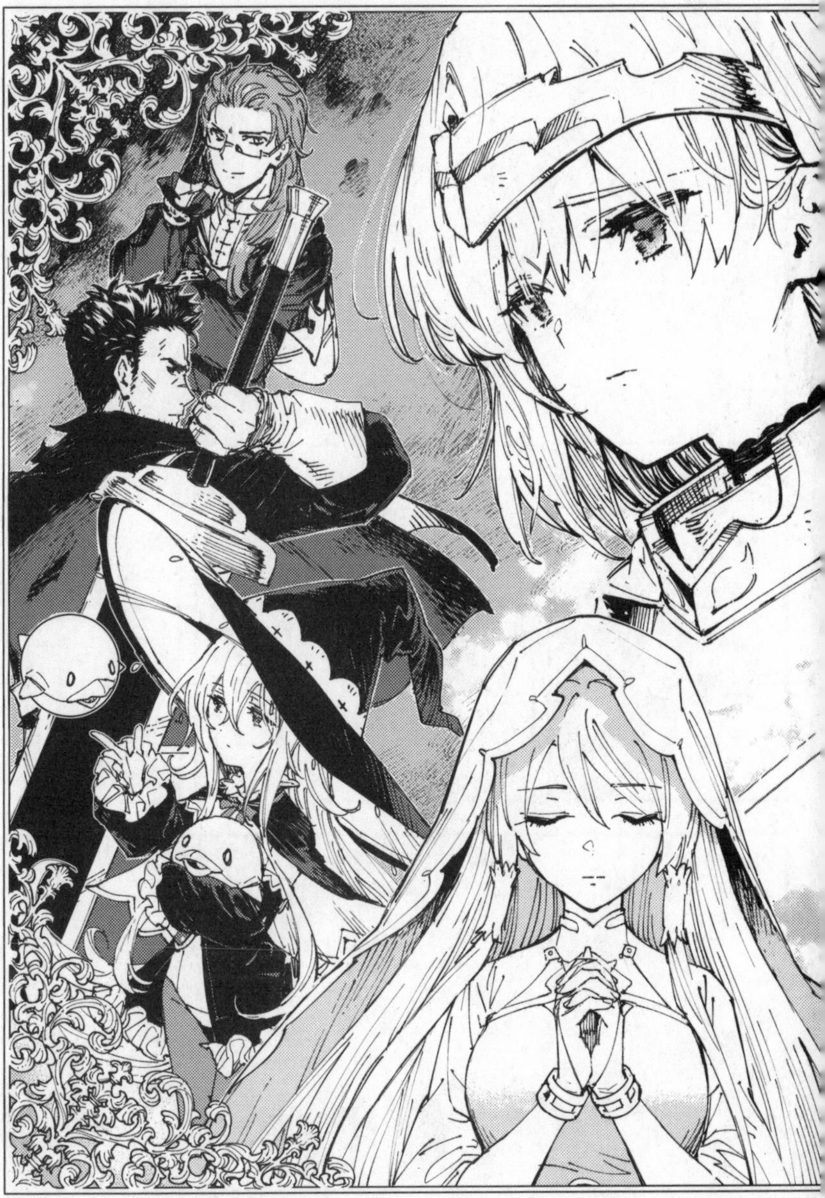

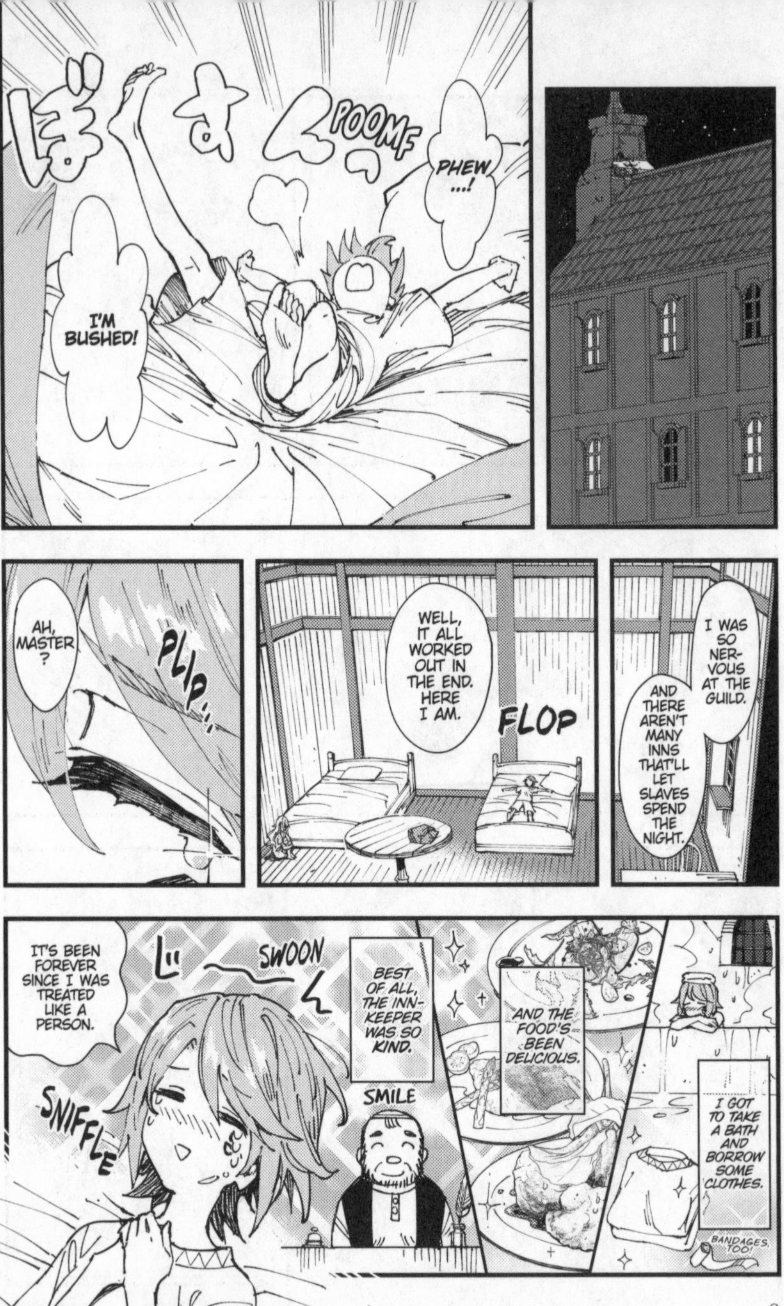
POOMF
PHEW ...!
I'M BUSHED!
I WAS SO NER-VOUS AT THE GUILD.
AND THERE AREN'T MANY INNS THAT'LL LET SLAVES SPEND THE NIGHT.
WELL, IT ALL WORKED OUT IN THE END. HERE I AM.
FLOP
AH, MASTER?
PLIP...
I GOT TO TAKE A BATH AND BORROW SOME CLOTHES.
BANDAGES, TOO!
AND THE FOOD'S BEEN DELICIOUS.
BEST OF ALL, THE INN-KEEPER WAS SO KIND.
SMILE
SWOON
IT'S BEEN FOREVER SINCE I WAS TREATED LIKE A PERSON.
SNIFFLE

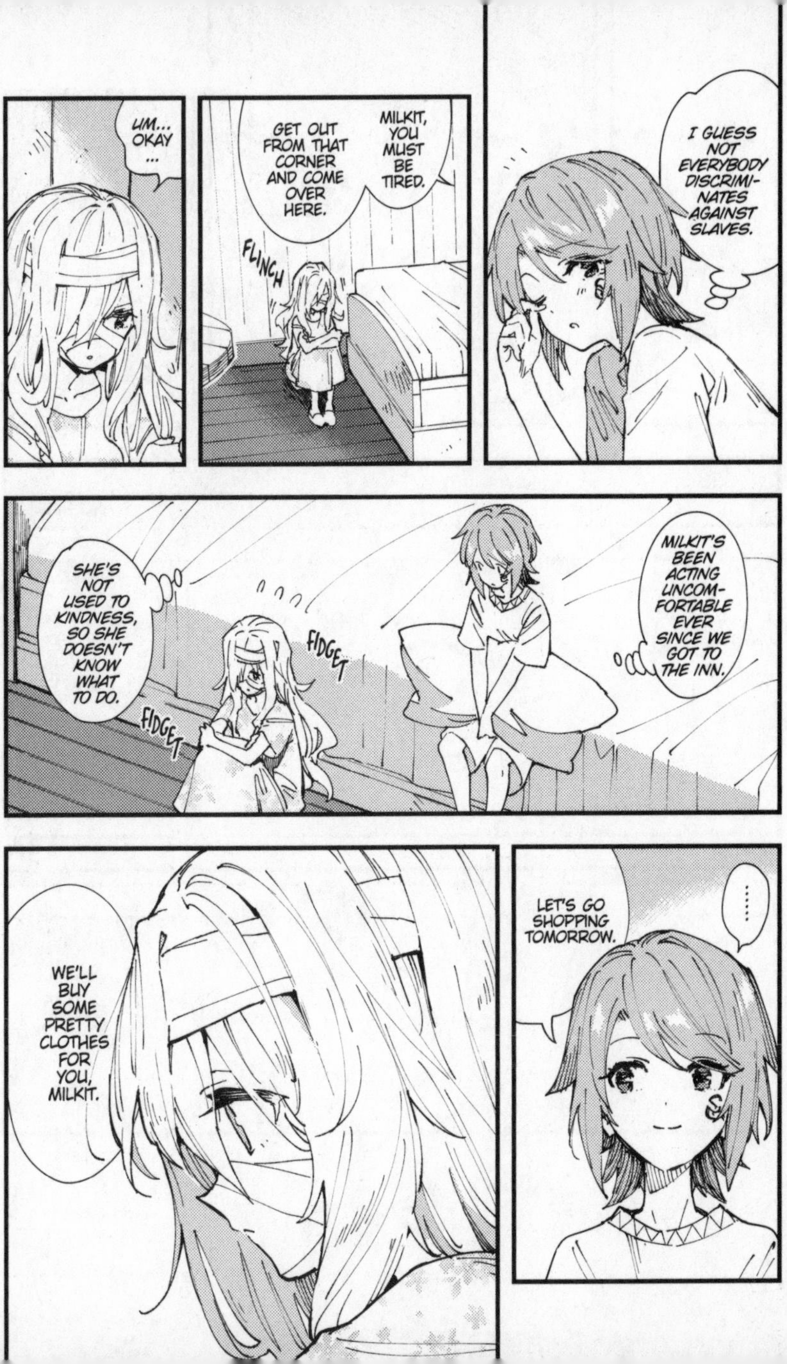
I GUESS NOT EVERYBODY DISCRIMI-NATES AGAINST SLAVES.
MILKIT, YOU MUST BE TIRED.
GET OUT FROM THAT CORNER AND COME OVER HERE.
FLINCH
UM... OKAY ...
MILKIT'S BEEN ACTING UNCOM-FORTABLE EVER SINCE WE GOT TO THE INN.
FIDGET
FIDGET
SHE'S NOT USED TO KINDNESS, SO SHE DOESN'T KNOW WHAT TO DO.
......
LET'S GO SHOPPING TOMORROW.
WE'LL BUY SOME PRETTY CLOTHES FOR YOU, MILKIT.

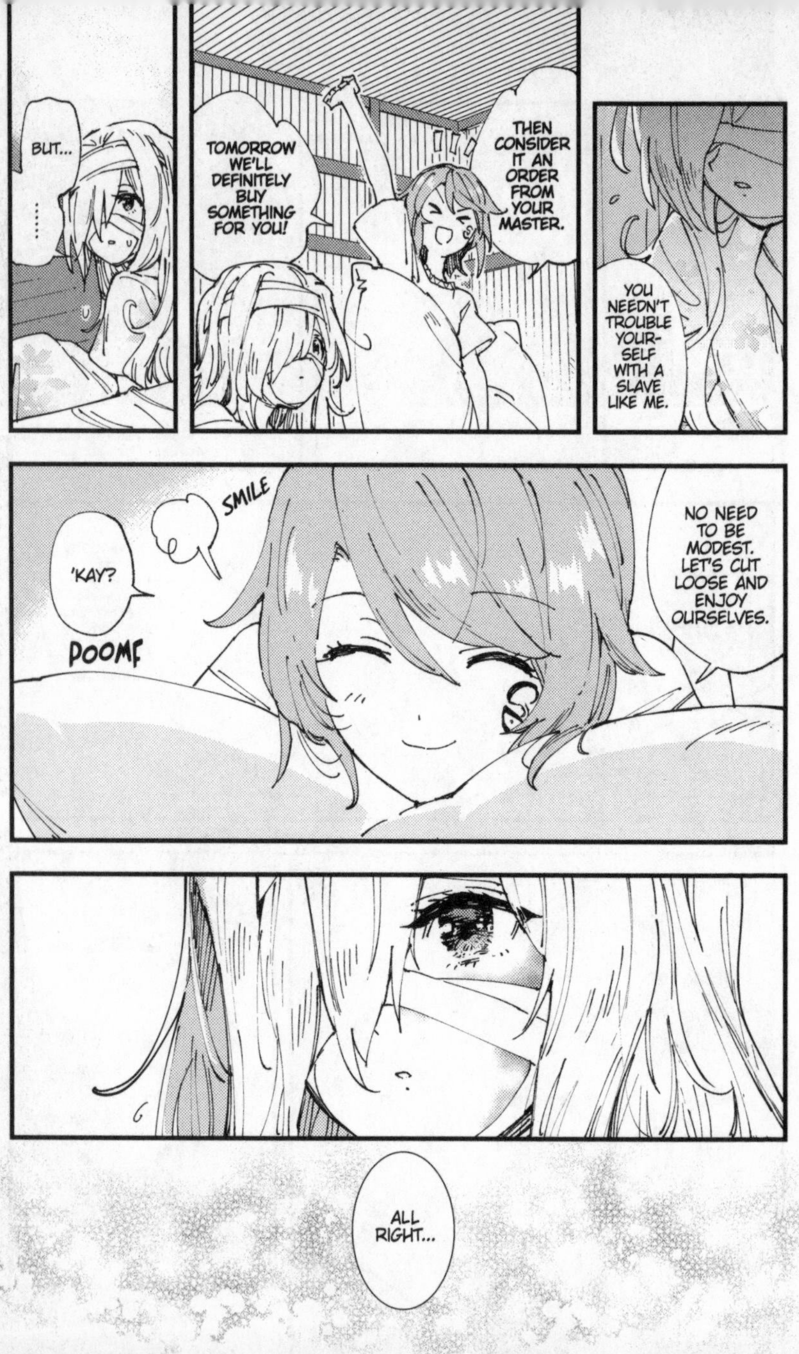
YOU NEEDN'T TROUBLE YOUR-SELF WITH A SLAVE LIKE ME.
THEN CONSIDER IT AN ORDER FROM YOUR MASTER.
TOMORROW WE'LL DEFINITELY BUY SOMETHING FOR YOU!
BUT...
......
NO NEED TO BE MODEST. LET'S CUT LOOSE AND ENJOY OURSELVES.
SMILE
'KAY?
POOMF
ALL RIGHT...

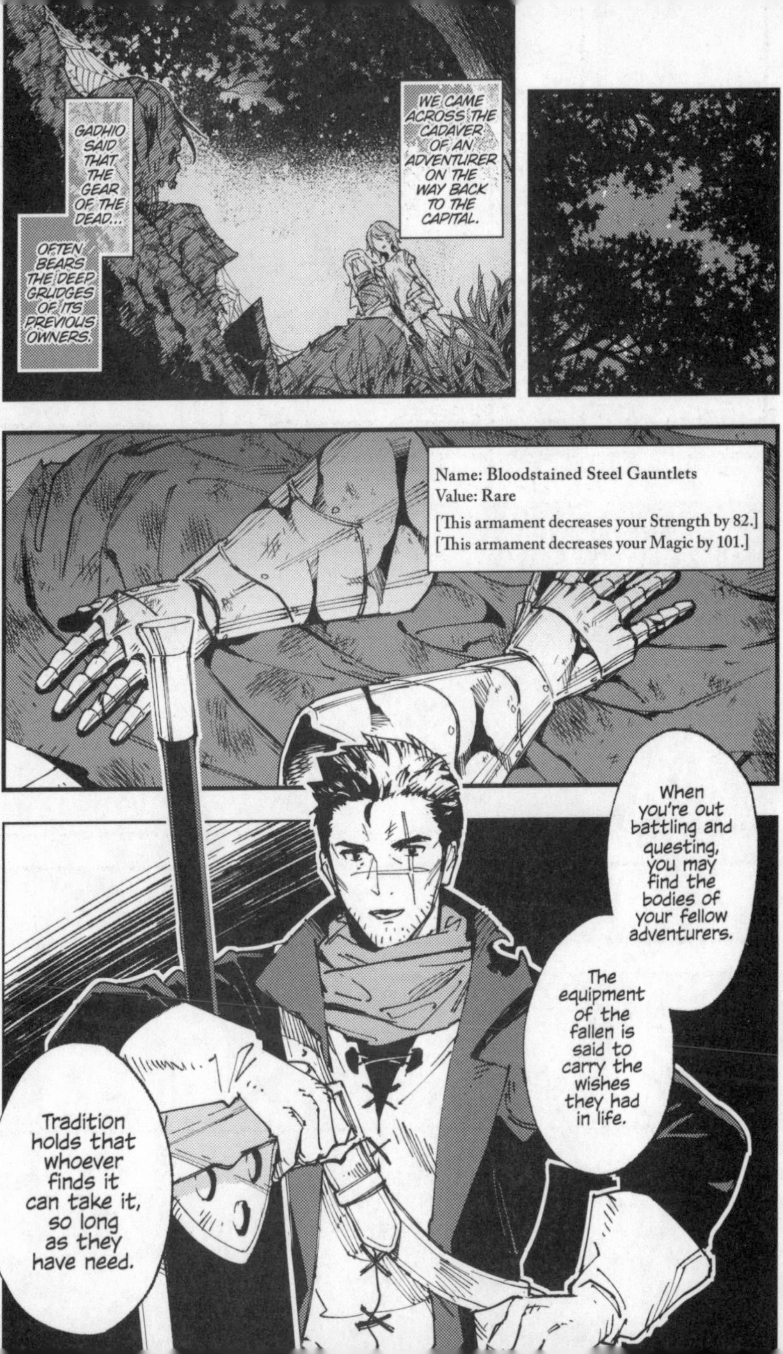
WE CAME ACROSS THE CADAVER OF AN ADVENTURER ON THE WAY BACK TO THE CAPITAL.
GADHIO SAID THAT THE GEAR OF THE DEAD...
OFTEN BEARS THE DEEP GRUDGES OF ITS PREVIOUS OWNERS.
Name: Bloodstained Steel Gauntlets
Value: Rare
[This armament decreases your Strength by 82.]
[This armament decreases your Magic by 101.]
When you're out battling and questing, you may find the bodies of your fellow adventurers.
The equipment of the fallen is said to carry the wishes they had in life.
Tradition holds that whoever finds it can take it, so long as they have need.

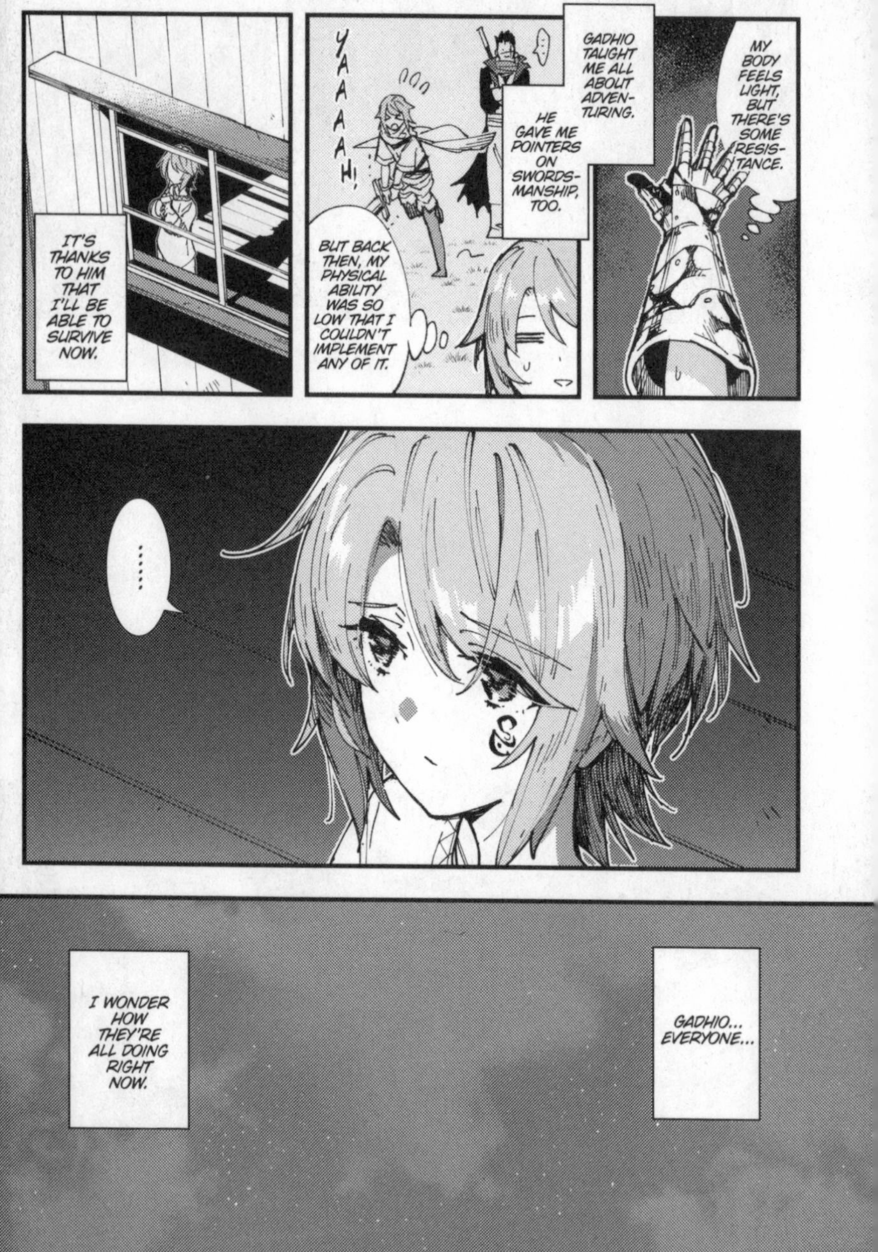
MY BODY FEELS LIGHT, BUT THERE'S SOME RESISTANCE.
GADHIO TAUGHT ME ALL ABOUT ADVENTURING.
...
YAAAAAH!
HE GAVE ME POINTERS ON SWORDSMANSHIP, TOO.
BUT BACK THEN, MY PHYSICAL ABILITY WAS SO LOW THAT I COULDN'T IMPLEMENT ANY OF IT.
IT'S THANKS TO HIM THAT I'LL BE ABLE TO SURVIVE NOW.
......
GADHIO... EVERYONE...
I WONDER HOW THEY'RE ALL DOING RIGHT NOW.

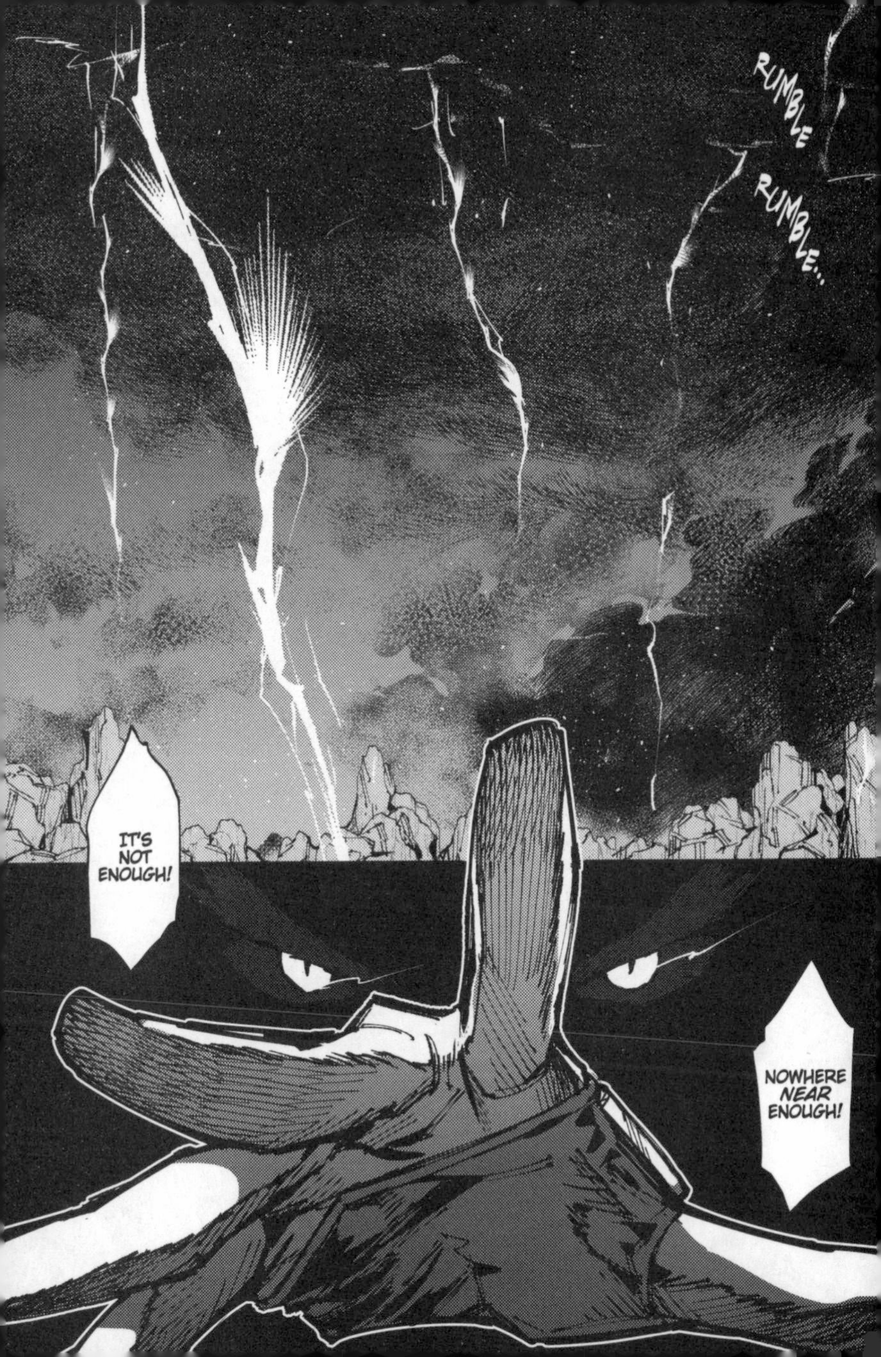
RUMBLE
RUMBLE...
NOWHERE NEAR ENOUGH!
IT'S NOT ENOUGH!

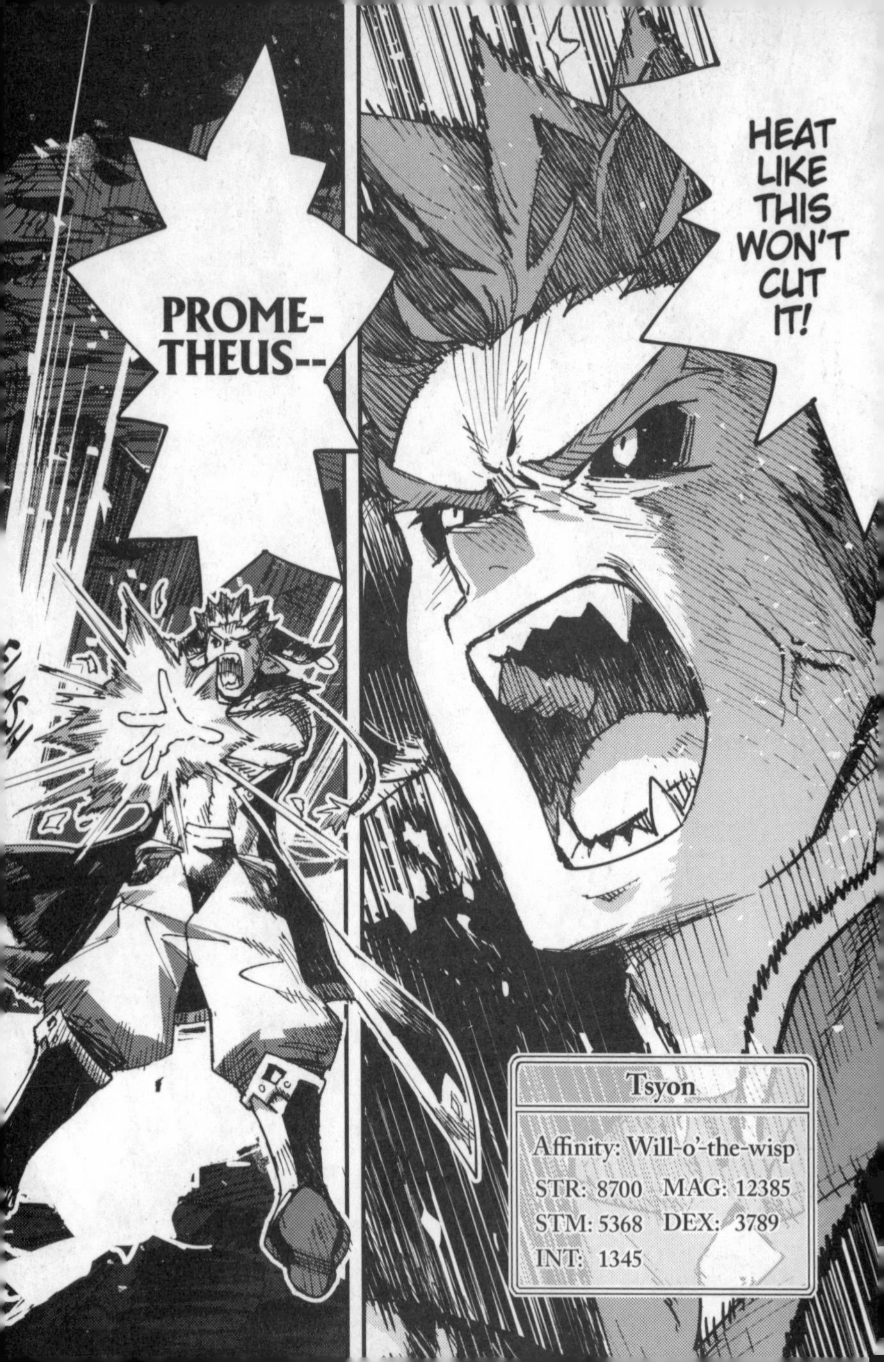

HEAT LIKE THIS WON'T CUT IT!
Tsyon
Affinity: Will-o'-the-wisp
STR: 8700 MAG: 12385
STM: 5368 DEX: 3789
INT: 1345
PROME-THEUS--
CLASH

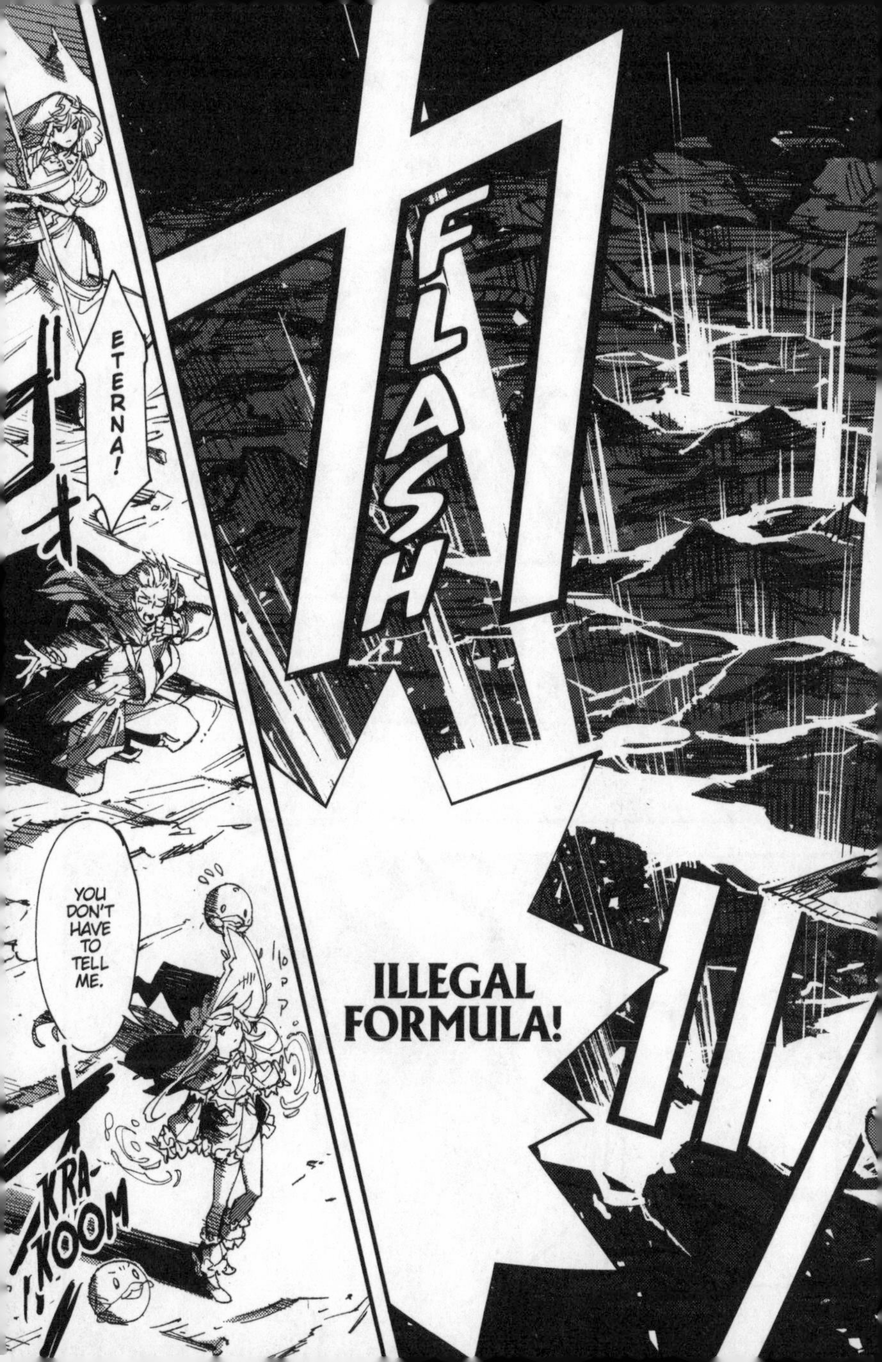
FLASH
ILLEGAL FORMULA!
ETERNA!
YOU DON'T HAVE TO TELL ME.
KRA-KOOM

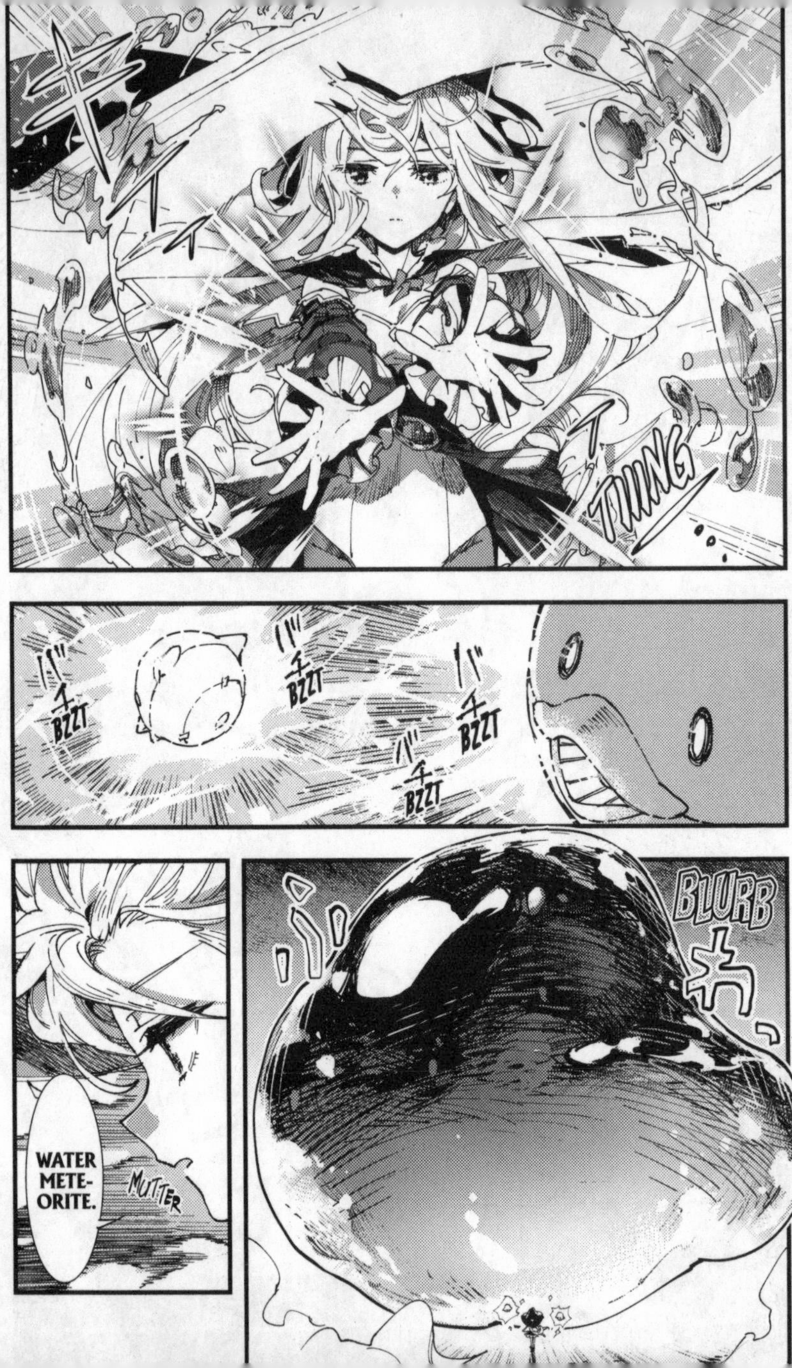
TIIING
BZZT
BZZT
BZZT
BZZT
BLURB
WATER METE-ORITE.
MUTTER

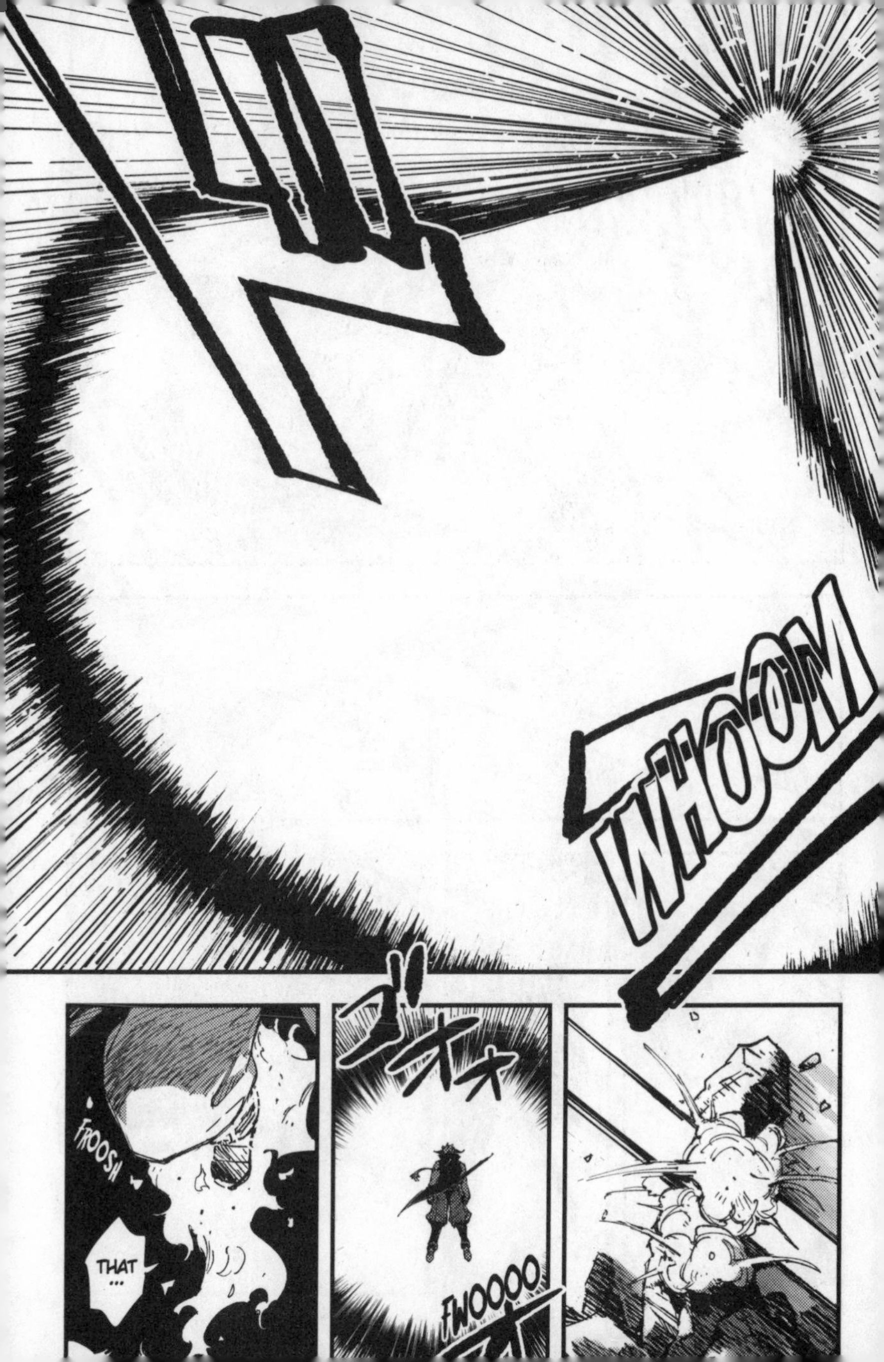
WHOOM
FWOOOO
FROOSH
THAT ...

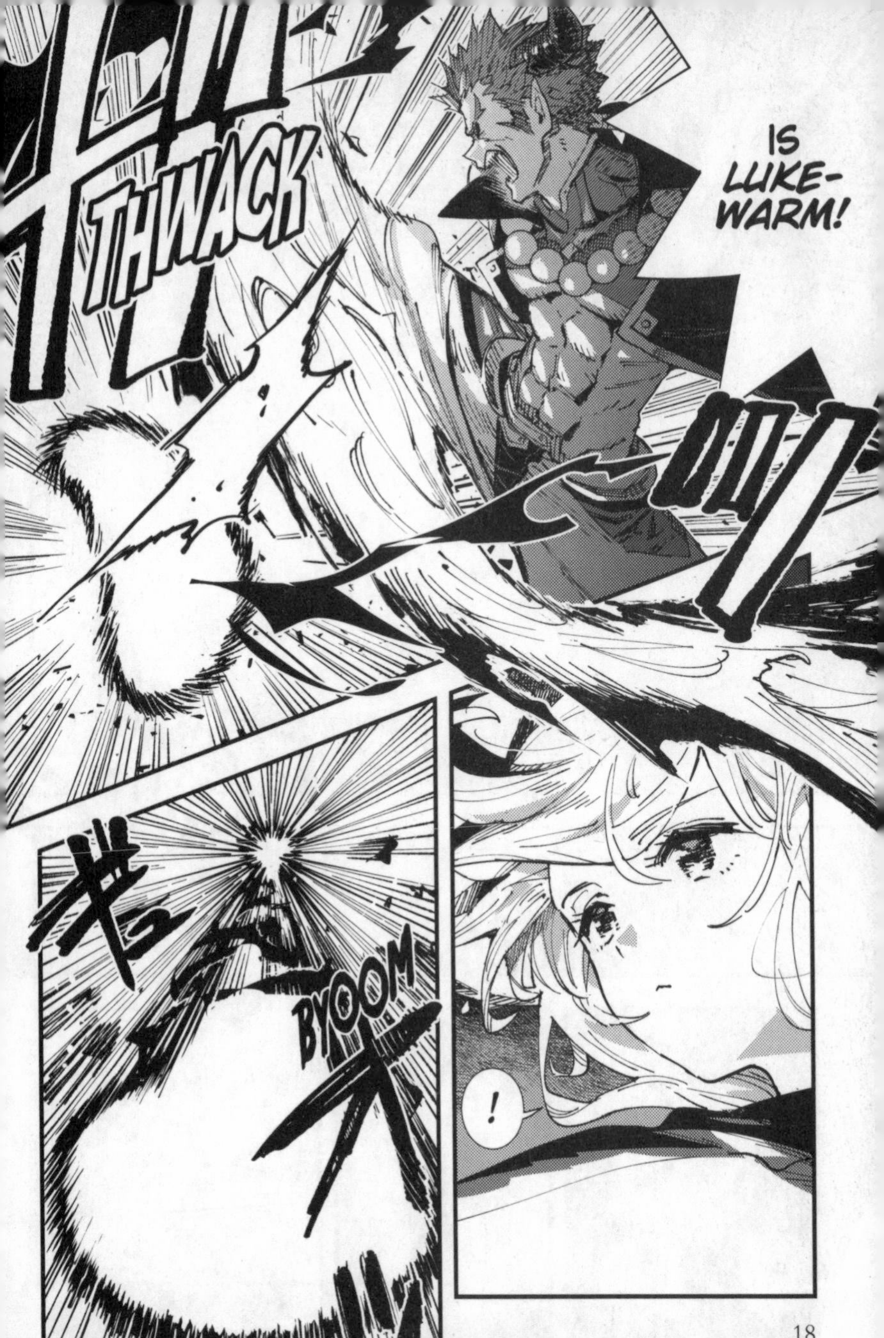
IS LUKE-WARM!
THWACK
!
BYOOM

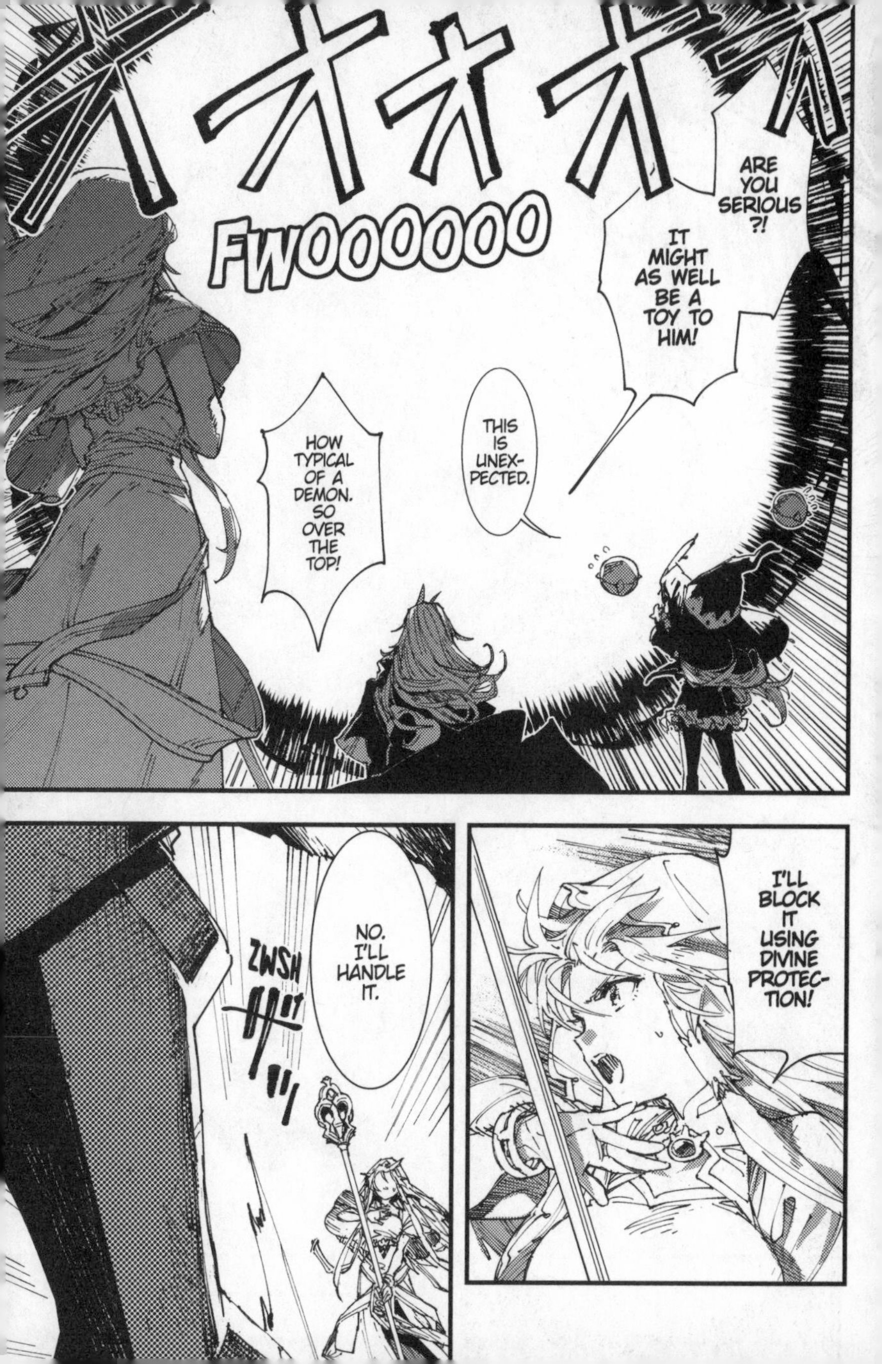
ARE YOU SERIOUS?!
IT MIGHT AS WELL BE A TOY TO HIM!
FWOOOOOO
THIS IS UNEXPECTED.
HOW TYPICAL OF A DEMON. SO OVER THE TOP!
I'LL BLOCK IT USING DIVINE PROTECTION!
NO. I'LL HANDLE IT.
ZWSH

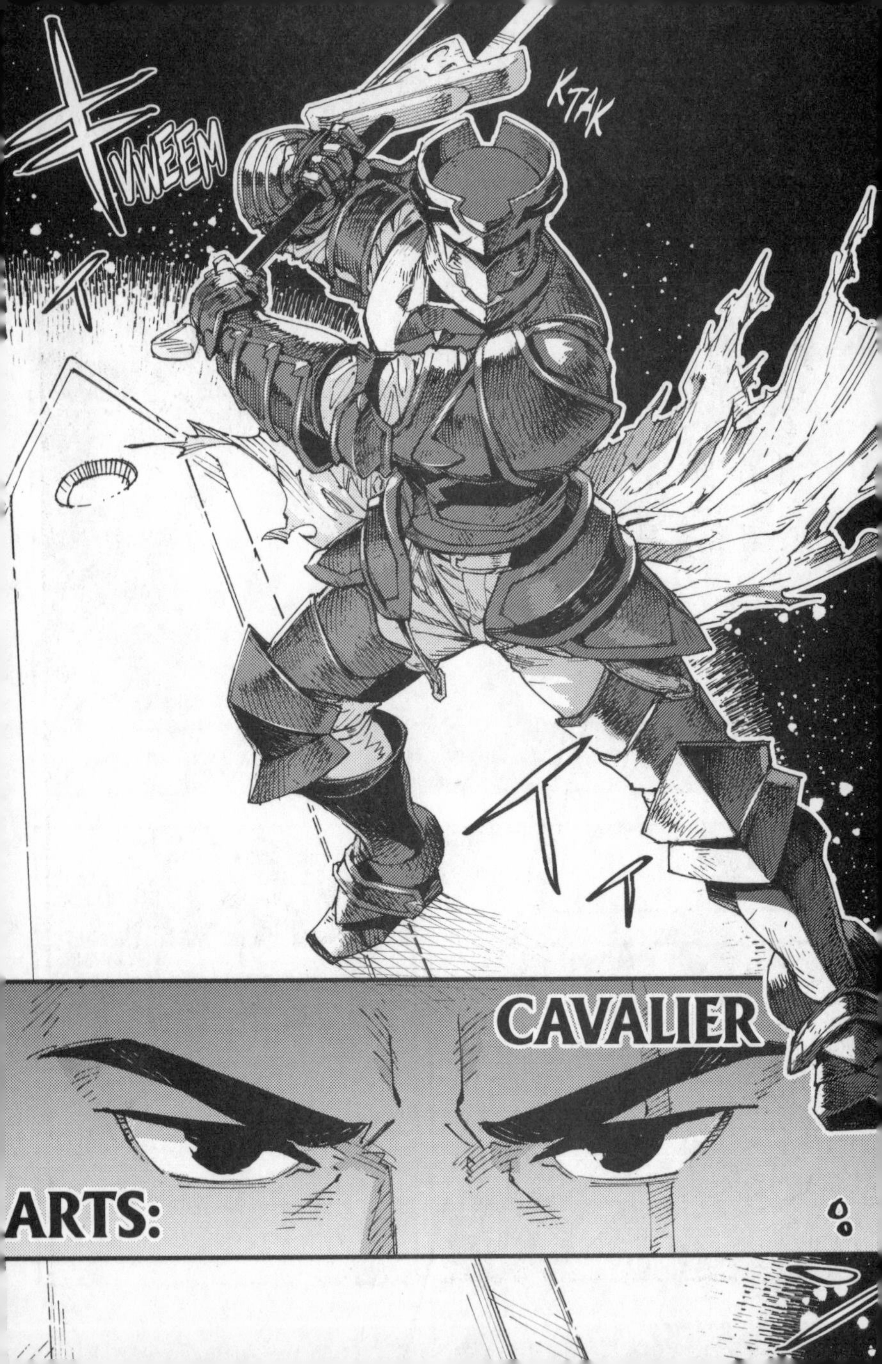
KTAK
VWEEM
CAVALIER
ARTS:

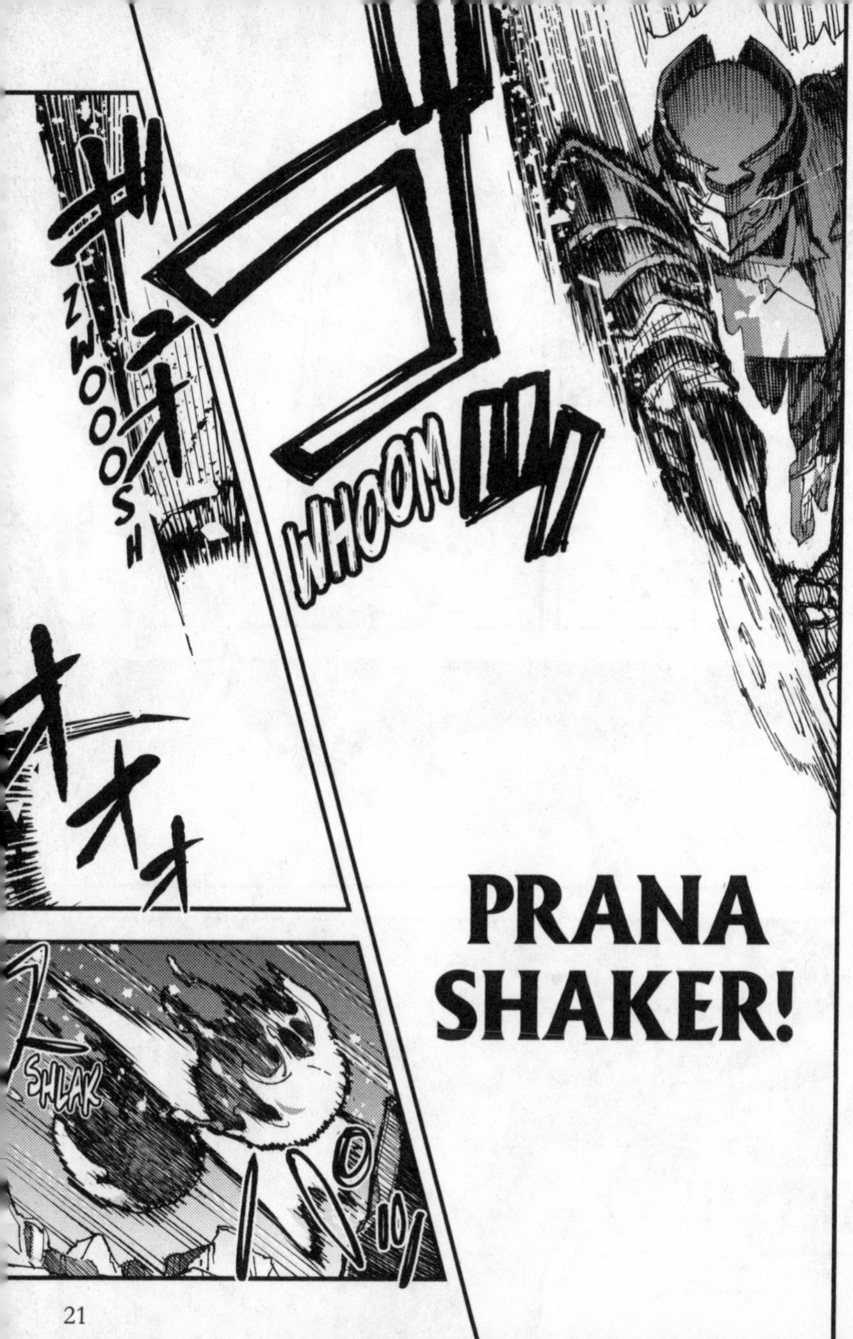
WHOOM
PRANA SHAKER!
ZWOOOOSH
SHLAK

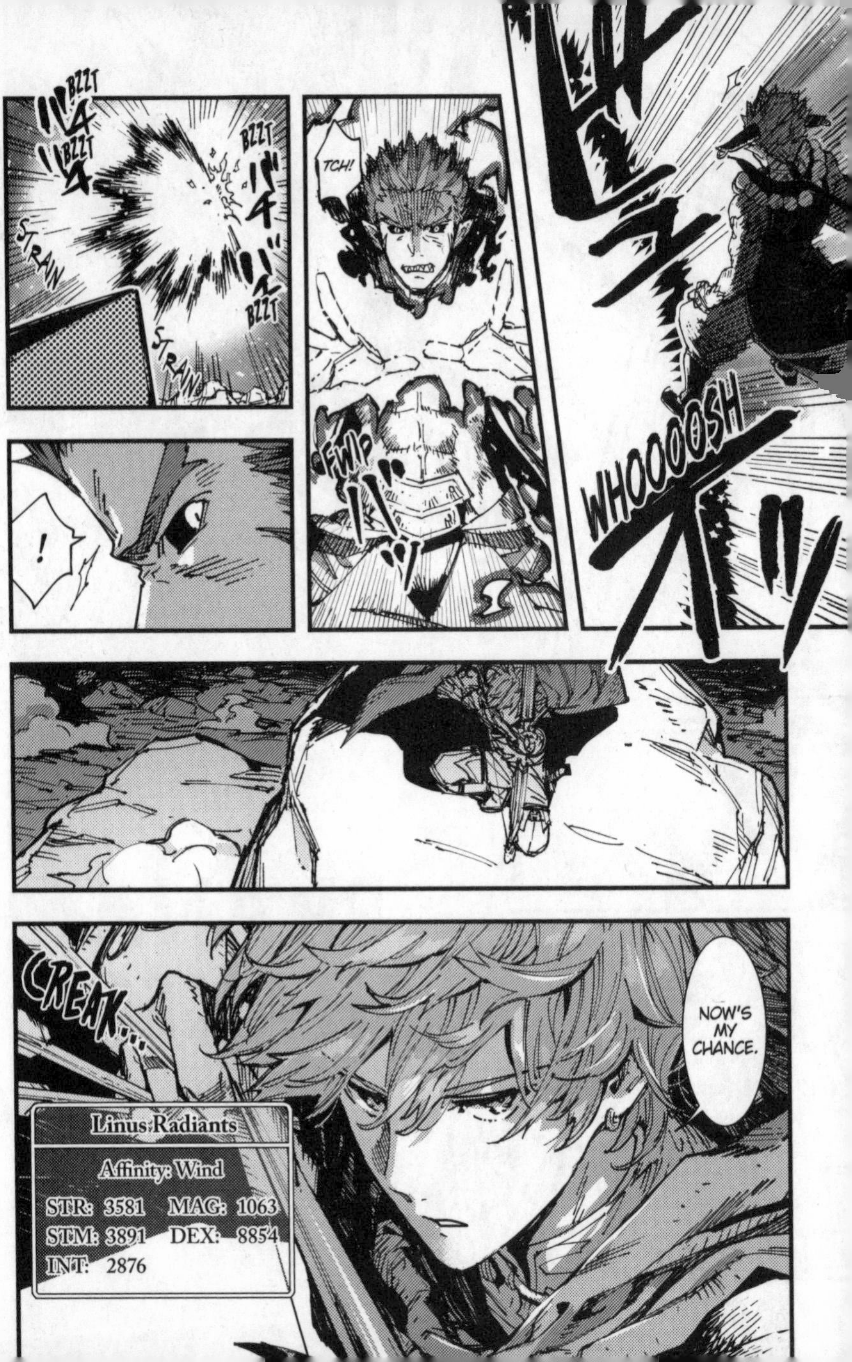
WHOOOOSH
TCH!
FWIP
BZZT
BZZT
BZZT
BZZT
STRAIN
STRAIN
!
CREAK...
NOW'S MY CHANCE.
Linus Radiants
Affinity: Wind
STR: 3581 MAG: 1063
STM: 3891 DEX: 8854
INT: 2876

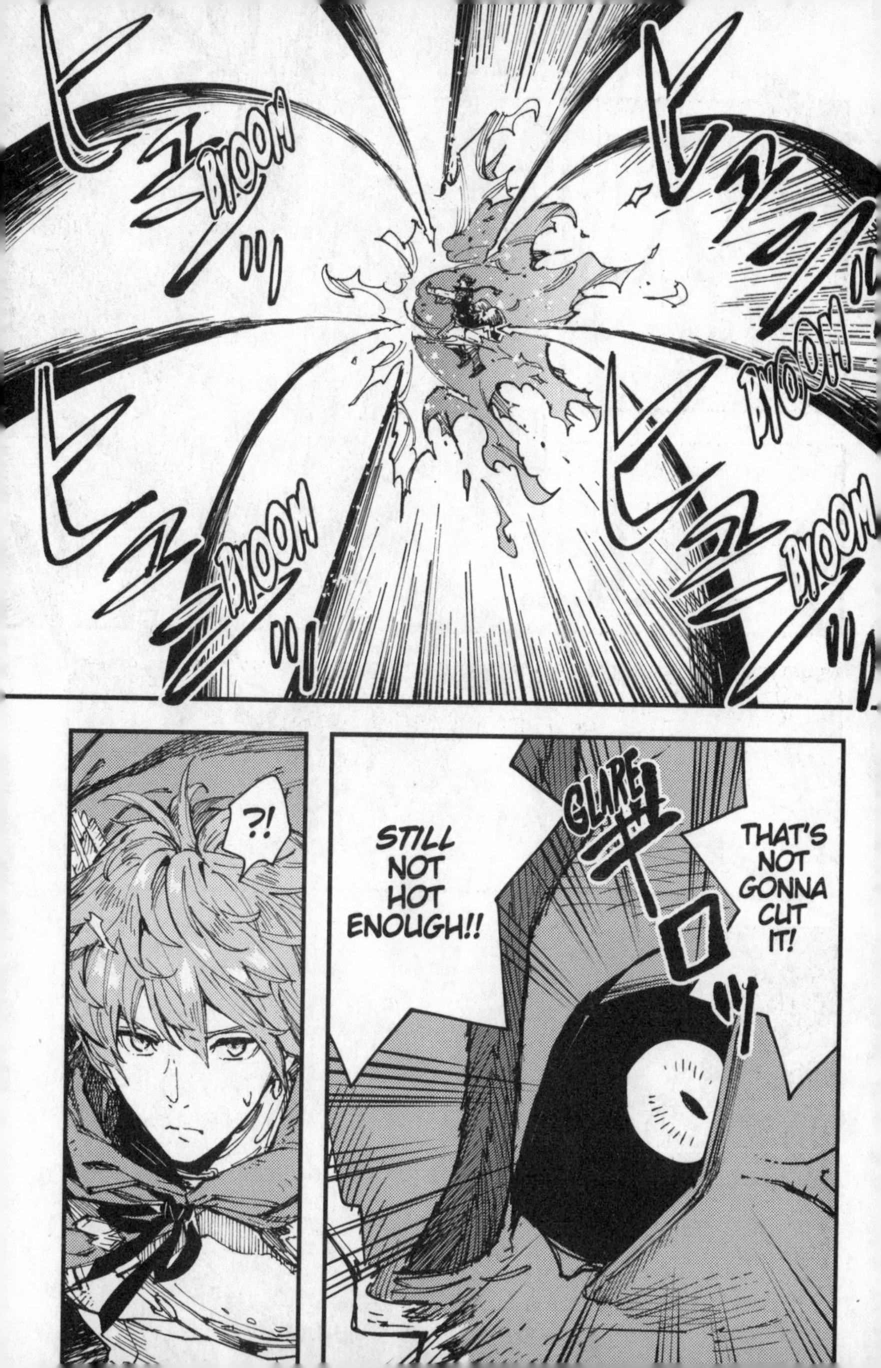
BYOOM
BYOOM
BYOOM
BYOOM
GLARE
THAT'S NOT GONNA CUT IT!
STILL NOT HOT ENOUGH!!
?!

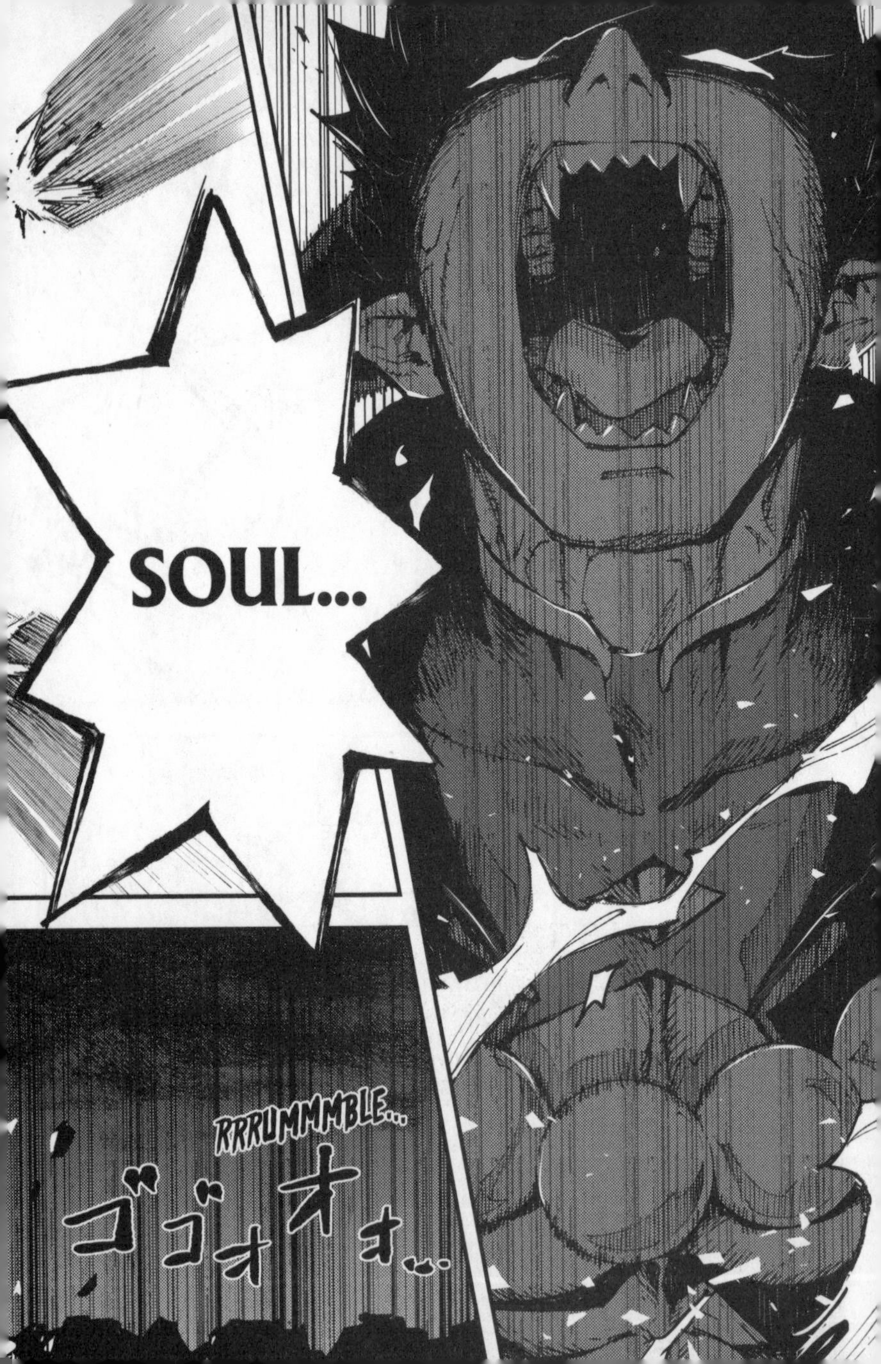
SOUL...
RRRUMMMBLE...
ゴゴオオォ…

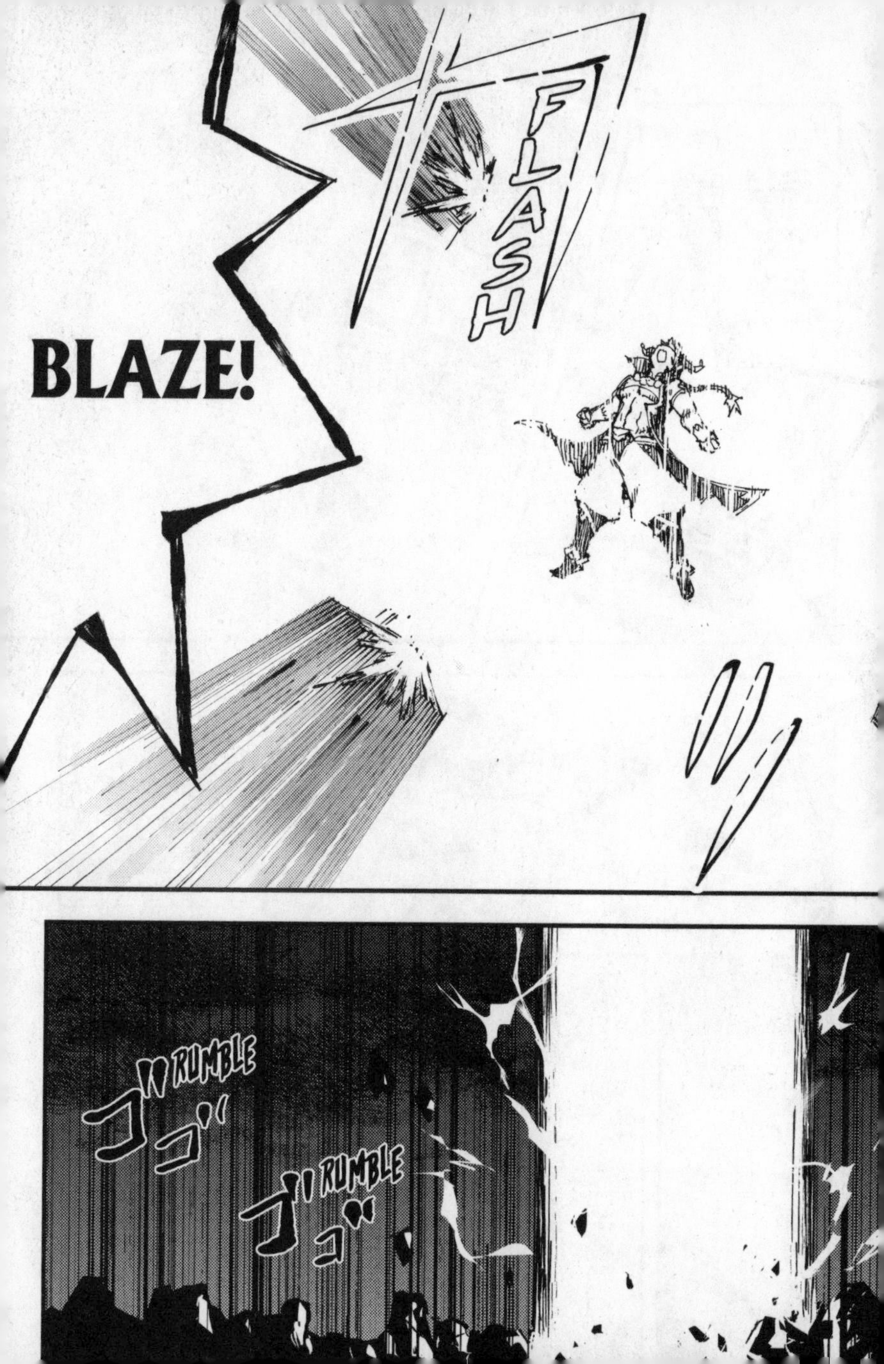
FLASH
BLAZE!
ゴゴ RUMBLE
ゴゴ RUMBLE

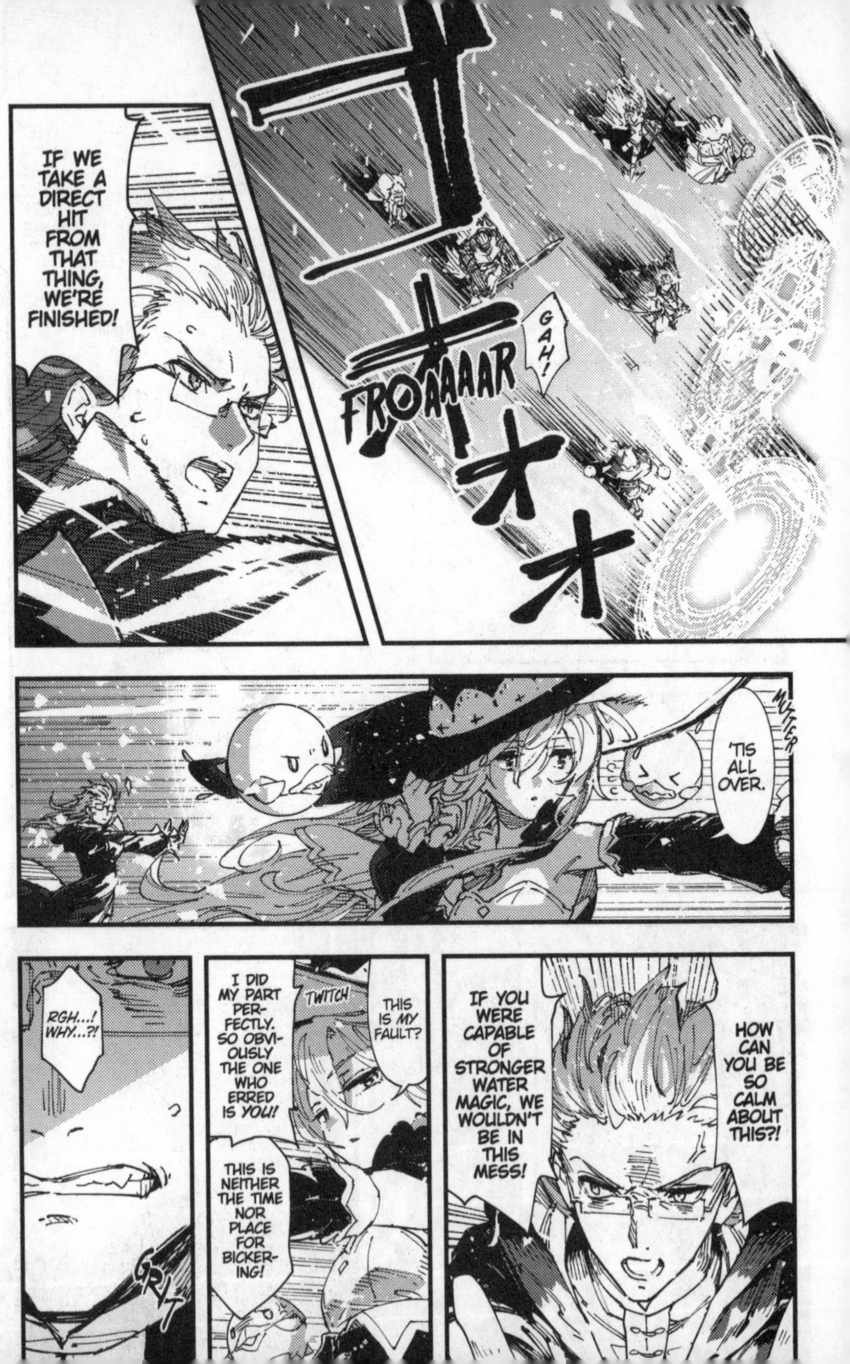
GAH!
FROAAAAR
IF WE TAKE A DIRECT HIT FROM THAT THING, WE'RE FINISHED!
MUTTER
'TIS ALL OVER.
HOW CAN YOU BE SO CALM ABOUT THIS?!
IF YOU WERE CAPABLE OF STRONGER WATER MAGIC, WE WOULDN'T BE IN THIS MESS!
THIS IS MY FAULT?
TWITCH
I DID MY PART PER-FECTLY. SO OBVI-OUSLY THE ONE WHO ERRED IS YOU!
THIS IS NEITHER THE TIME NOR PLACE FOR BICKER-ING!
RGH...! WHY...?!
GRIT

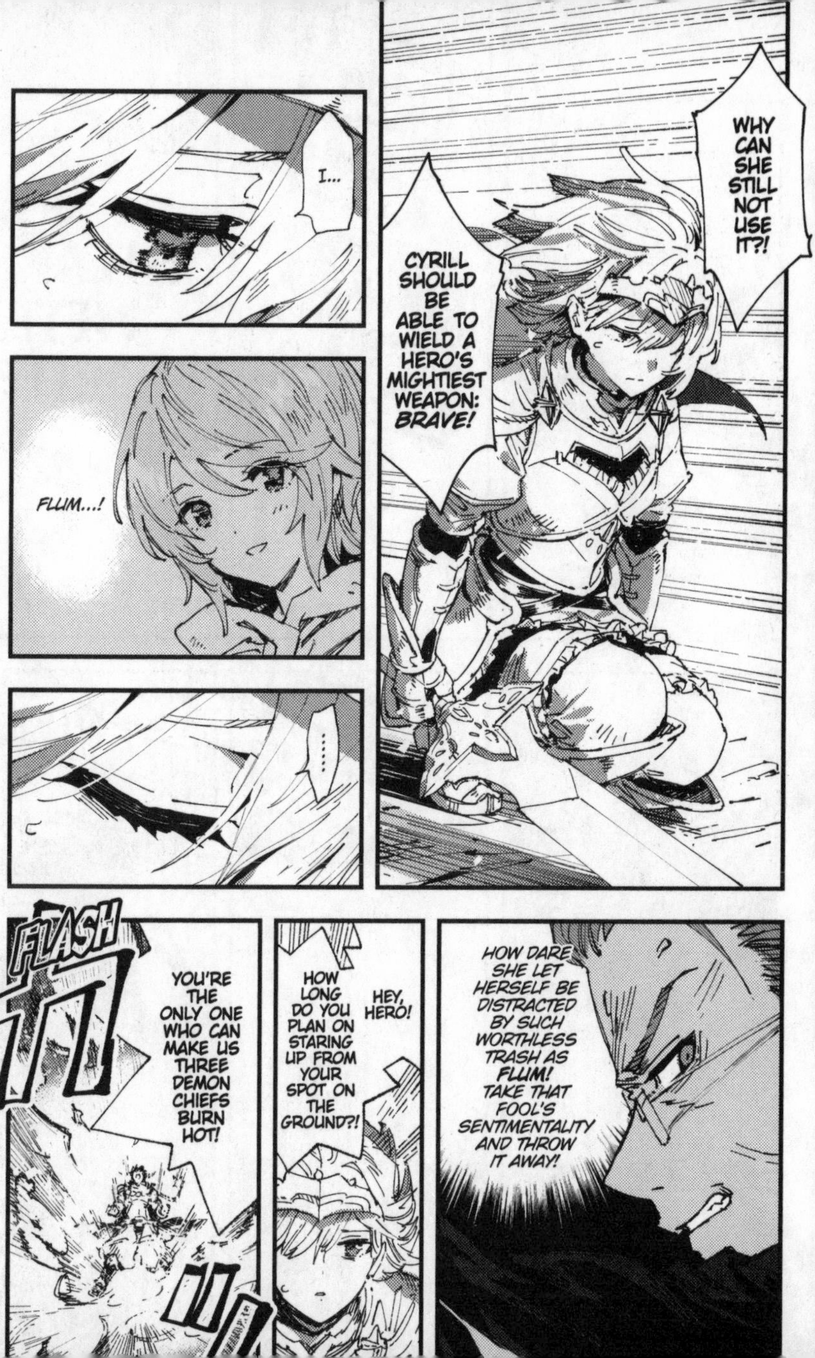
WHY CAN SHE STILL NOT USE IT?!
CYRILL SHOULD BE ABLE TO WIELD A HERO'S MIGHTIEST WEAPON: BRAVE!
I...
FLUM...!
......
HOW DARE SHE LET HERSELF BE DISTRACTED BY SUCH WORTHLESS TRASH AS FLUM! TAKE THAT FOOL'S SENTIMENTALITY AND THROW IT AWAY!
HEY, HERO!
HOW LONG DO YOU PLAN ON STARING UP FROM YOUR SPOT ON THE GROUND?!
YOU'RE THE ONLY ONE WHO CAN MAKE US THREE DEMON CHIEFS BURN HOT!
FLASH

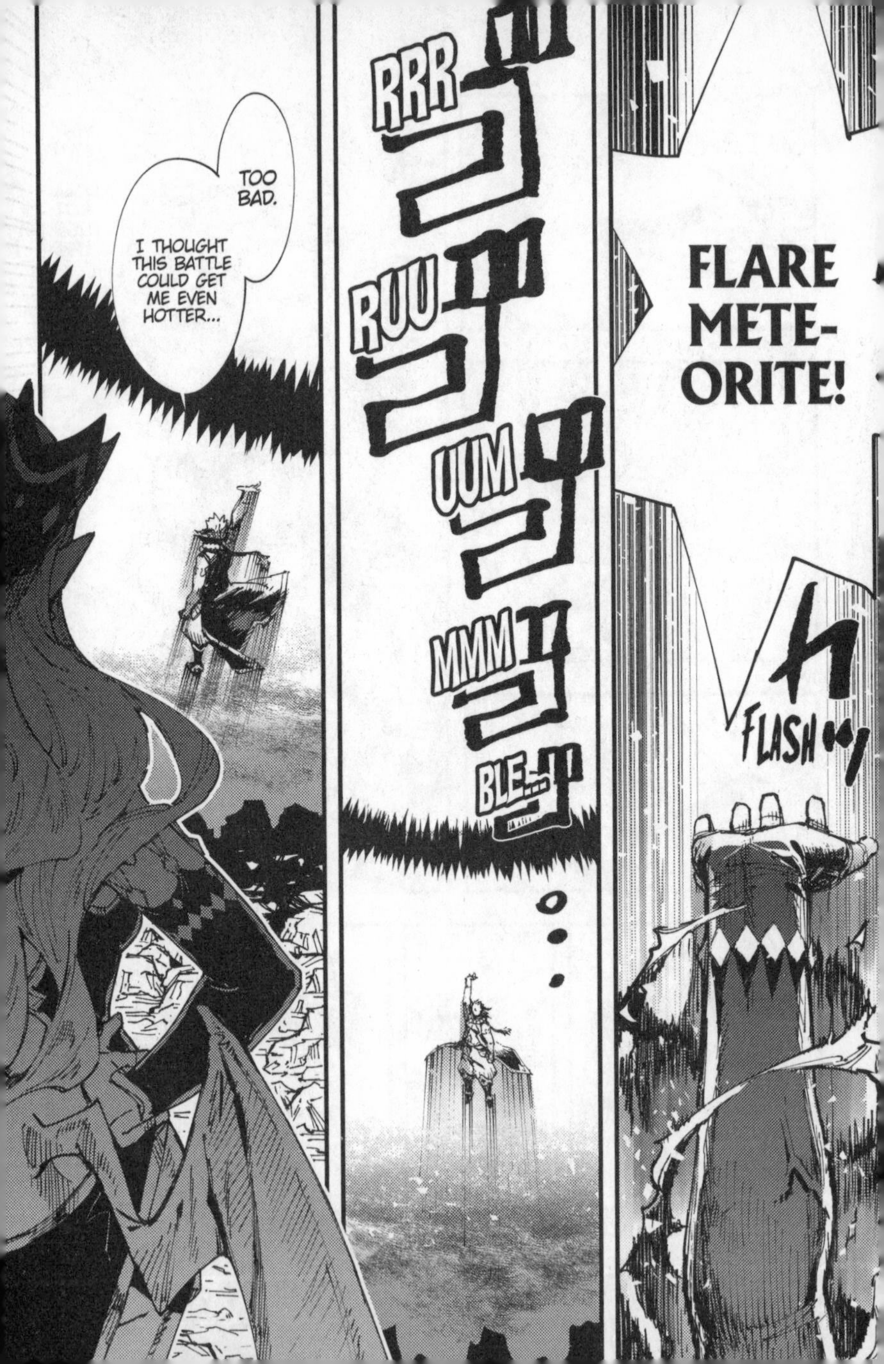
FLARE METE-ORITE!
FLASH
RRR RUU UUM MMM BLE...
TOO BAD.
I THOUGHT THIS BATTLE COULD GET ME EVEN HOTTER...

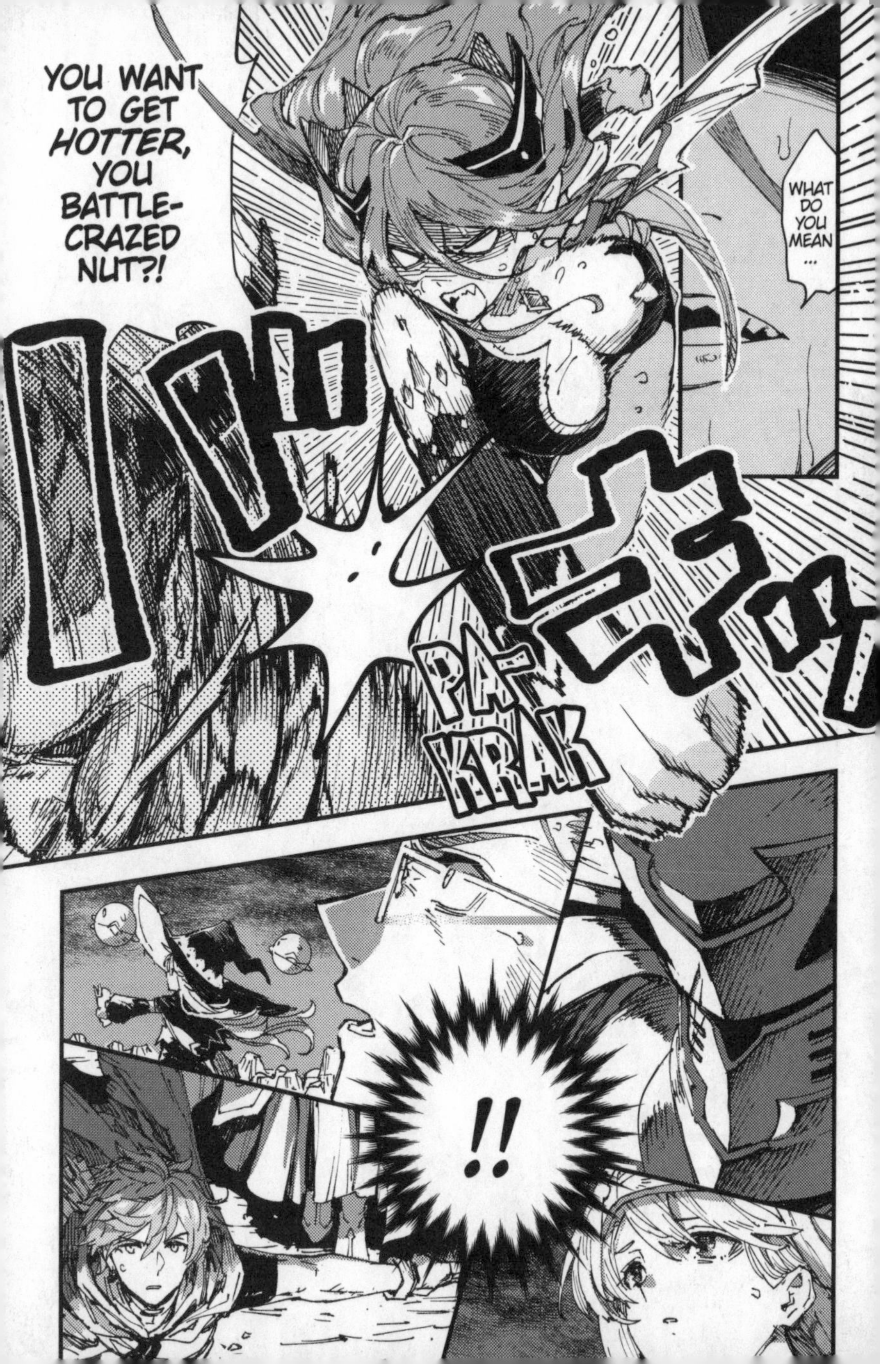
WHAT DO YOU MEAN ...
YOU WANT TO GET HOTTER, YOU BATTLE-CRAZED NUT?!
PA-KRAK
!!

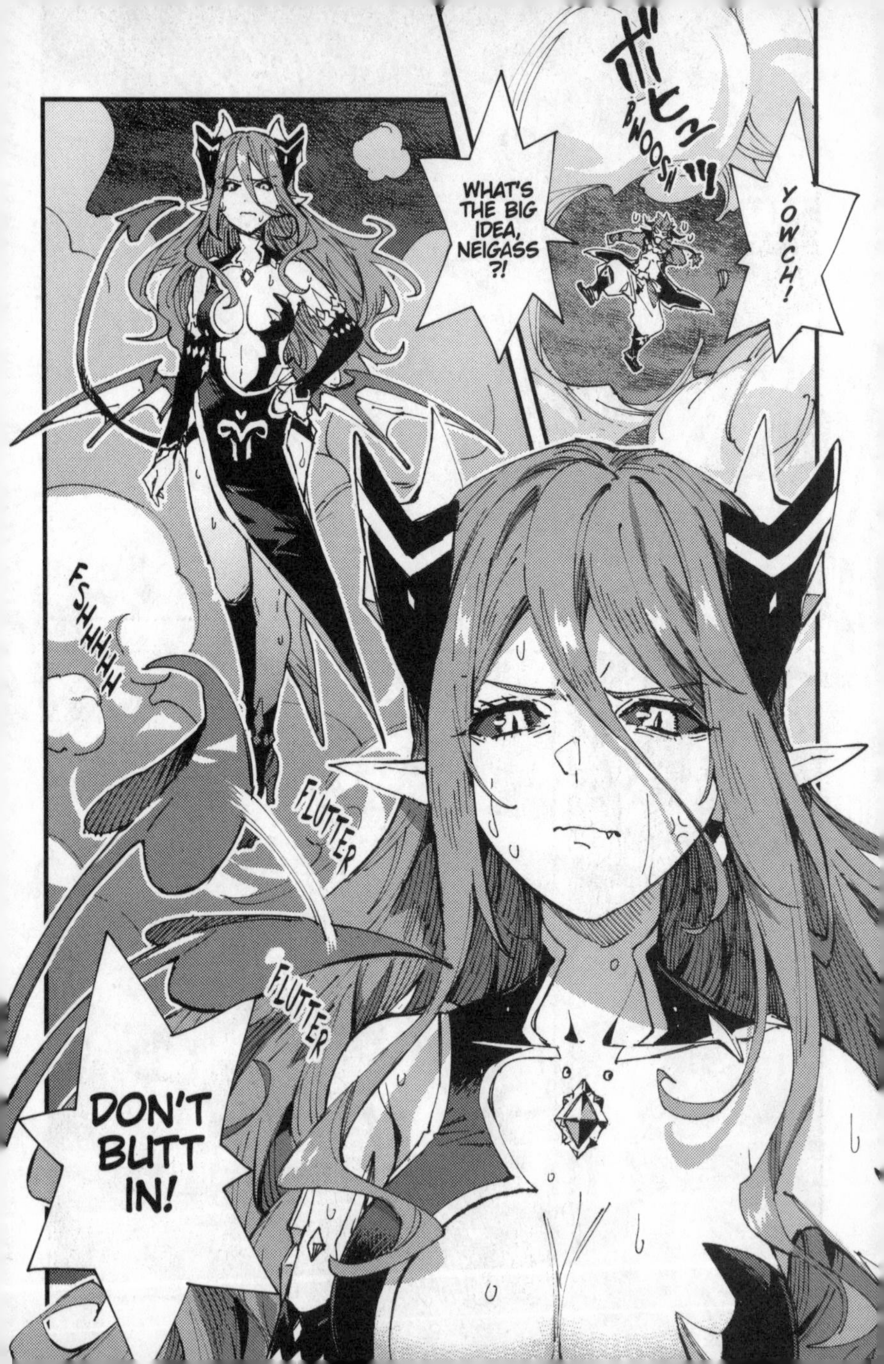
BWOOSH
YOWCH!
WHAT'S THE BIG IDEA, NEIGASS?!
FSHHHHH
FLUTTER
FLUTTER
DON'T BUTT IN!

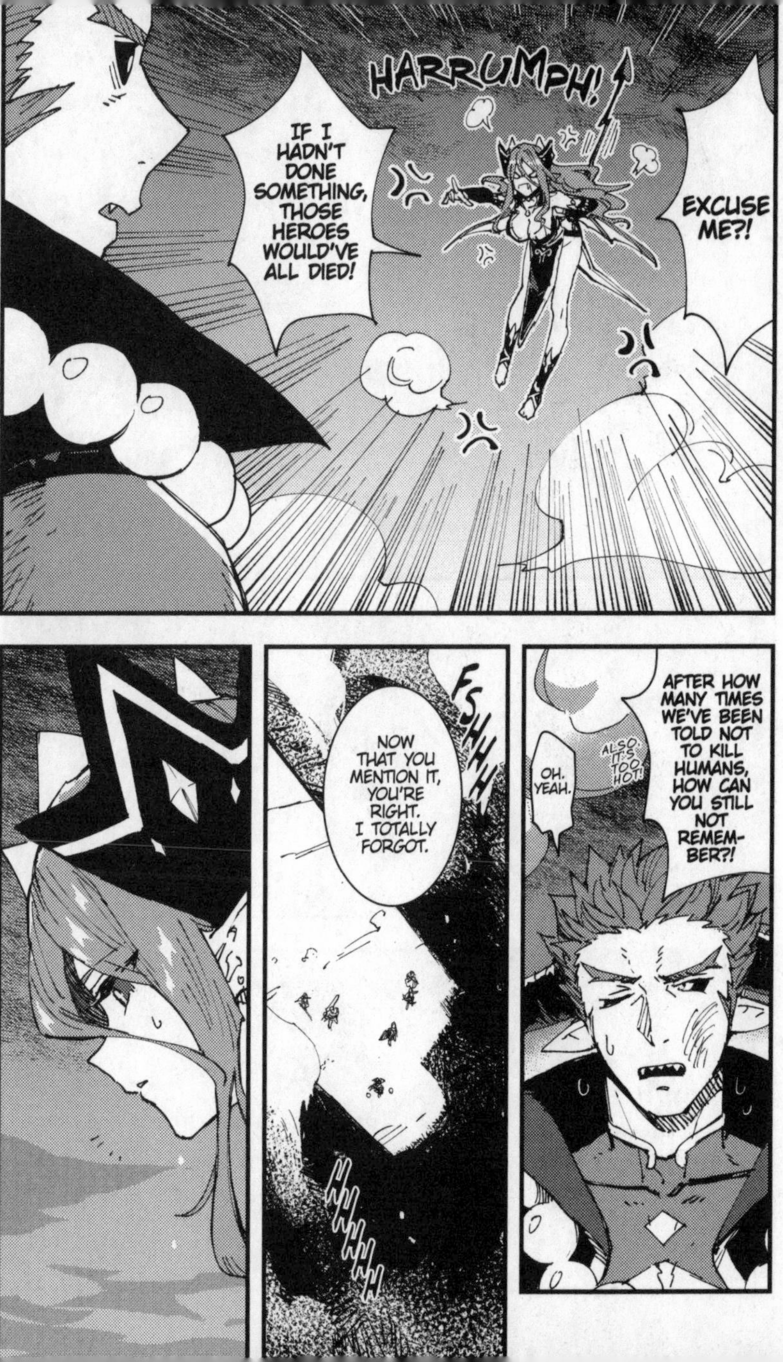
HARRUMPH!
EXCUSE ME?!
IF I HADN'T DONE SOMETHING, THOSE HEROES WOULD'VE ALL DIED!
AFTER HOW MANY TIMES WE'VE BEEN TOLD NOT TO KILL HUMANS, HOW CAN YOU STILL NOT REMEM-BER?!
ALSO, IT'S TOO HOT!
OH. YEAH.
FSHHH
NOW THAT YOU MENTION IT, YOU'RE RIGHT. I TOTALLY FORGOT.
HHHHH

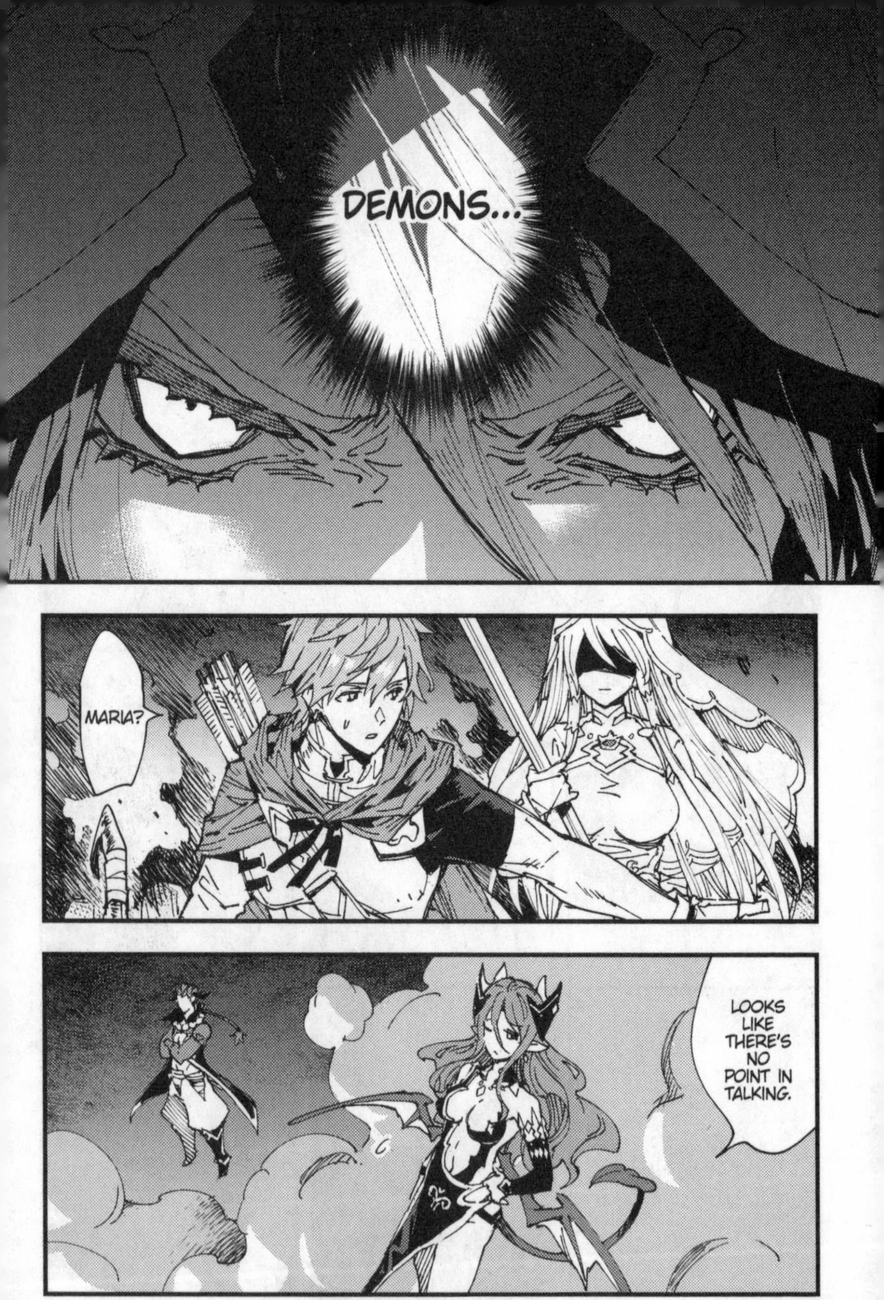
DEMONS...
MARIA?
LOOKS LIKE THERE'S NO POINT IN TALKING.

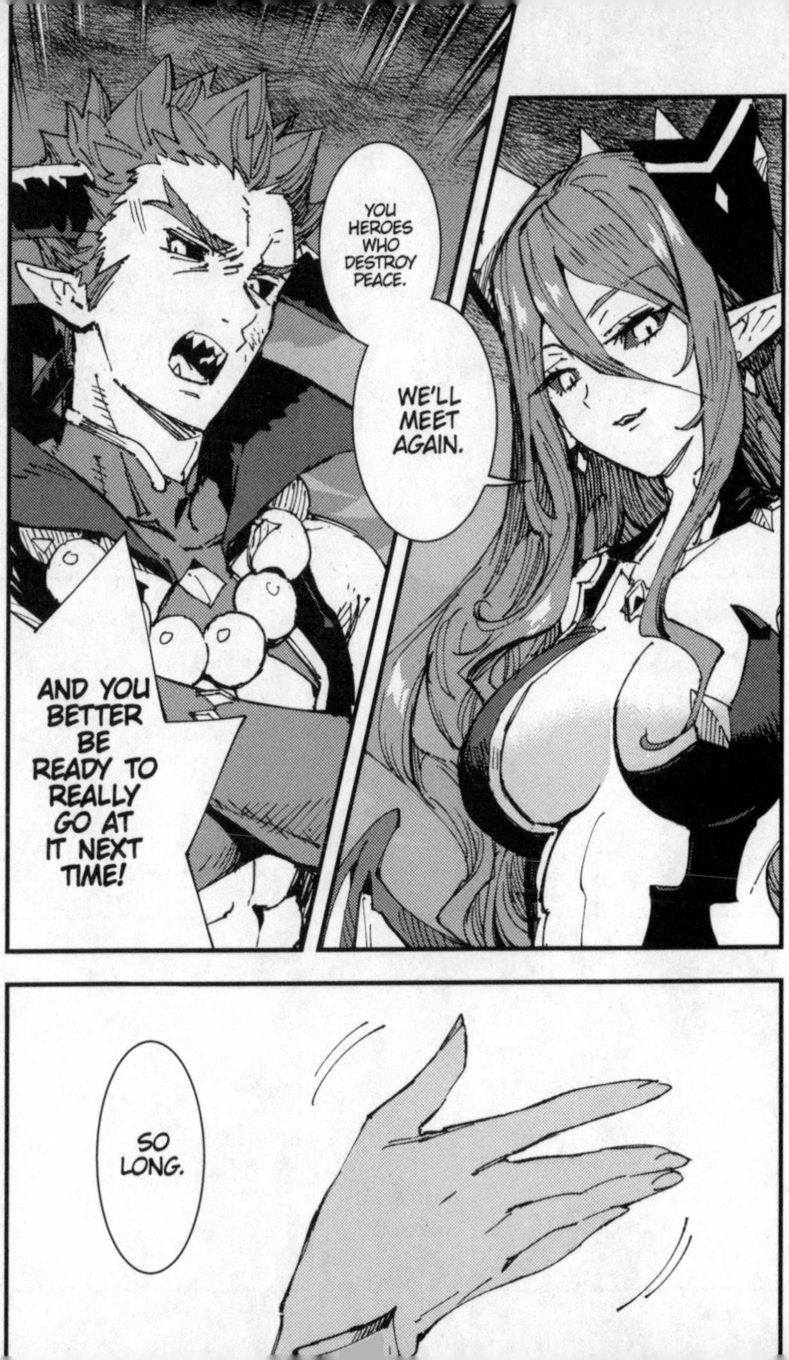
YOU HEROES WHO DESTROY PEACE.
WE'LL MEET AGAIN.
AND YOU BETTER BE READY TO REALLY GO AT IT NEXT TIME!
SO LONG.

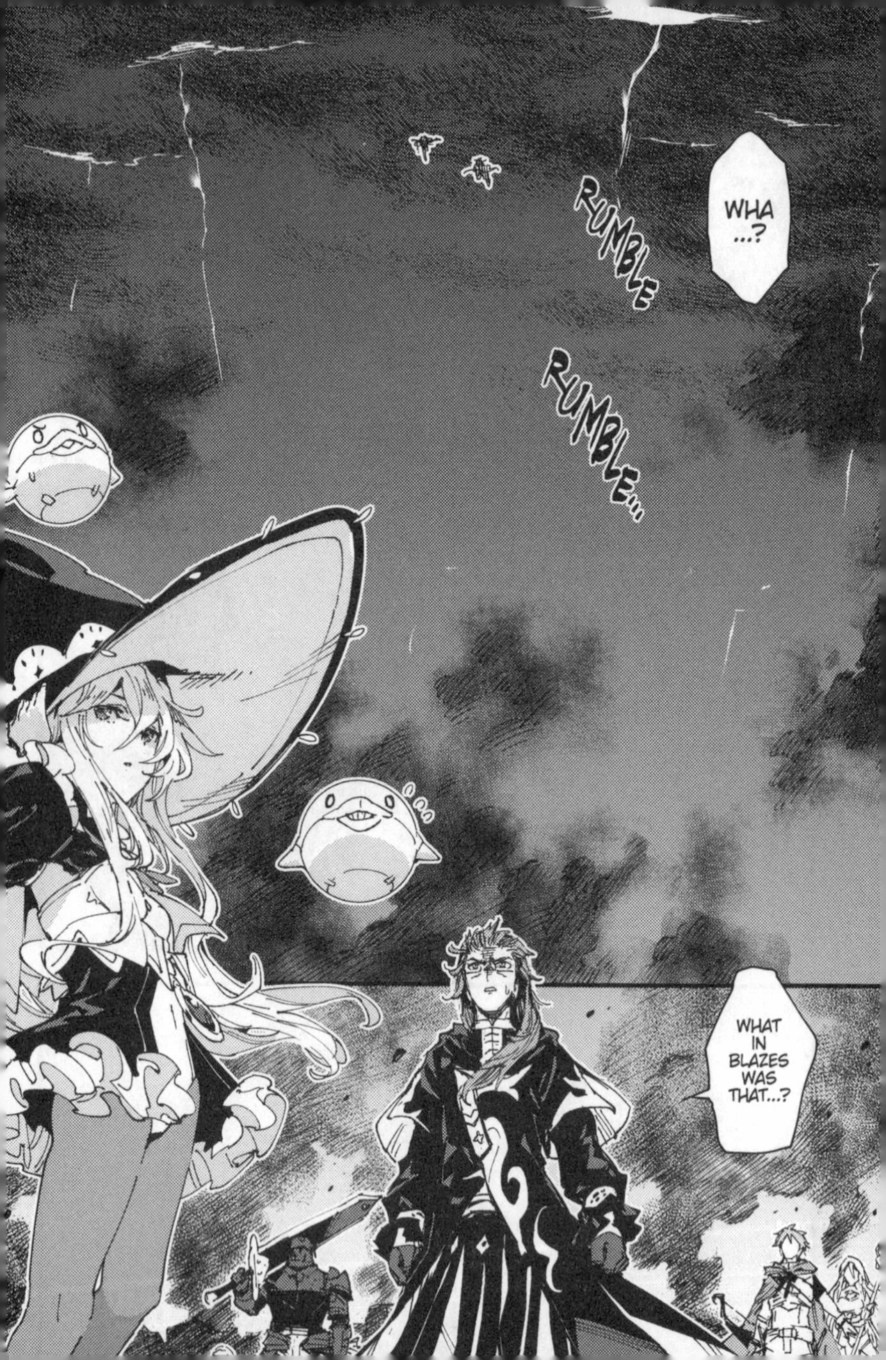
WHA ...?
RUMBLE
RUMBLE...
WHAT IN BLAZES WAS THAT...?

Chapter 6: The Starting Signal

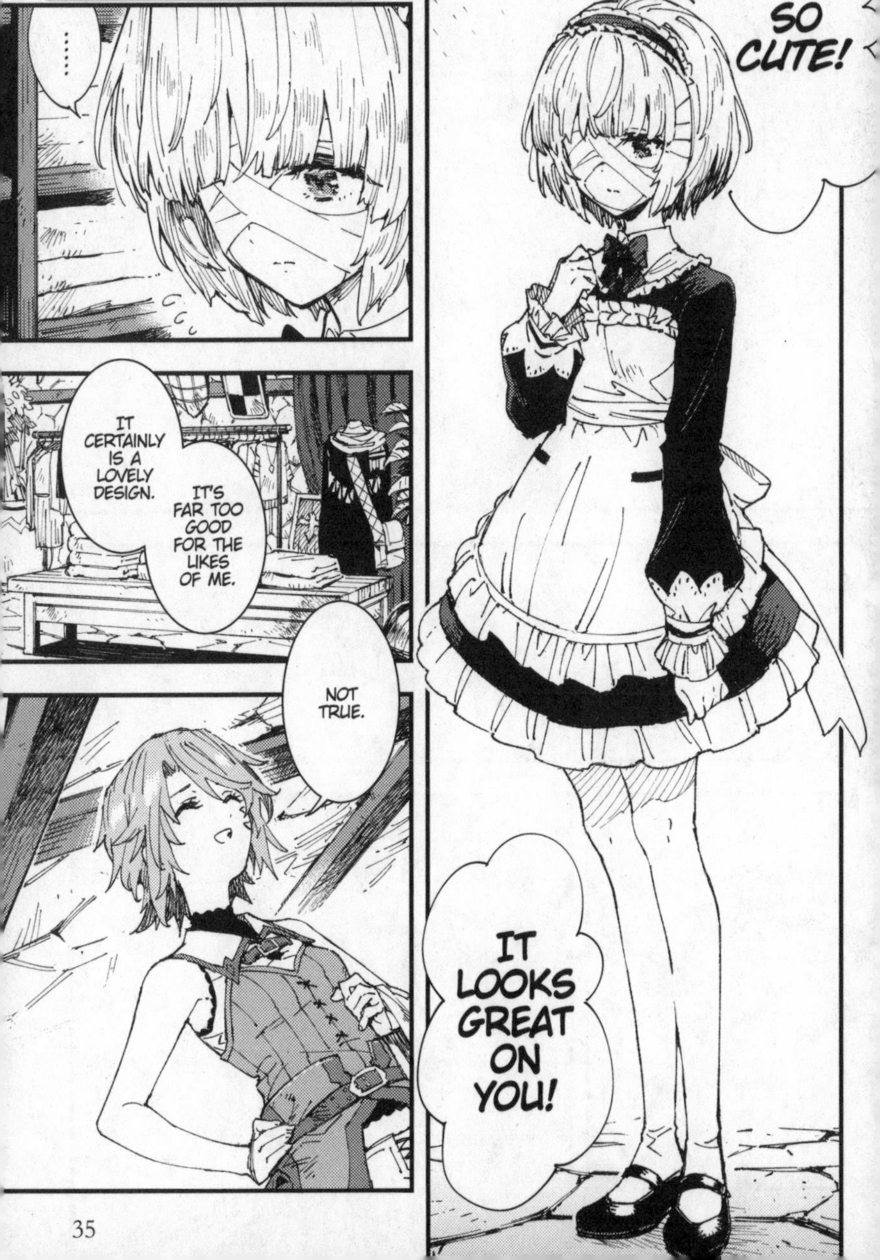
SO CUTE!
IT LOOKS GREAT ON YOU!
......
IT CERTAINLY IS A LOVELY DESIGN.
IT'S FAR TOO GOOD FOR THE LIKES OF ME.
NOT TRUE.

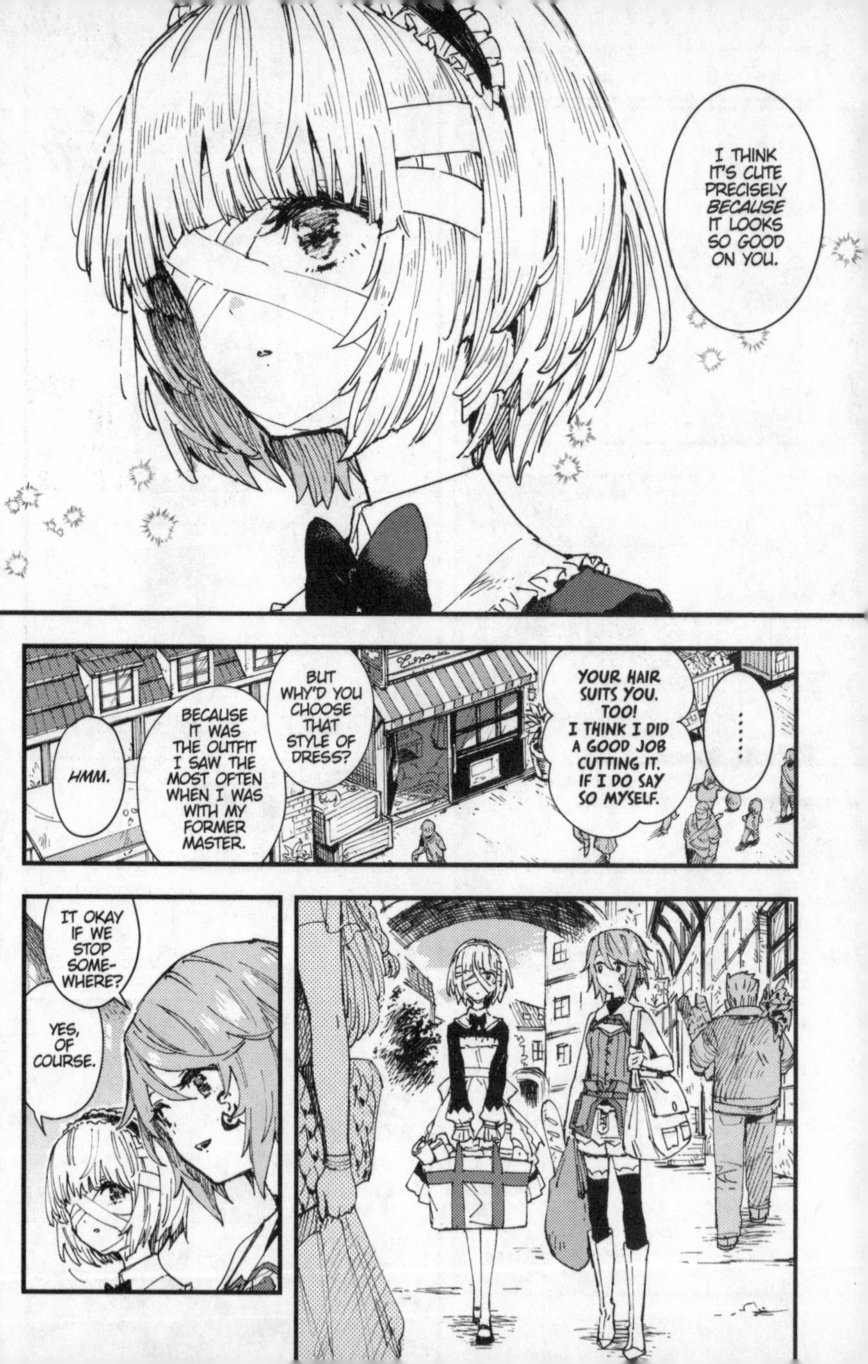
I THINK IT'S CUTE PRECISELY BECAUSE IT LOOKS SO GOOD ON YOU.
......
YOUR HAIR SUITS YOU, TOO! I THINK I DID A GOOD JOB CUTTING IT, IF I DO SAY SO MYSELF.
BUT WHY'D YOU CHOOSE THAT STYLE OF DRESS?
BECAUSE IT WAS THE OUTFIT I SAW THE MOST OFTEN WHEN I WAS WITH MY FORMER MASTER.
HMM.
IT OKAY IF WE STOP SOME-WHERE?
YES, OF COURSE.

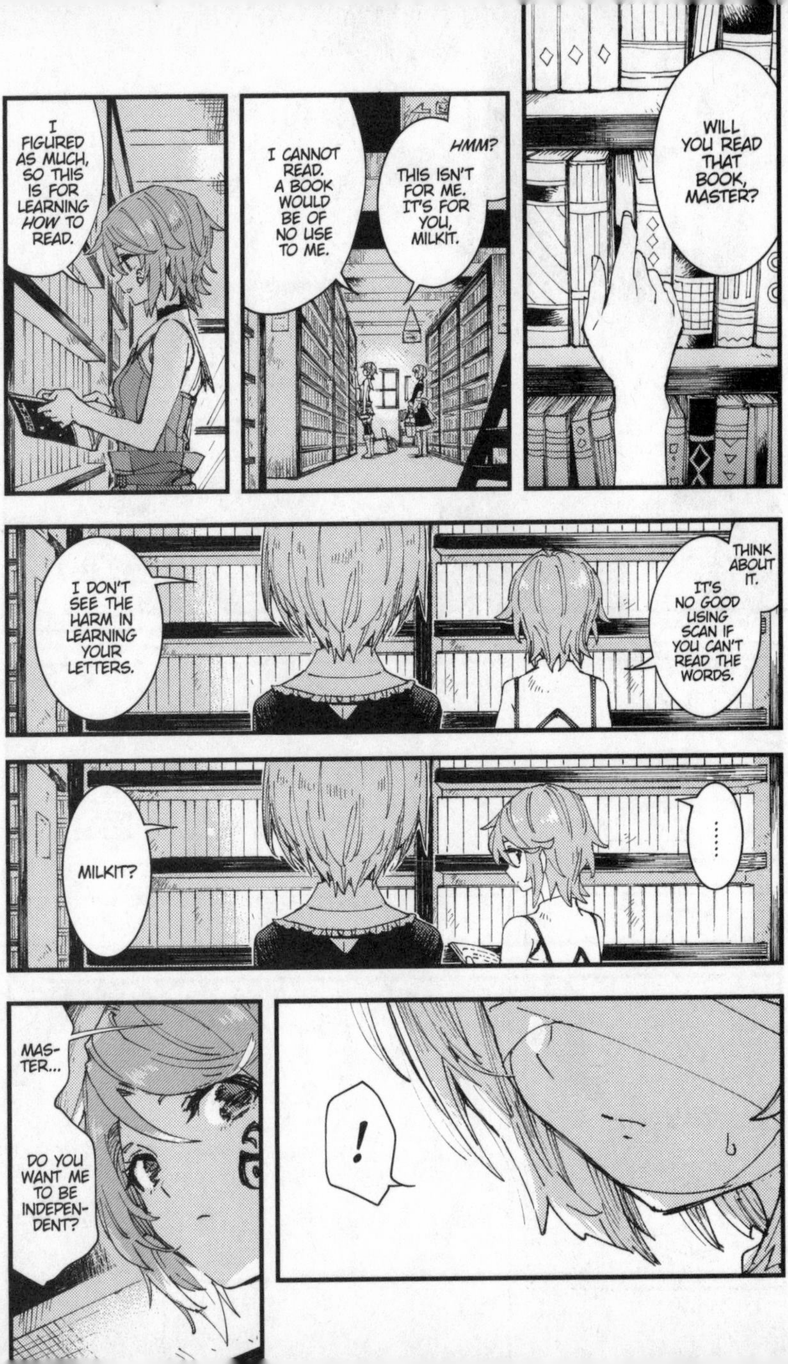
WILL YOU READ THAT BOOK, MASTER?
HMM?
THIS ISN'T FOR ME. IT'S FOR YOU, MILKIT.
I CANNOT READ. A BOOK WOULD BE OF NO USE TO ME.
I FIGURED AS MUCH, SO THIS IS FOR LEARNING *HOW* TO READ.
THINK ABOUT IT.
IT'S NO GOOD USING SCAN IF YOU CAN'T READ THE WORDS.
I DON'T SEE THE HARM IN LEARNING YOUR LETTERS.
......
MILKIT?
!
MAS-TER...
DO YOU WANT ME TO BE INDEPEN-DENT?

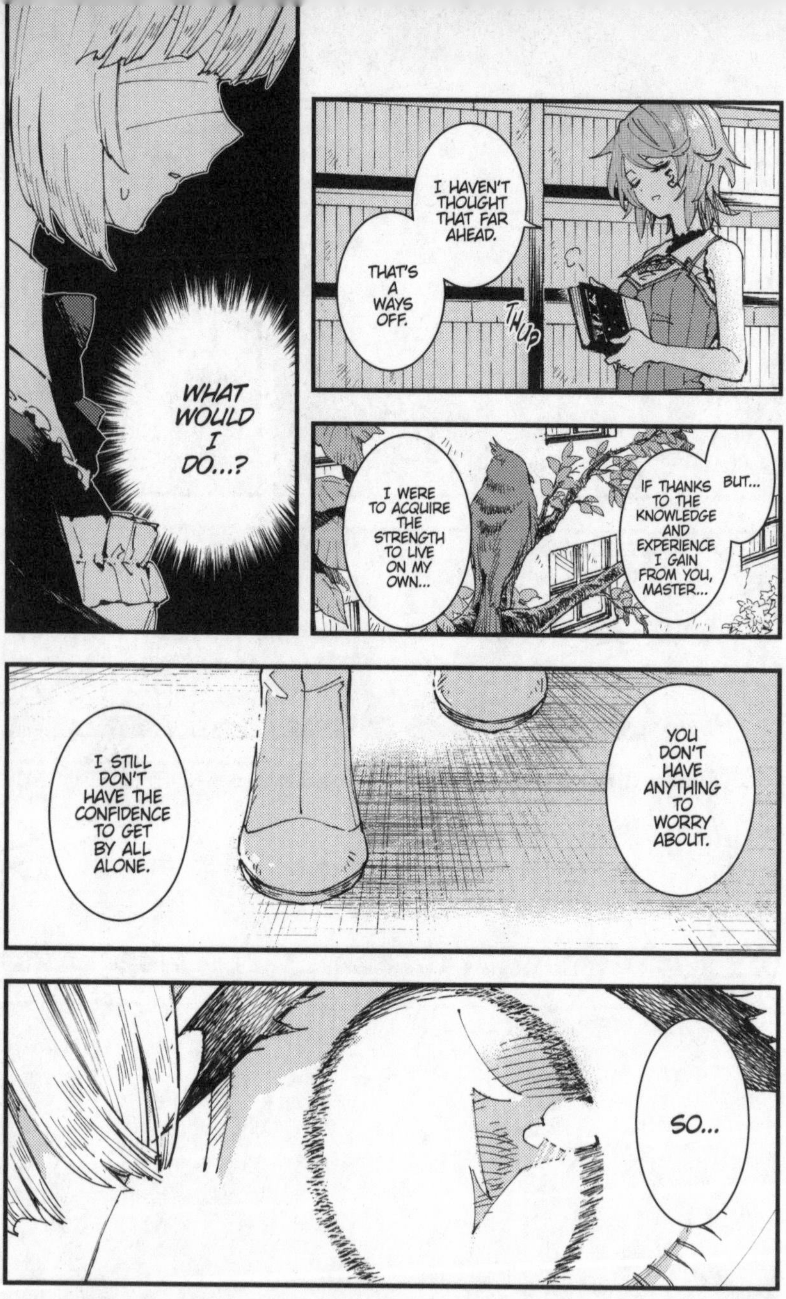
I HAVEN'T THOUGHT THAT FAR AHEAD.
THAT'S A WAYS OFF.
THUP
BUT...
IF THANKS TO THE KNOWLEDGE AND EXPERIENCE I GAIN FROM YOU, MASTER...
I WERE TO ACQUIRE THE STRENGTH TO LIVE ON MY OWN...
WHAT WOULD I DO...?
YOU DON'T HAVE ANYTHING TO WORRY ABOUT.
I STILL DON'T HAVE THE CONFIDENCE TO GET BY ALL ALONE.
SO...

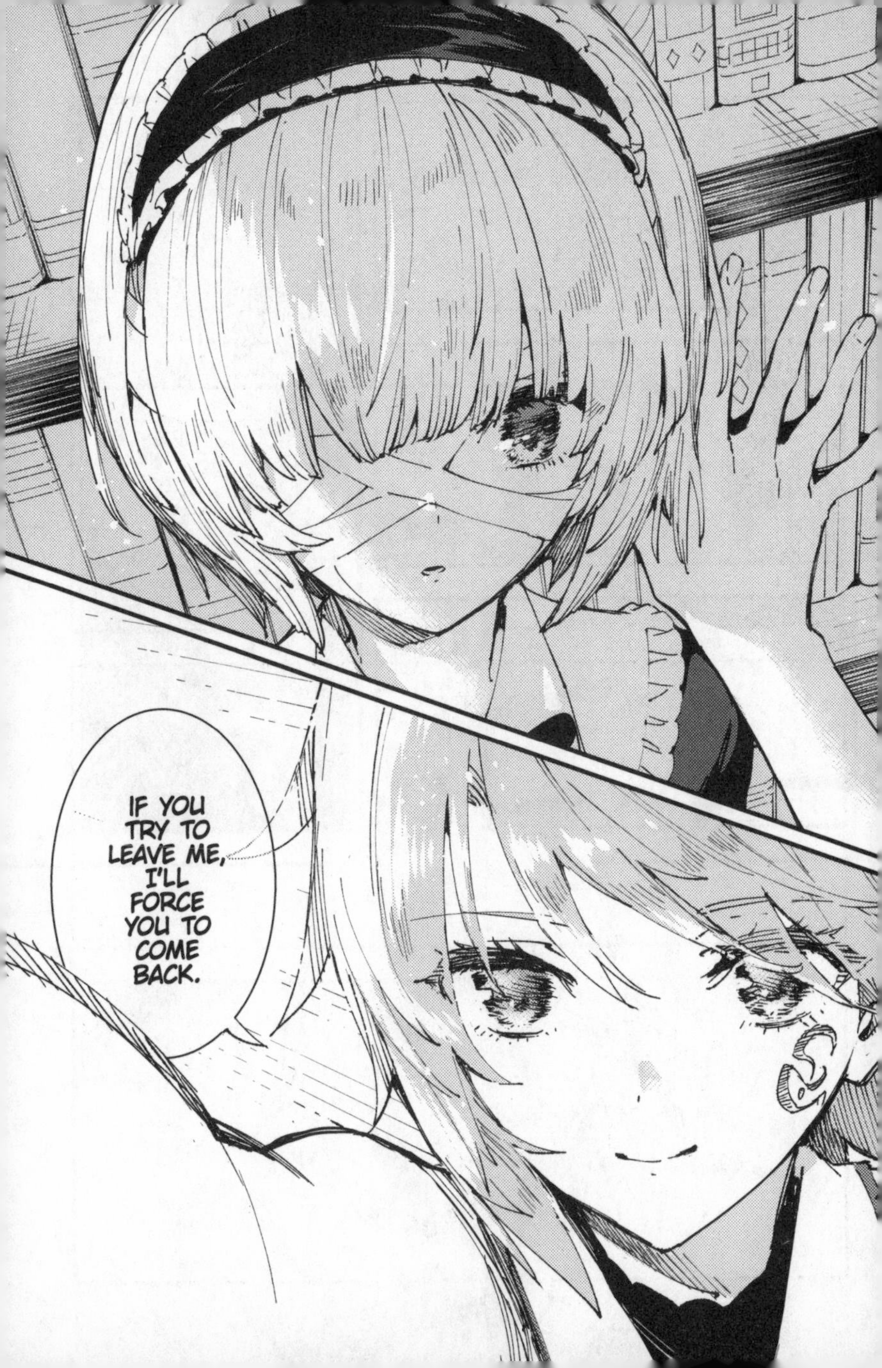
IF YOU TRY TO LEAVE ME, I'LL FORCE YOU TO COME BACK.

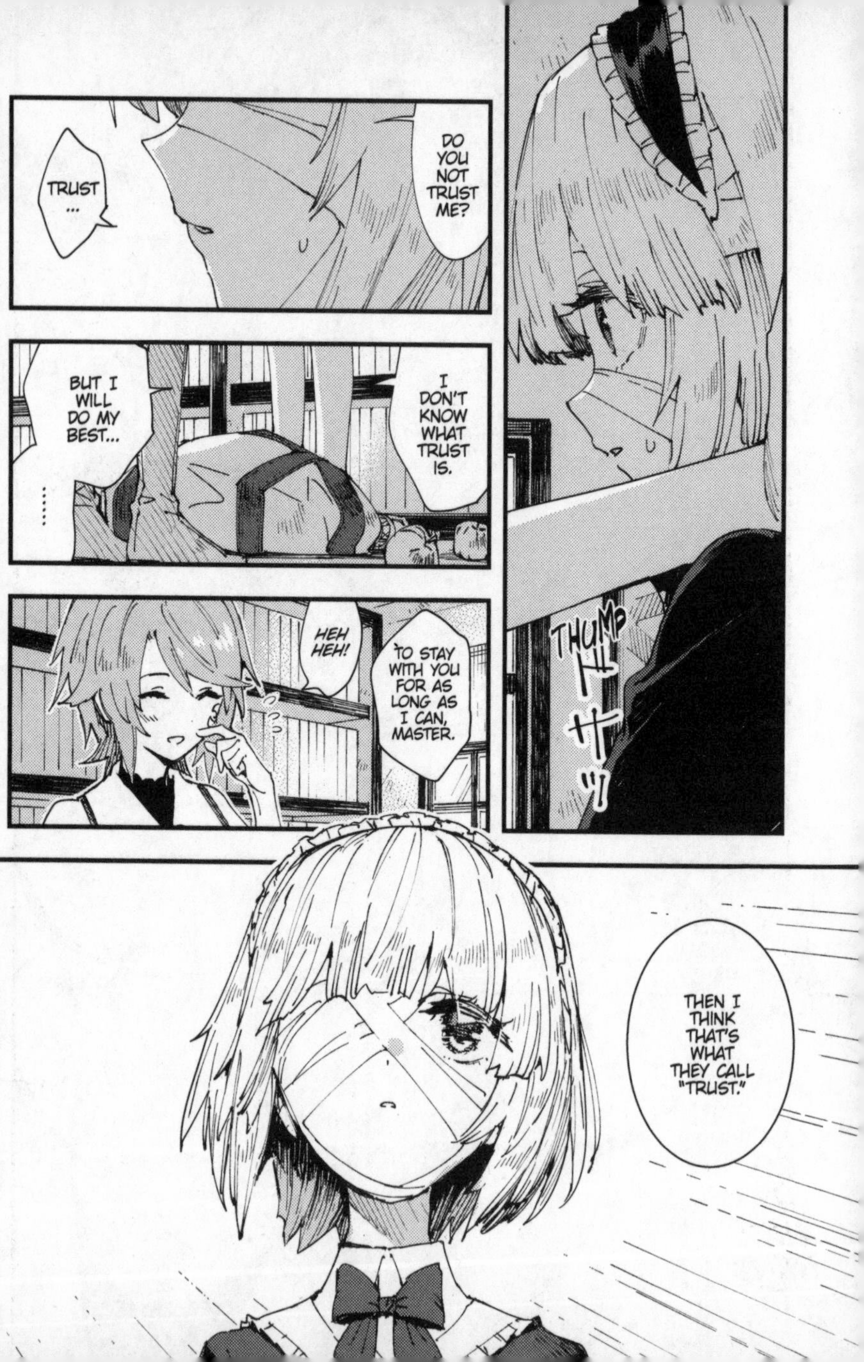

THUMP
DO YOU NOT TRUST ME?
TRUST ...
I DON'T KNOW WHAT TRUST IS.
BUT I WILL DO MY BEST...
......
TO STAY WITH YOU FOR AS LONG AS I CAN, MASTER.
HEH HEH!
THEN I THINK THAT'S WHAT THEY CALL "TRUST."

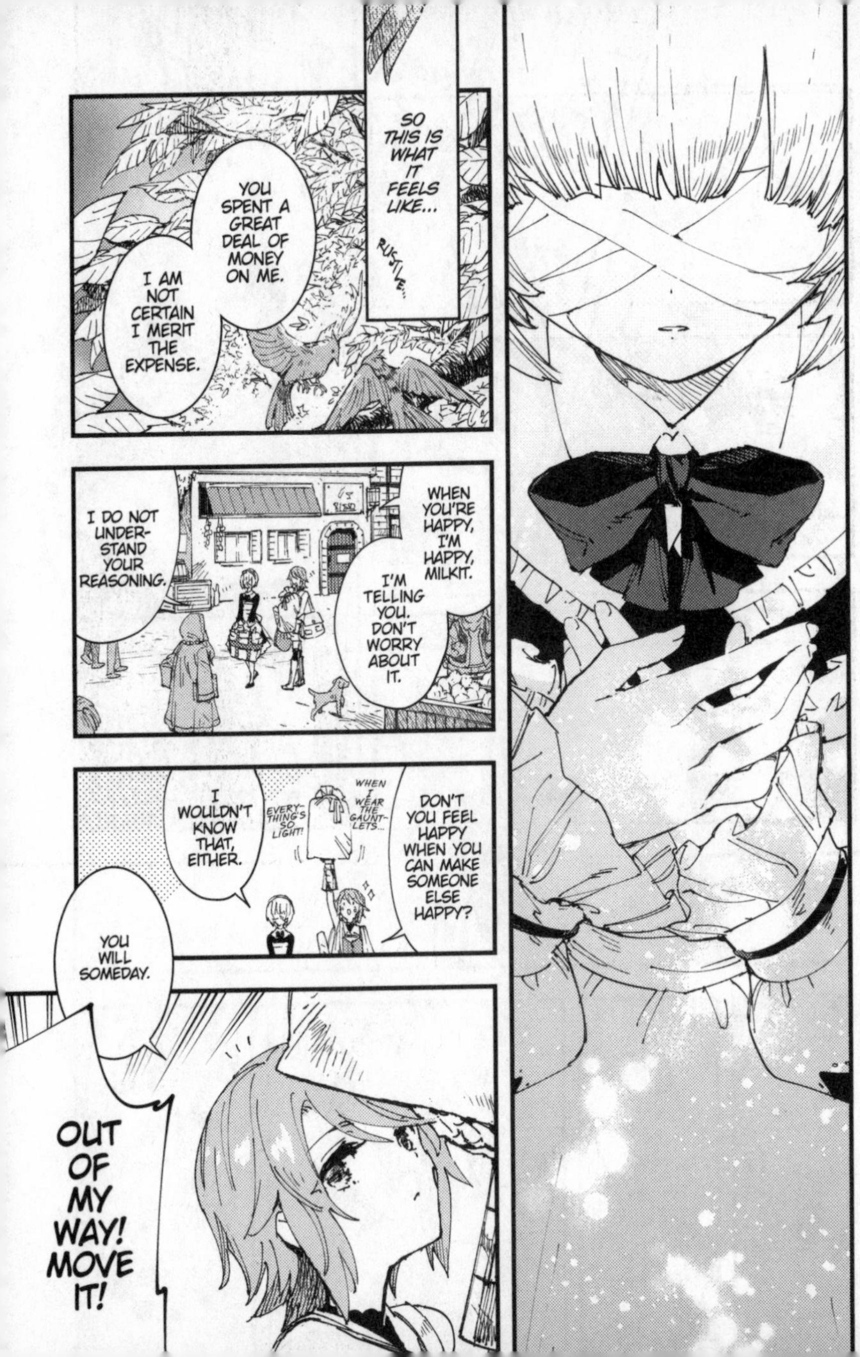
SO THIS IS WHAT IT FEELS LIKE...
RUSTLE...
YOU SPENT A GREAT DEAL OF MONEY ON ME.
I AM NOT CERTAIN I MERIT THE EXPENSE.
WHEN YOU'RE HAPPY, I'M HAPPY, MILKIT.
I'M TELLING YOU. DON'T WORRY ABOUT IT.
I DO NOT UNDER-STAND YOUR REASONING.
DON'T YOU FEEL HAPPY WHEN YOU CAN MAKE SOMEONE ELSE HAPPY?
WHEN I WEAR THE GAUNT-LETS...
EVERY-THING'S SO LIGHT!
I WOULDN'T KNOW THAT, EITHER.
YOU WILL SOMEDAY.
OUT OF MY WAY! MOVE IT!

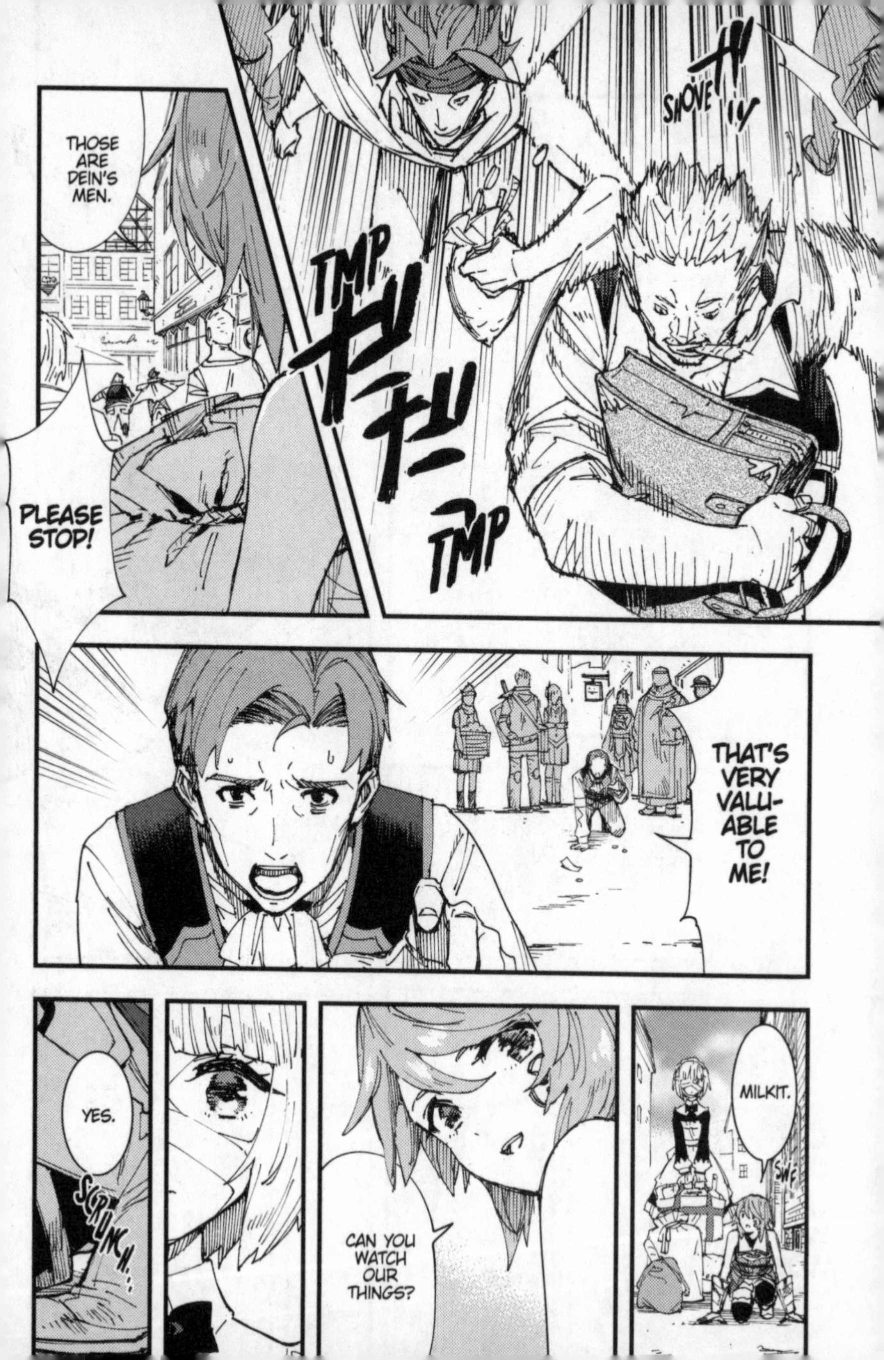
SHOVE
TMP
TMP
THOSE ARE DEIN'S MEN.
PLEASE STOP!
THAT'S VERY VALUABLE TO ME!
MILKIT.
SWF
CAN YOU WATCH OUR THINGS?
YES.
SCRUNCH..

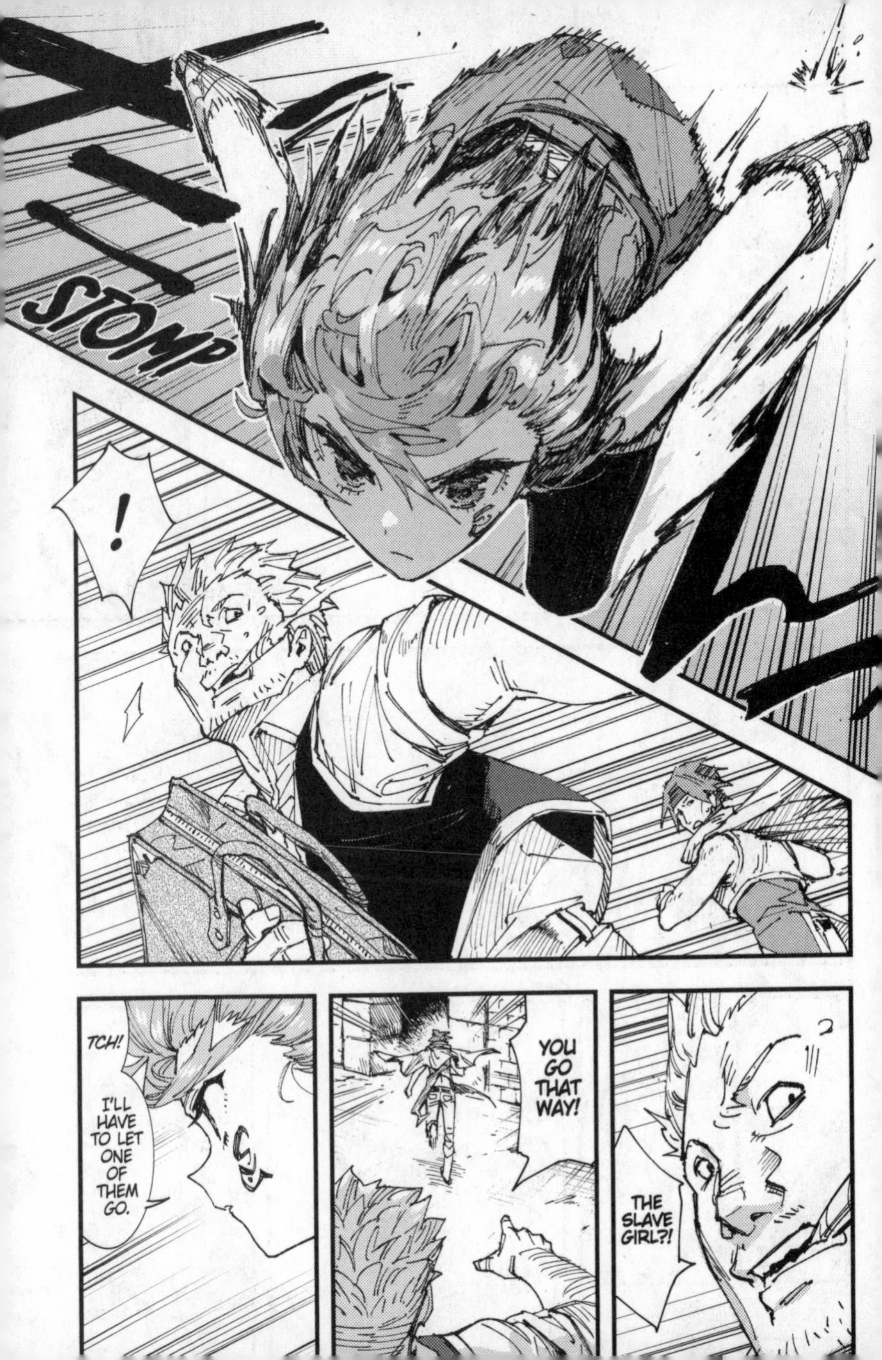
STOMP
!
THE SLAVE GIRL?!
YOU GO THAT WAY!
TCH!
I'LL HAVE TO LET ONE OF THEM GO.

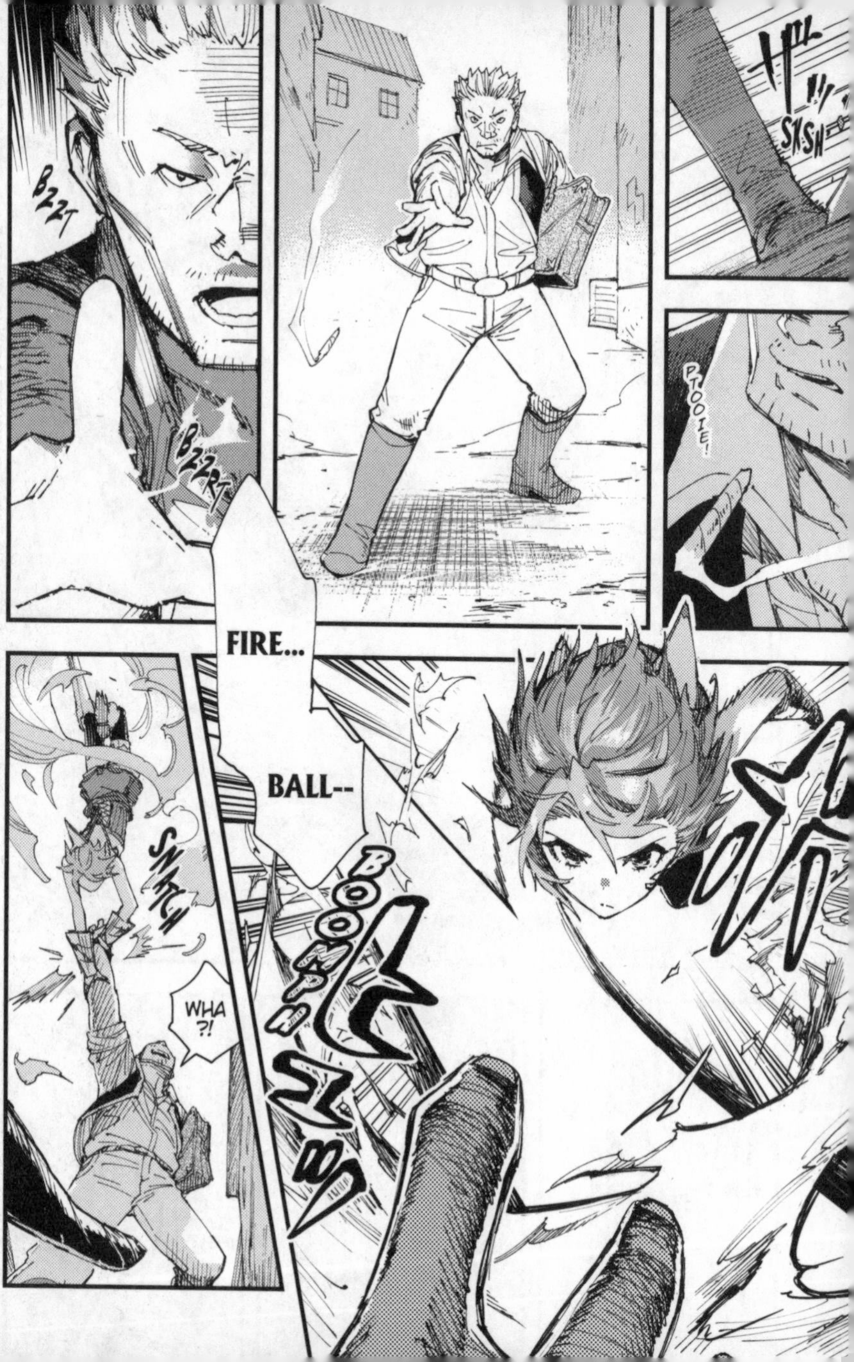
SKSH
PTOOIE!
BZZT
BZZRT
FIRE...
BALL--
BOOM
SNATCH
WHA?!

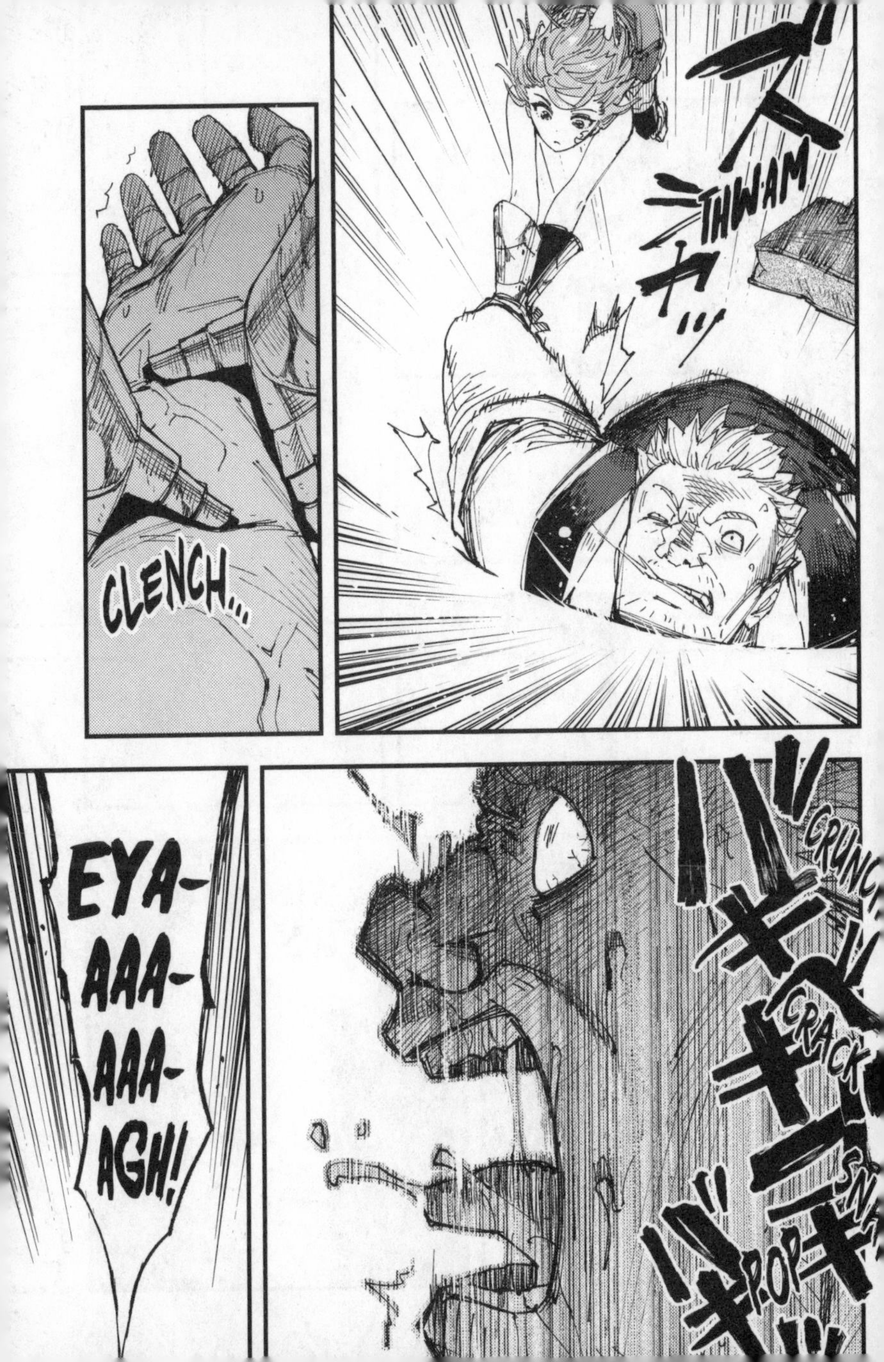
THWAM
CLENCH...
CRUNC
CRACK
SNA
POP
EYA-AAA-AAA-AGH!

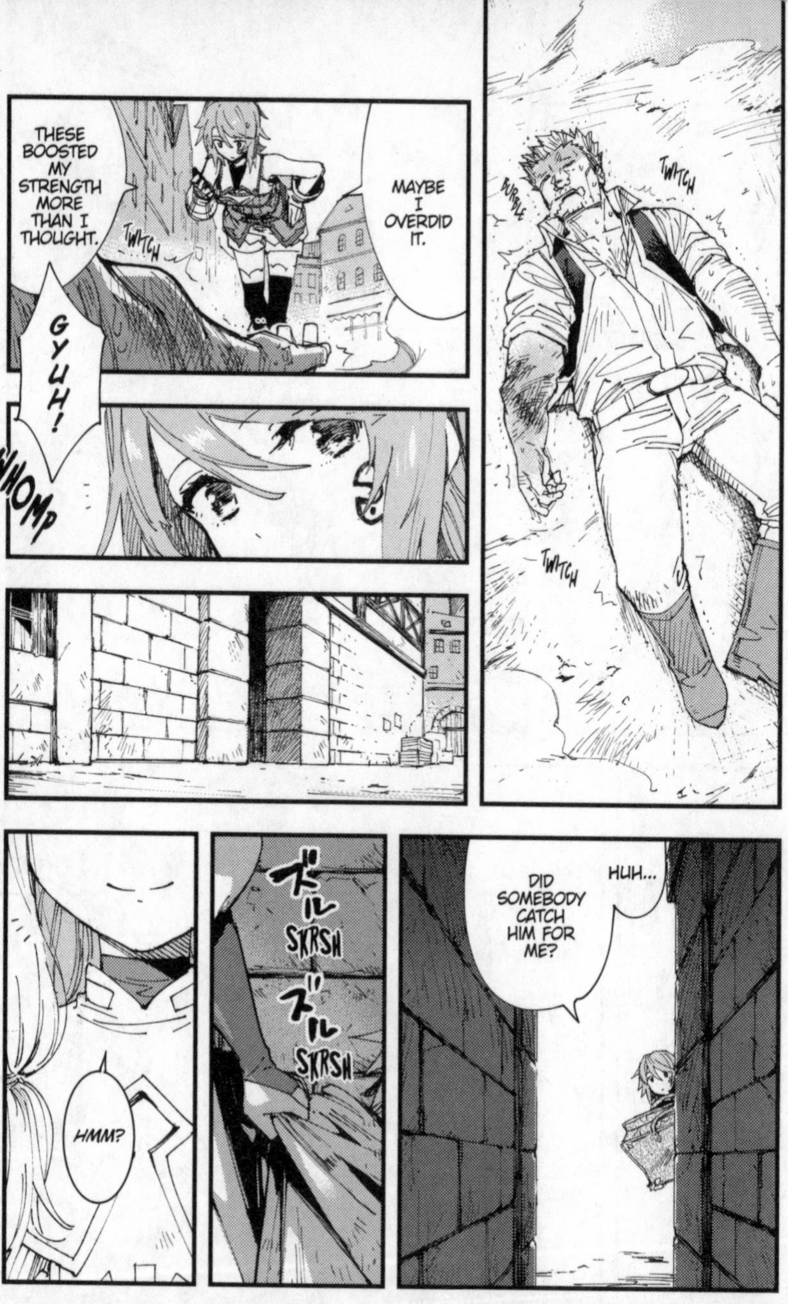
BURBLE
TWITCH
TWITCH
MAYBE I OVERDID IT.
THESE BOOSTED MY STRENGTH MORE THAN I THOUGHT.
TWITCH
GYUH!
WHOMP
HUH...
DID SOMEBODY CATCH HIM FOR ME?
ズル
SKRSH
ズル
SKRSH
HMM?

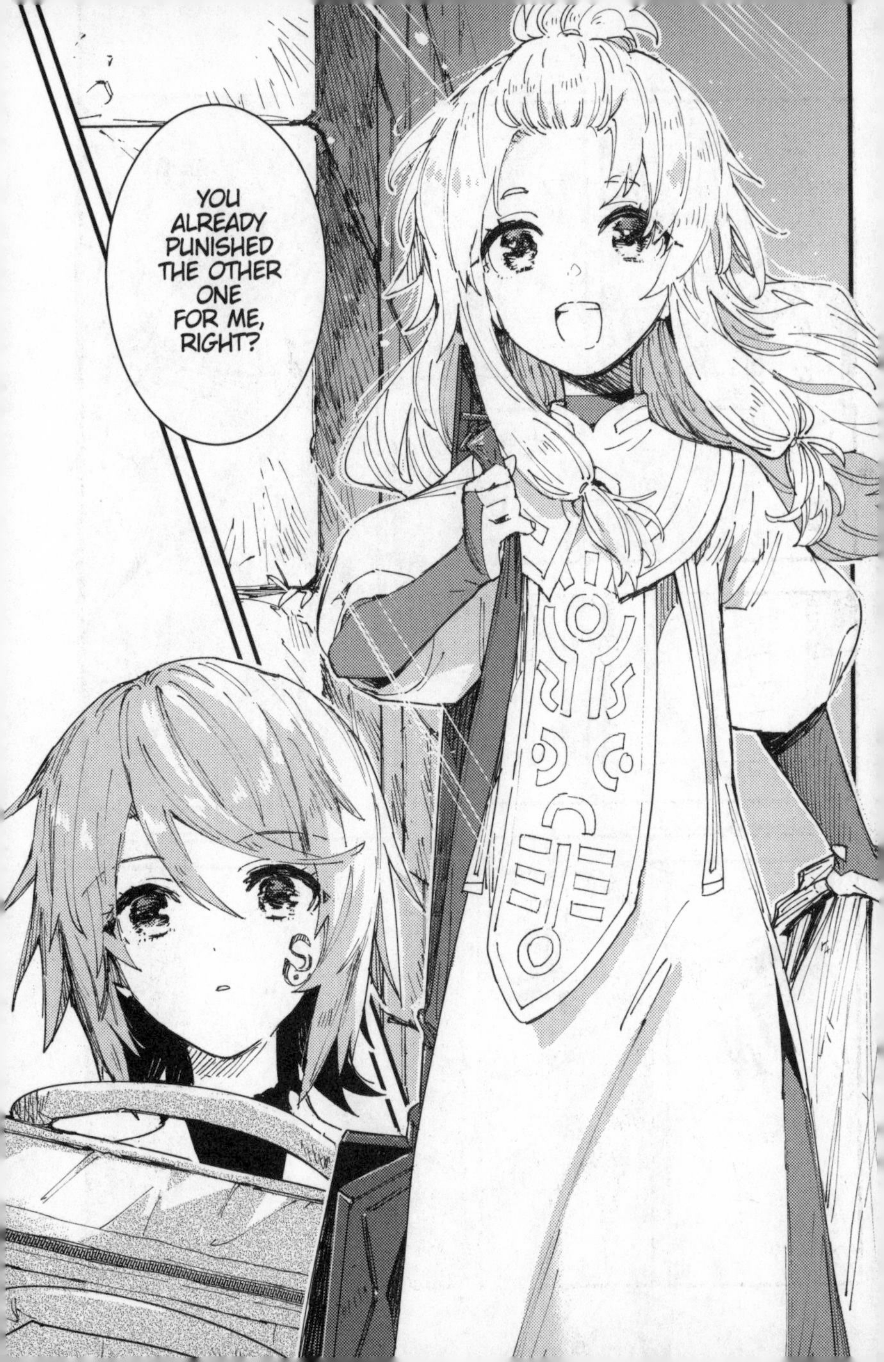
YOU ALREADY PUNISHED THE OTHER ONE FOR ME, RIGHT?

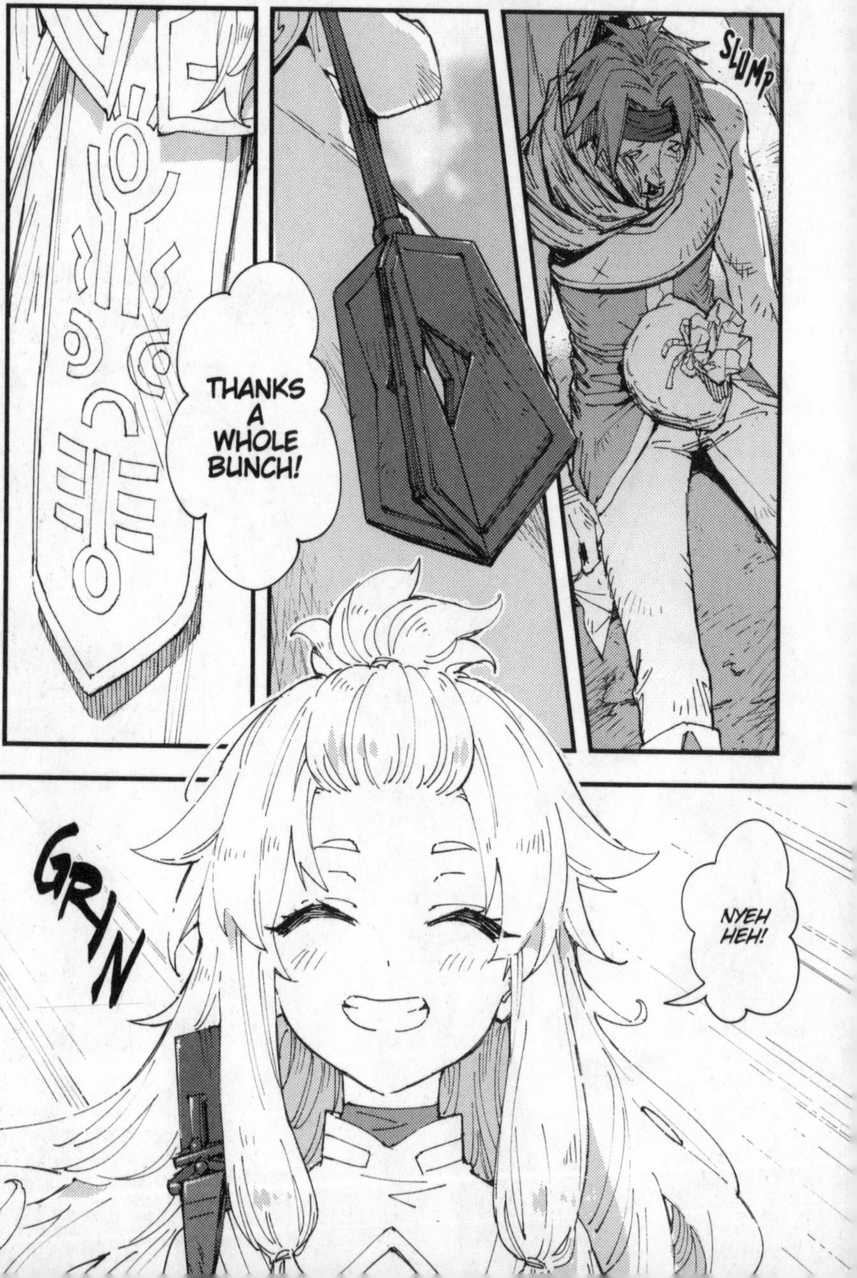
SLUMP
THANKS A WHOLE BUNCH!
NYEH HEH!
GRIN

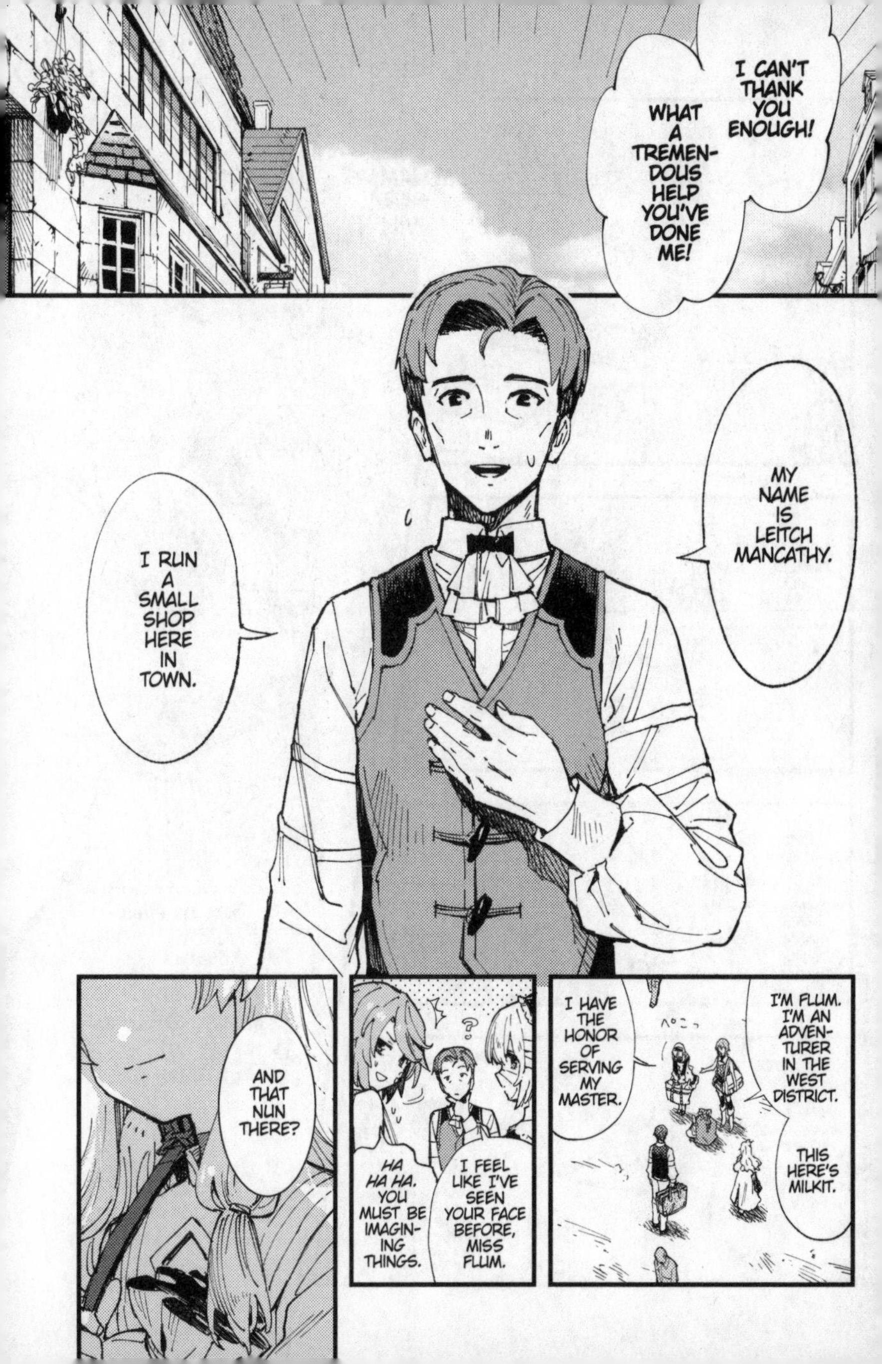
I CAN'T THANK YOU ENOUGH!
WHAT A TREMENDOUS HELP YOU'VE DONE ME!
MY NAME IS LEITCH MANCATHY.
I RUN A SMALL SHOP HERE IN TOWN.
I'M FLUM. I'M AN ADVENTURER IN THE WEST DISTRICT.
THIS HERE'S MILKIT.
I HAVE THE HONOR OF SERVING MY MASTER.
I FEEL LIKE I'VE SEEN YOUR FACE BEFORE, MISS FLUM.
HA HA HA. YOU MUST BE IMAGINING THINGS.
AND THAT NUN THERE?

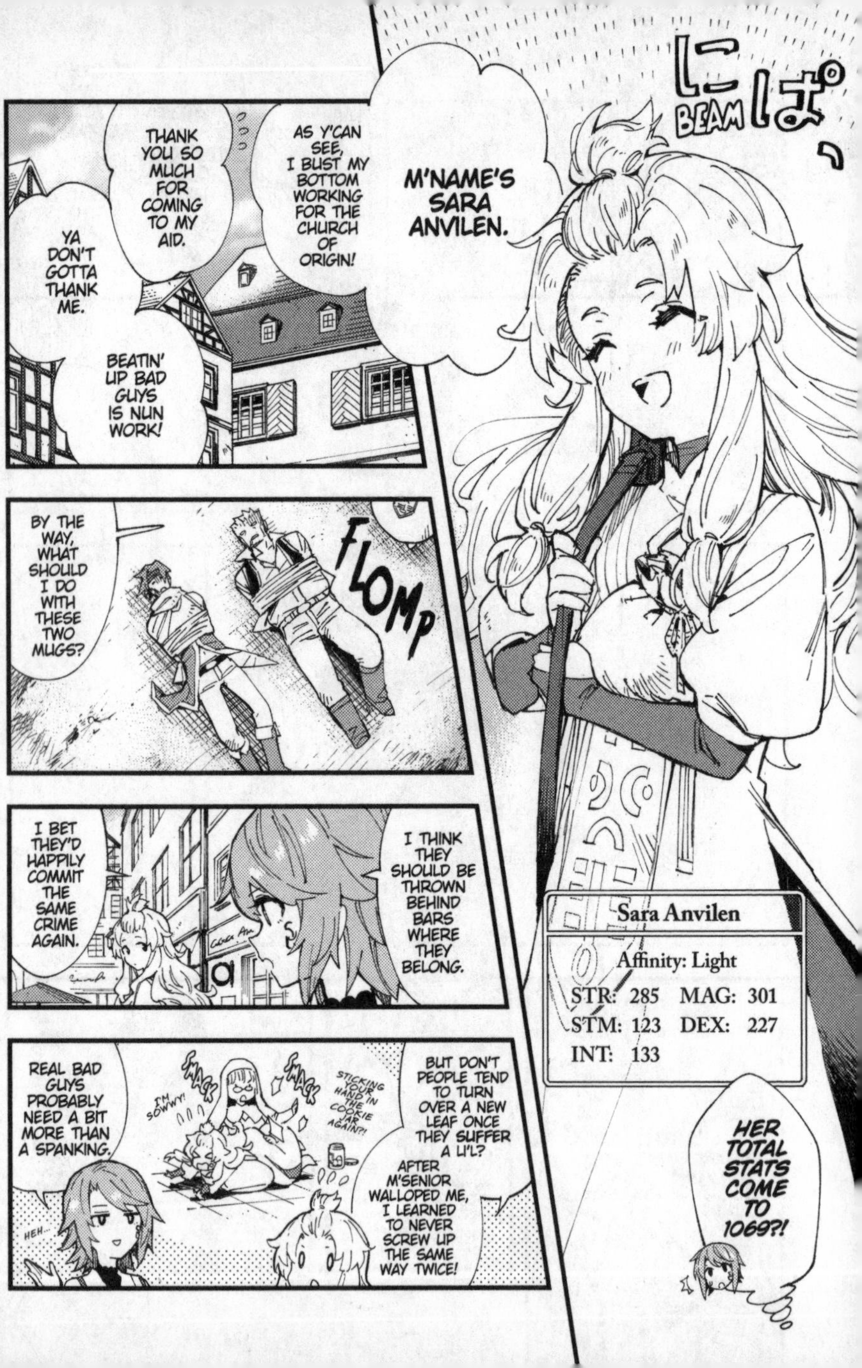
にぱっ
BEAM
M'NAME'S SARA ANVILEN.
Sara Anvilen
Affinity: Light
STR: 285 MAG: 301
STM: 123 DEX: 227
INT: 133
HER TOTAL STATS COME TO 1069?!
AS Y'CAN SEE, I BUST MY BOTTOM WORKING FOR THE CHURCH OF ORIGIN!
THANK YOU SO MUCH FOR COMING TO MY AID.
YA DON'T GOTTA THANK ME.
BEATIN' UP BAD GUYS IS NUN WORK!
FLOMP
BY THE WAY, WHAT SHOULD I DO WITH THESE TWO MUGS?
I THINK THEY SHOULD BE THROWN BEHIND BARS WHERE THEY BELONG.
I BET THEY'D HAPPILY COMMIT THE SAME CRIME AGAIN.
BUT DON'T PEOPLE TEND TO TURN OVER A NEW LEAF ONCE THEY SUFFER A LI'L?
SMACK
SMACK
STICKING YOUR HAND IN THE COOKIE JAR AGAIN?!
I'M SOWWY!
AFTER M'SENIOR WALLOPED ME, I LEARNED TO NEVER SCREW UP THE SAME WAY TWICE!
REAL BAD GUYS PROBABLY NEED A BIT MORE THAN A SPANKING.
HEH...

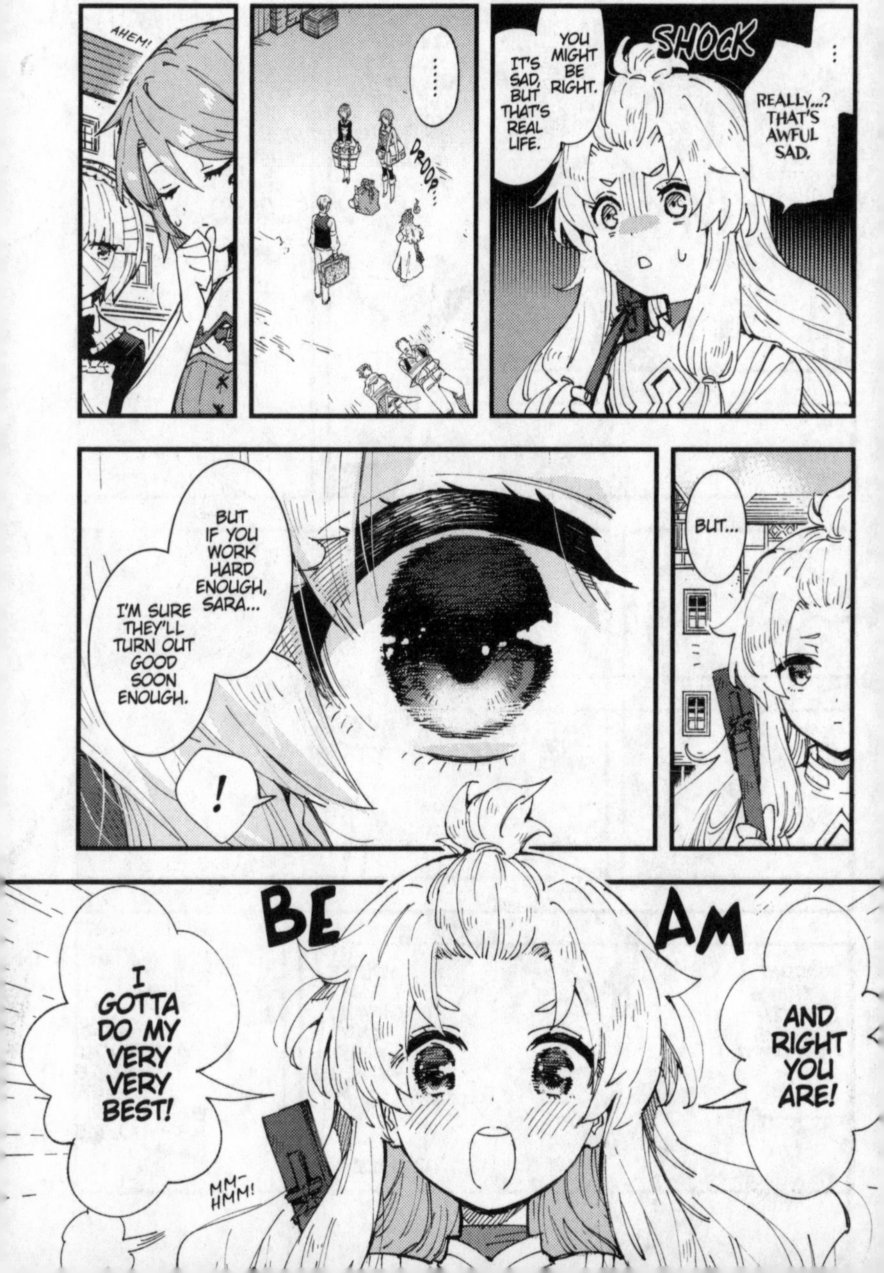
...
REALLY...? THAT'S AWFUL SAD.
SHOCK
YOU MIGHT BE RIGHT.
IT'S SAD, BUT THAT'S REAL LIFE.
......
DROOP...
AHEM!
BUT...
BUT IF YOU WORK HARD ENOUGH, SARA...
I'M SURE THEY'LL TURN OUT GOOD SOON ENOUGH.
!
BE
AM
AND RIGHT YOU ARE!
I GOTTA DO MY VERY VERY BEST!
MM-HMM!

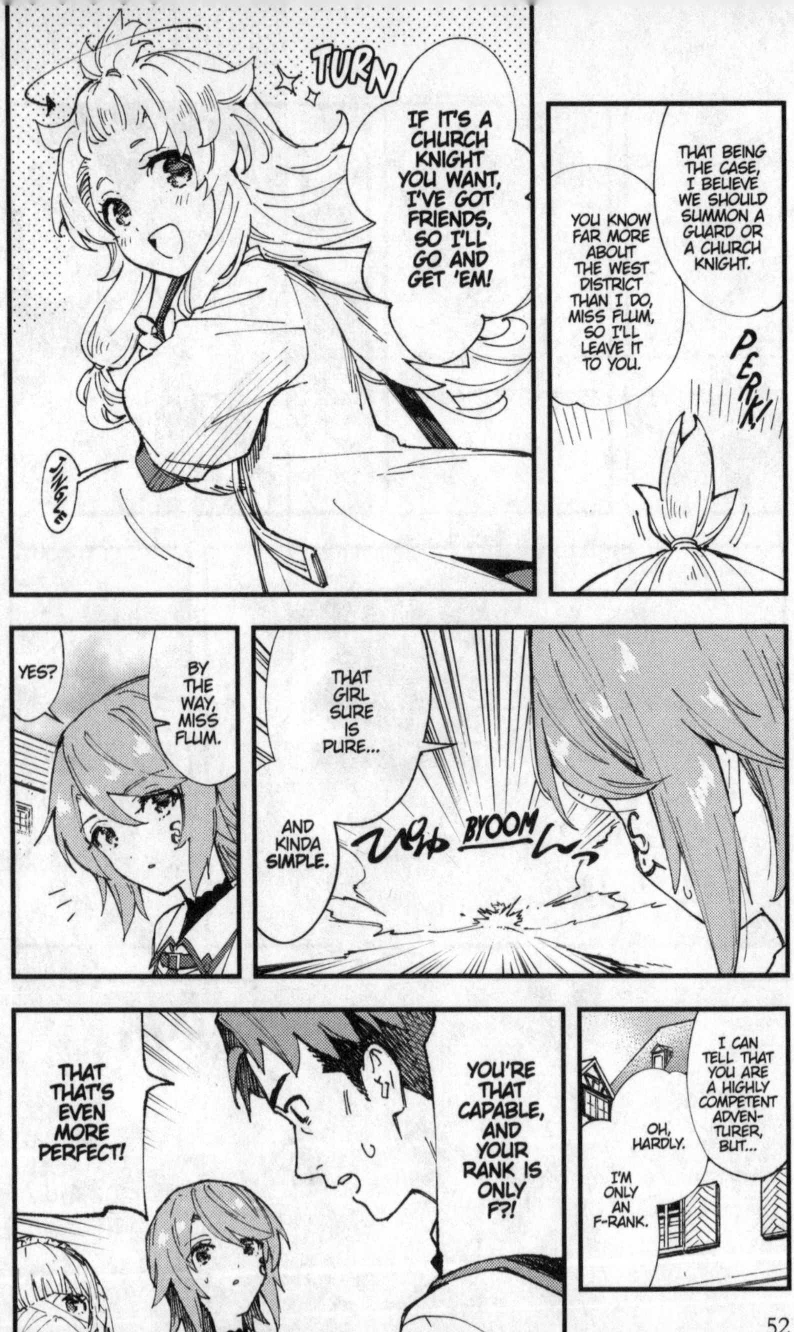
THAT BEING THE CASE, I BELIEVE WE SHOULD SUMMON A GUARD OR A CHURCH KNIGHT.
YOU KNOW FAR MORE ABOUT THE WEST DISTRICT THAN I DO, MISS FLUM, SO I'LL LEAVE IT TO YOU.
PERK!
TURN
IF IT'S A CHURCH KNIGHT YOU WANT, I'VE GOT FRIENDS, SO I'LL GO AND GET 'EM!
JINGLE
THAT GIRL SURE IS PURE...
AND KINDA SIMPLE.
BYOOM
BY THE WAY, MISS FLUM.
YES?
I CAN TELL THAT YOU ARE A HIGHLY COMPETENT ADVEN-TURER, BUT...
OH, HARDLY.
I'M ONLY AN F-RANK.
YOU'RE THAT CAPABLE, AND YOUR RANK IS ONLY F?!
THAT THAT'S EVEN MORE PERFECT!

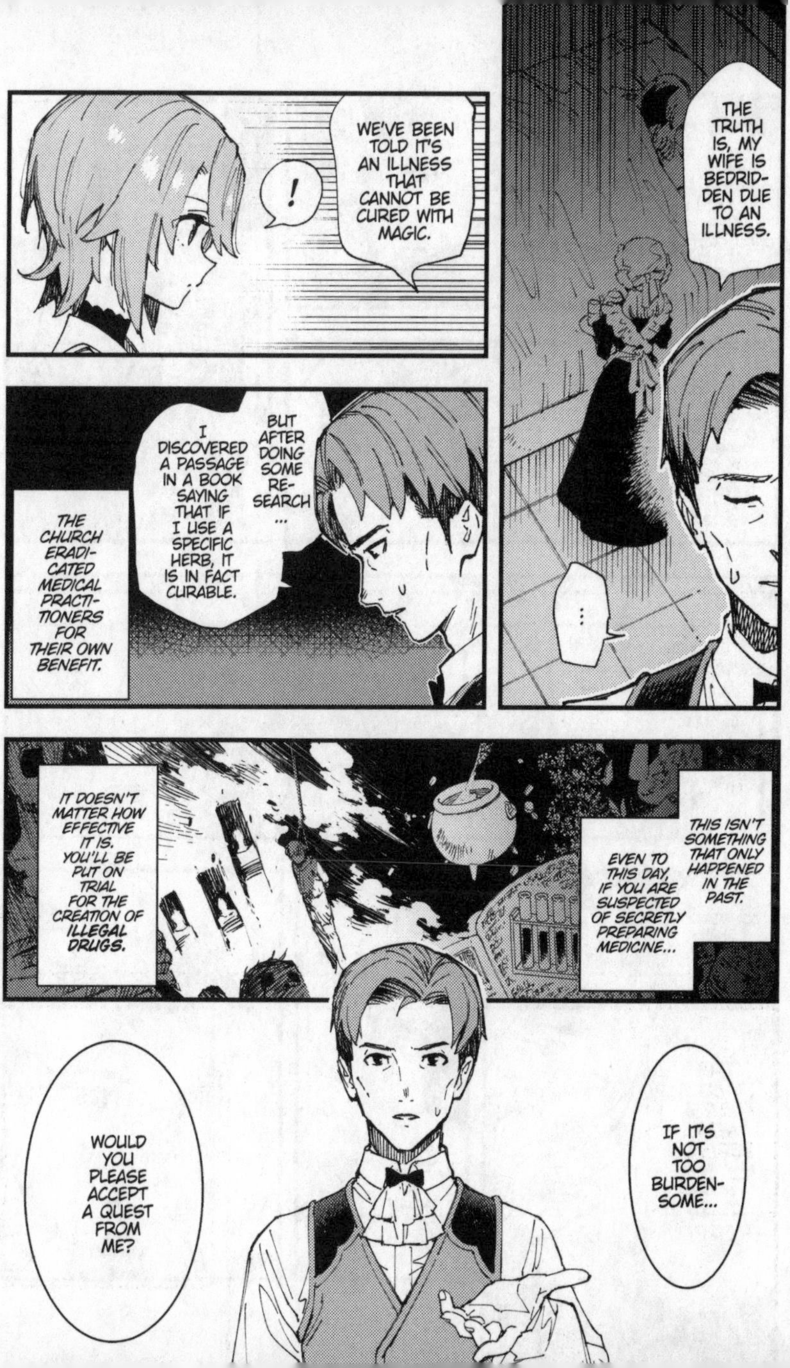
THE TRUTH IS, MY WIFE IS BEDRIDDEN DUE TO AN ILLNESS.
...
WE'VE BEEN TOLD IT'S AN ILLNESS THAT CANNOT BE CURED WITH MAGIC.
!
BUT AFTER DOING SOME RESEARCH...
I DISCOVERED A PASSAGE IN A BOOK SAYING THAT IF I USE A SPECIFIC HERB, IT IS IN FACT CURABLE.
THE CHURCH ERADICATED MEDICAL PRACTITIONERS FOR THEIR OWN BENEFIT.
THIS ISN'T SOMETHING THAT ONLY HAPPENED IN THE PAST.
EVEN TO THIS DAY, IF YOU ARE SUSPECTED OF SECRETLY PREPARING MEDICINE...
IT DOESN'T MATTER HOW EFFECTIVE IT IS. YOU'LL BE PUT ON TRIAL FOR THE CREATION OF ILLEGAL DRUGS.
IF IT'S NOT TOO BURDENSOME...
WOULD YOU PLEASE ACCEPT A QUEST FROM ME?

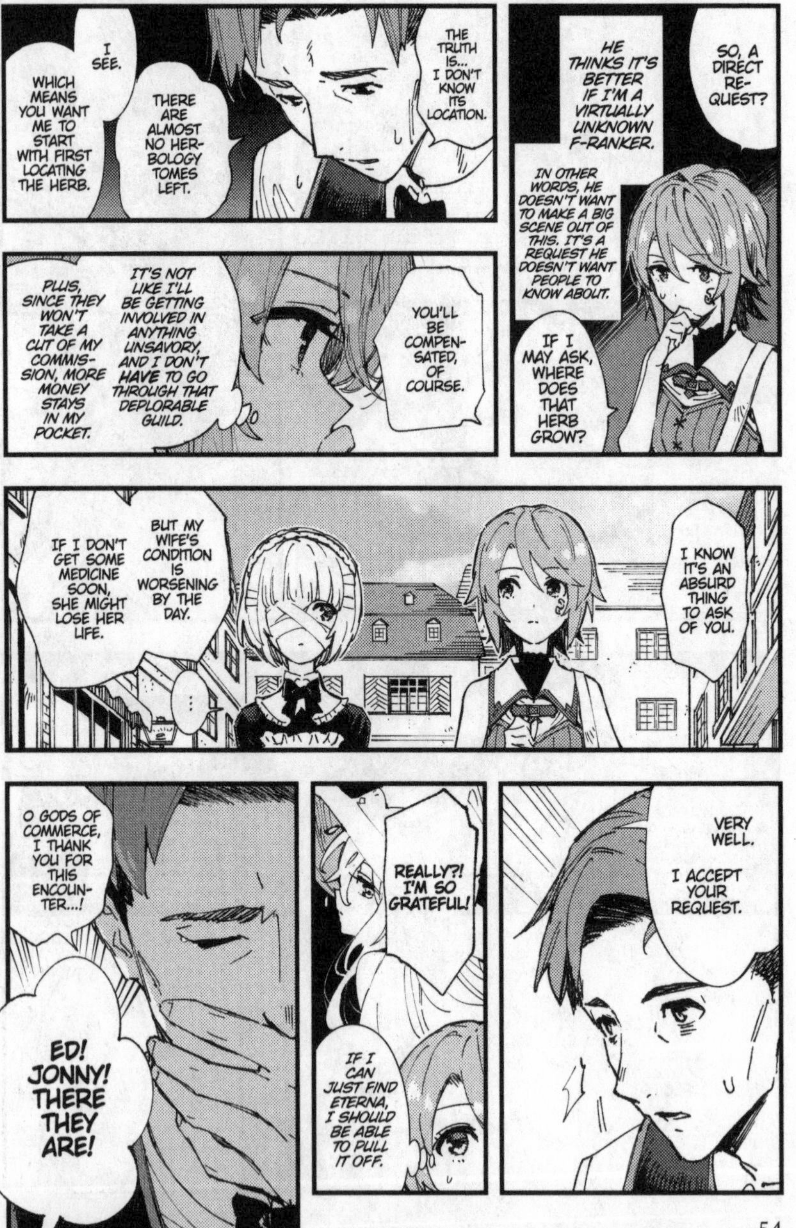
SO, A DIRECT RE-QUEST?
HE THINKS IT'S BETTER IF I'M A VIRTUALLY UNKNOWN F-RANKER.
IN OTHER WORDS, HE DOESN'T WANT TO MAKE A BIG SCENE OUT OF THIS. IT'S A REQUEST HE DOESN'T WANT PEOPLE TO KNOW ABOUT.
IF I MAY ASK, WHERE DOES THAT HERB GROW?
THE TRUTH IS... I DON'T KNOW ITS LOCATION.
THERE ARE ALMOST NO HER-BOLOGY TOMES LEFT.
I SEE.
WHICH MEANS YOU WANT ME TO START WITH FIRST LOCATING THE HERB.
YOU'LL BE COMPEN-SATED, OF COURSE.
IT'S NOT LIKE I'LL BE GETTING INVOLVED IN ANYTHING UNSAVORY, AND I DON'T HAVE TO GO THROUGH THAT DEPLORABLE GUILD.
PLUS, SINCE THEY WON'T TAKE A CUT OF MY COMMIS-SION, MORE MONEY STAYS IN MY POCKET.
I KNOW IT'S AN ABSURD THING TO ASK OF YOU.
BUT MY WIFE'S CONDITION IS WORSENING BY THE DAY.
IF I DON'T GET SOME MEDICINE SOON, SHE MIGHT LOSE HER LIFE.
...
VERY WELL.
I ACCEPT YOUR REQUEST.
REALLY?! I'M SO GRATEFUL!
IF I CAN JUST FIND ETERNA, I SHOULD BE ABLE TO PULL IT OFF.
O GODS OF COMMERCE, I THANK YOU FOR THIS ENCOUN-TER...!
ED! JONNY! THERE THEY ARE!

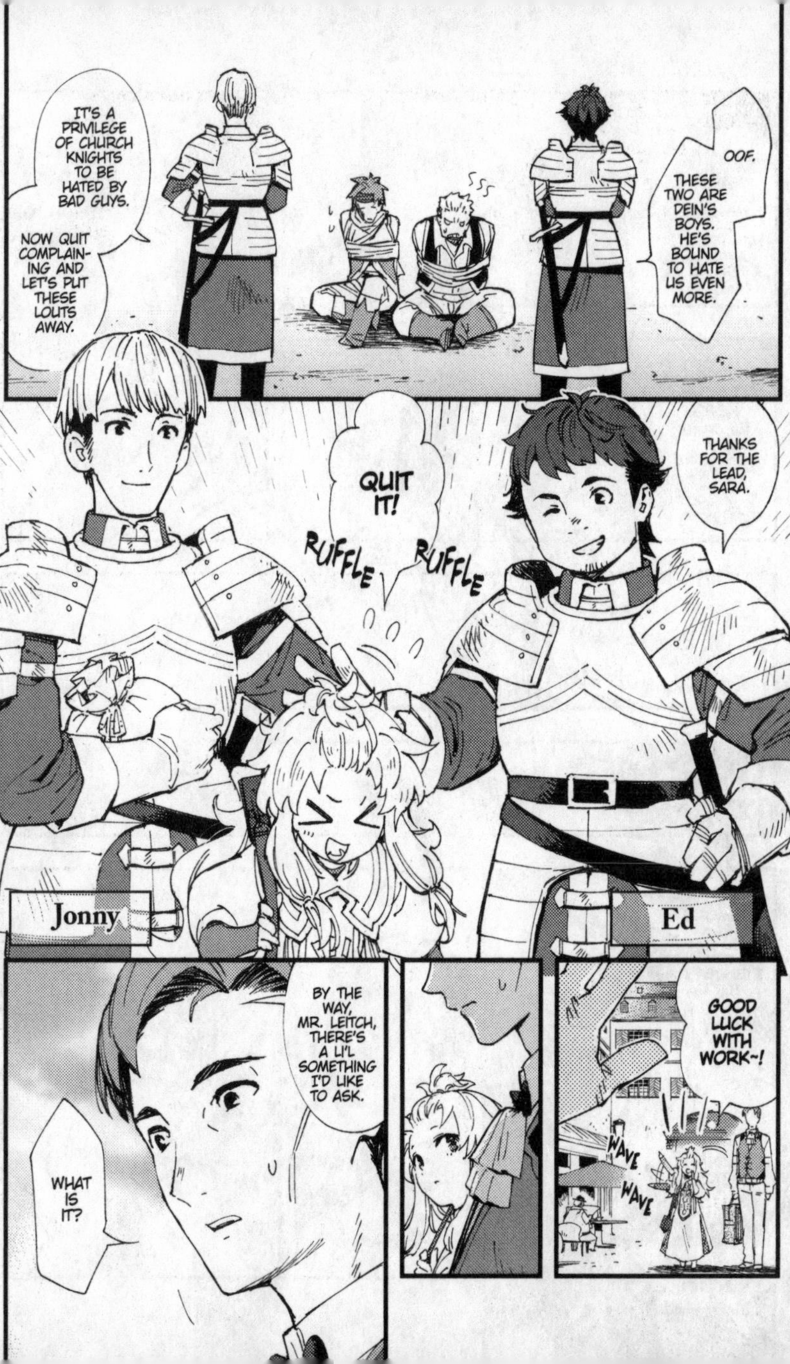
OOF.
THESE TWO ARE DEIN'S BOYS. HE'S BOUND TO HATE US EVEN MORE.
IT'S A PRIVILEGE OF CHURCH KNIGHTS TO BE HATED BY BAD GUYS.
NOW QUIT COMPLAINING AND LET'S PUT THESE LOUTS AWAY.
THANKS FOR THE LEAD, SARA.
RUFFLE RUFFLE
QUIT IT!
Ed
Jonny
GOOD LUCK WITH WORK~!
WAVE WAVE
BY THE WAY, MR. LEITCH, THERE'S A LI'L SOMETHING I'D LIKE TO ASK.
WHAT IS IT?

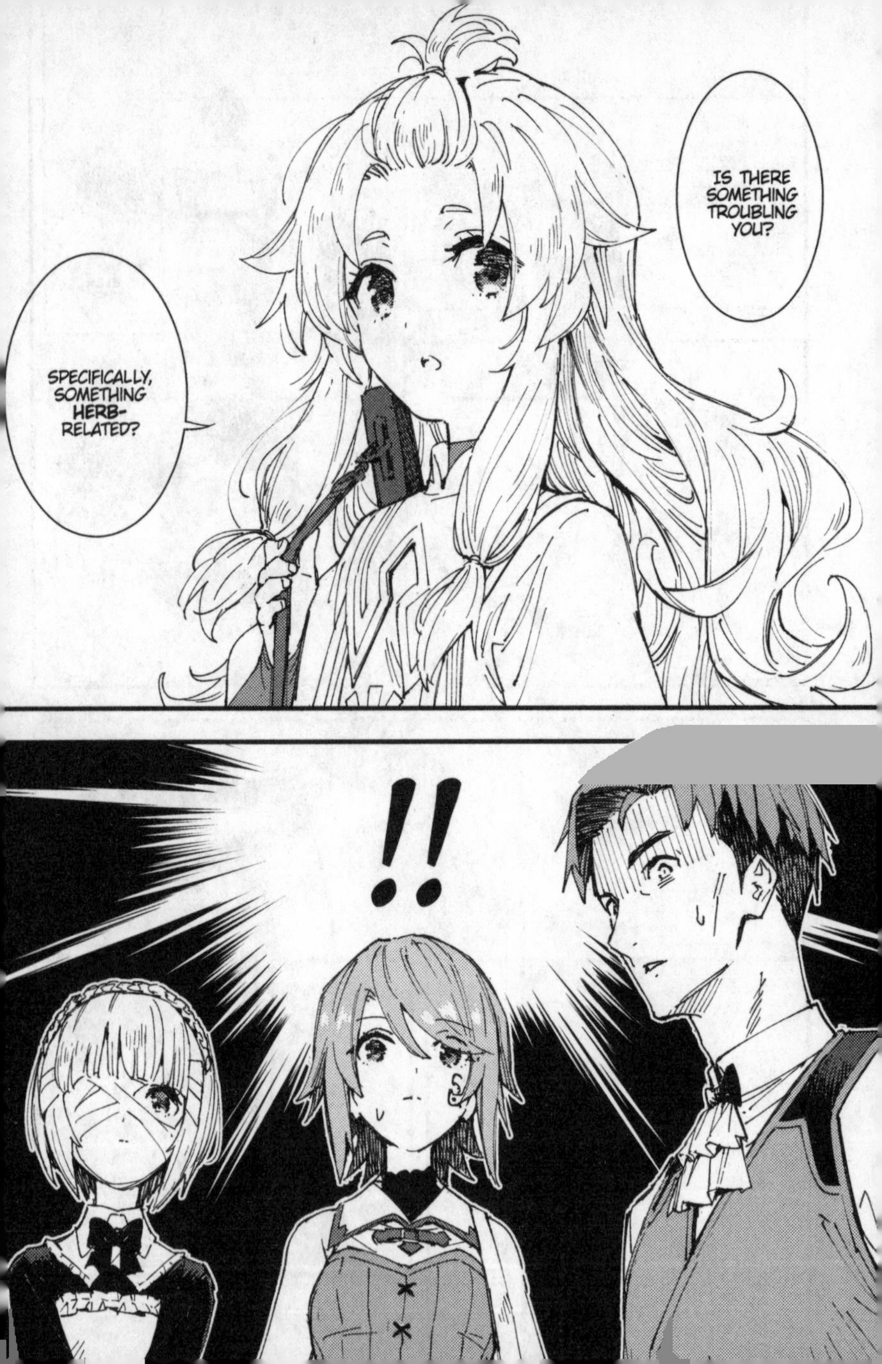
IS THERE SOMETHING TROUBLING YOU?
SPECIFICALLY, SOMETHING HERB-RELATED?
!!

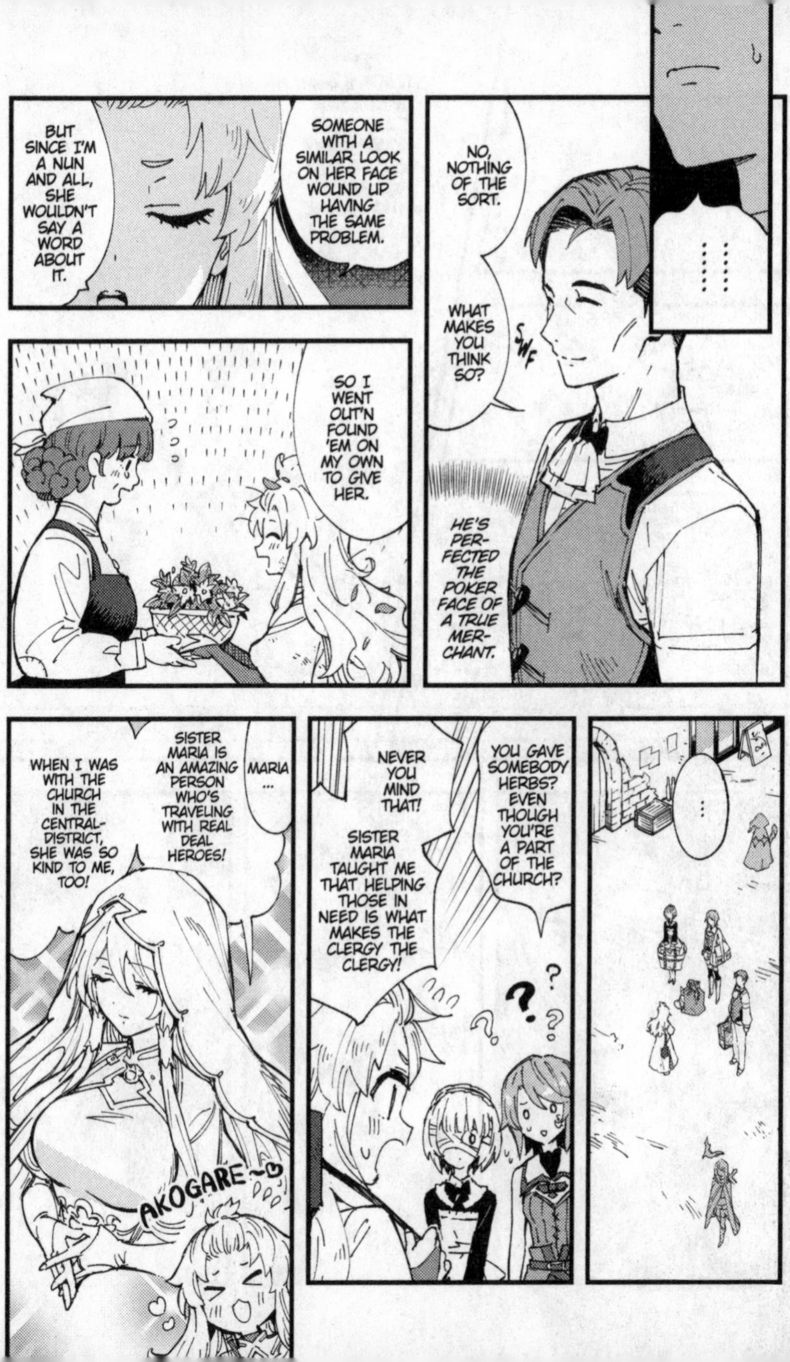
......
NO, NOTHING OF THE SORT.
WHAT MAKES YOU THINK SO?
SWF
HE'S PERFECTED THE POKER FACE OF A TRUE MERCHANT.
SOMEONE WITH A SIMILAR LOOK ON HER FACE WOUND UP HAVING THE SAME PROBLEM.
BUT SINCE I'M A NUN AND ALL, SHE WOULDN'T SAY A WORD ABOUT IT.
SO I WENT OUT'N FOUND 'EM ON MY OWN TO GIVE HER.
...
YOU GAVE SOMEBODY HERBS? EVEN THOUGH YOU'RE A PART OF THE CHURCH?
NEVER YOU MIND THAT!
SISTER MARIA TAUGHT ME THAT HELPING THOSE IN NEED IS WHAT MAKES THE CLERGY THE CLERGY!
MARIA...
SISTER MARIA IS AN AMAZING PERSON WHO'S TRAVELING WITH REAL DEAL HEROES!
WHEN I WAS WITH THE CHURCH IN THE CENTRAL-DISTRICT, SHE WAS SO KIND TO ME, TOO!
AKOGARE~♡

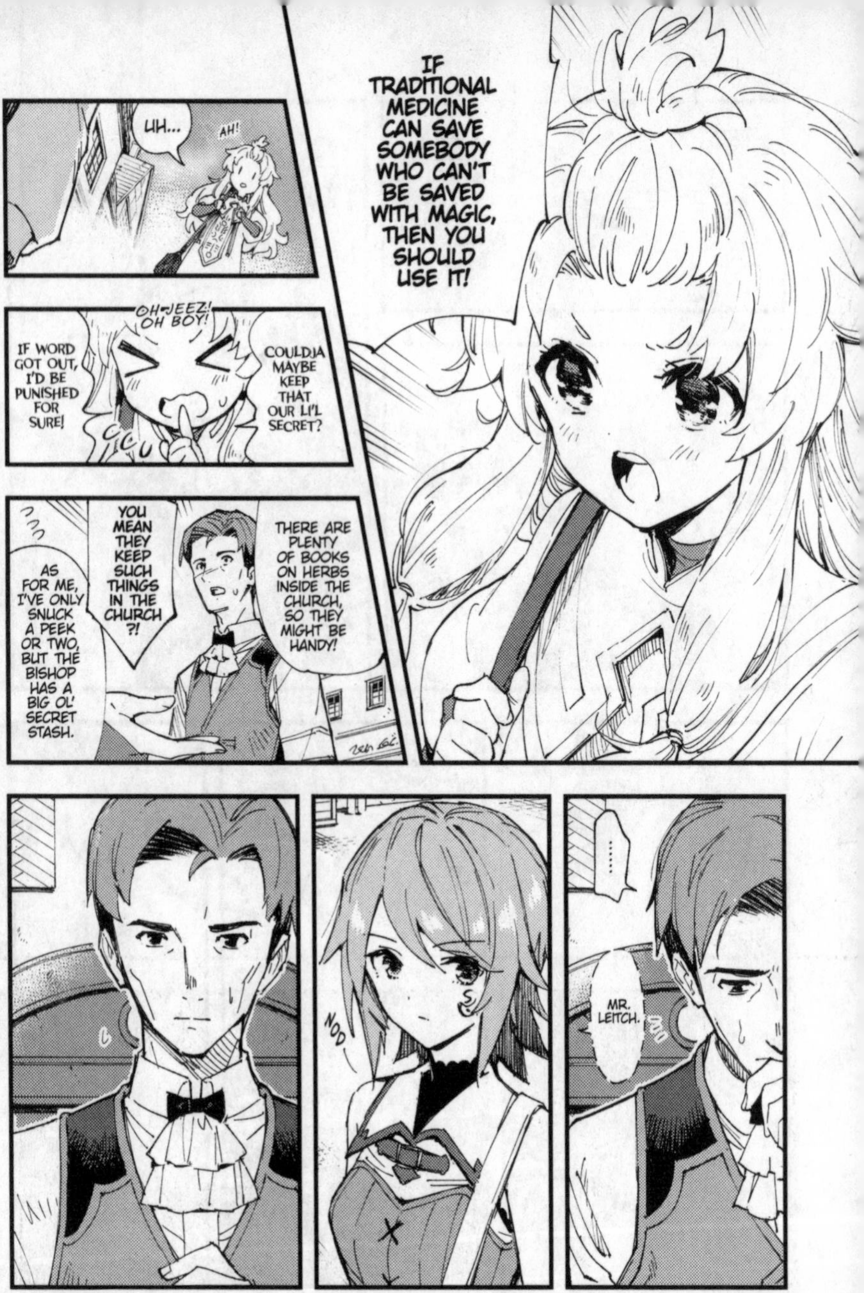
IF TRADITIONAL MEDICINE CAN SAVE SOMEBODY WHO CAN'T BE SAVED WITH MAGIC, THEN YOU SHOULD USE IT!
UH...
AH!
OH-JEEZ! OH BOY!
COULDJA MAYBE KEEP THAT OUR LI'L SECRET?
IF WORD GOT OUT, I'D BE PUNISHED FOR SURE!
THERE ARE PLENTY OF BOOKS ON HERBS INSIDE THE CHURCH, SO THEY MIGHT BE HANDY!
YOU MEAN THEY KEEP SUCH THINGS IN THE CHURCH ?!
AS FOR ME, I'VE ONLY SNUCK A PEEK OR TWO, BUT THE BISHOP HAS A BIG OL' SECRET STASH.
......
MR. LEITCH.
NOD

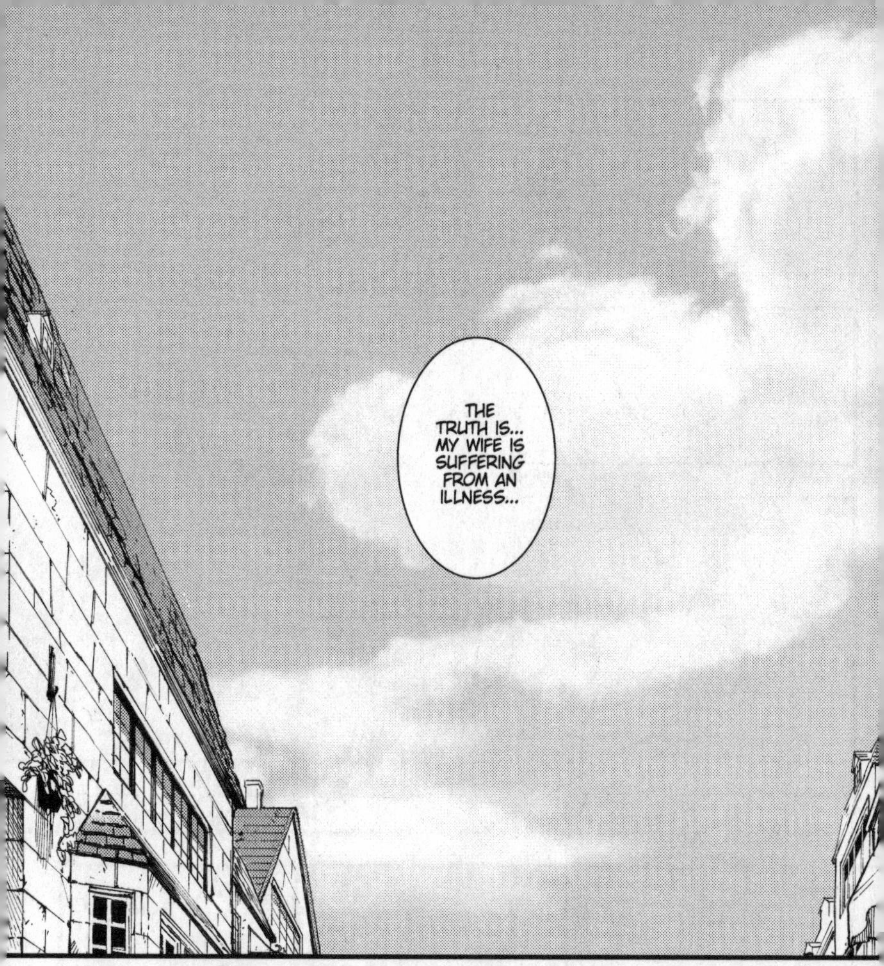
THE TRUTH IS... MY WIFE IS SUFFERING FROM AN ILLNESS...
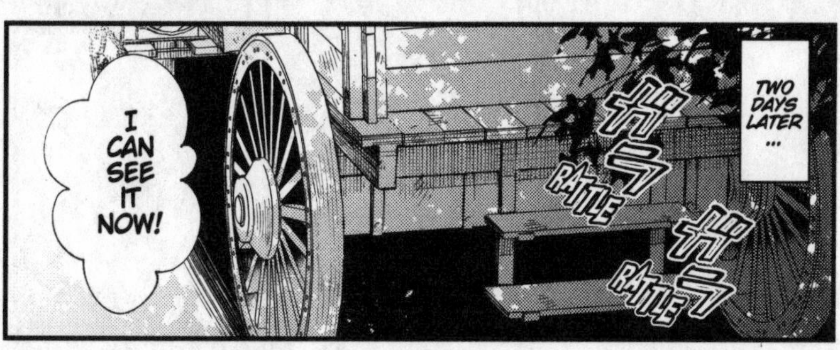
TWO DAYS LATER ...
RATTLE
RATTLE
I CAN SEE IT NOW!

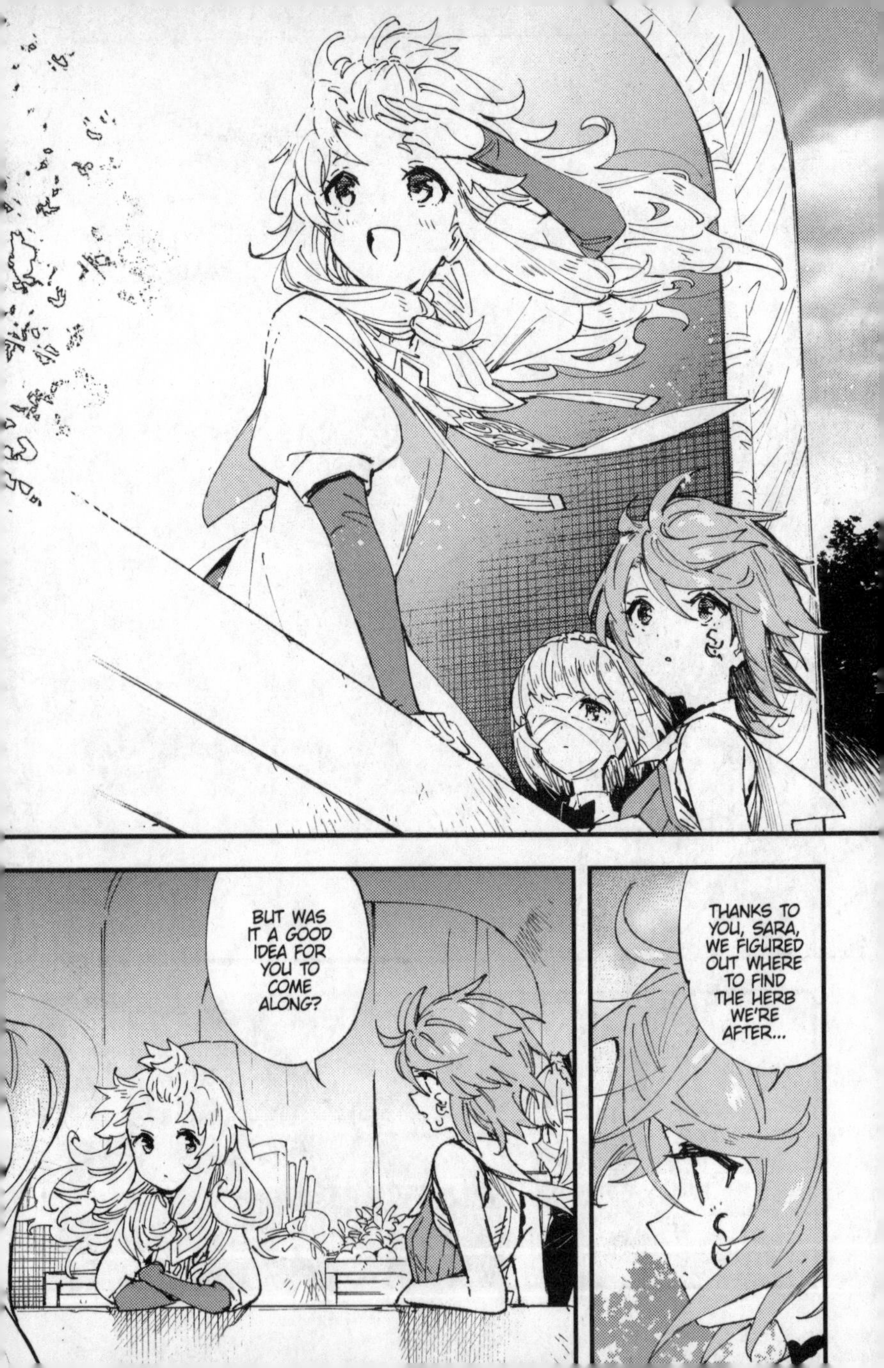
THANKS TO YOU, SARA, WE FIGURED OUT WHERE TO FIND THE HERB WE'RE AFTER...
BUT WAS IT A GOOD IDEA FOR YOU TO COME ALONG?

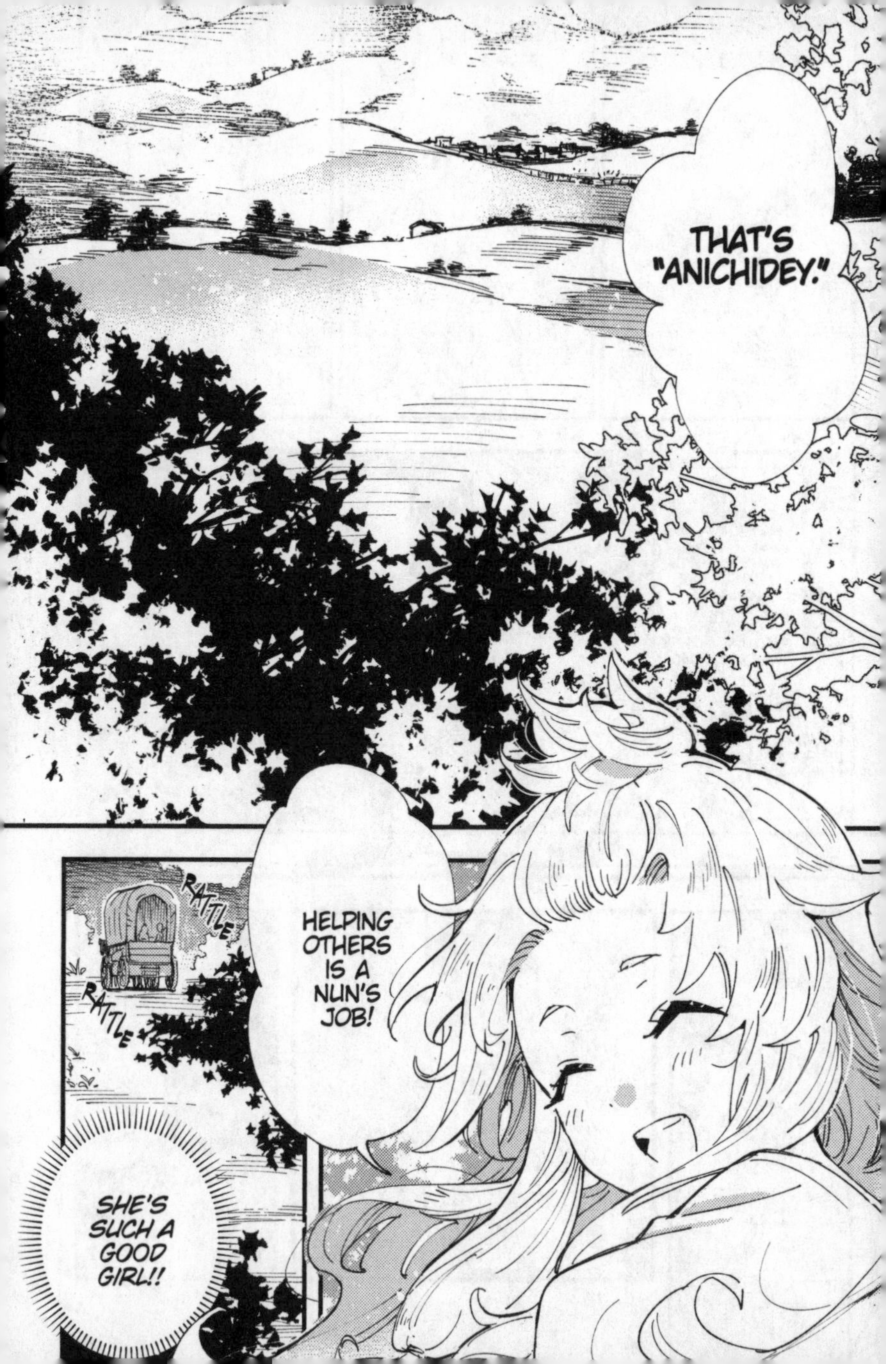
THAT'S "ANICHIDEY."
HELPING OTHERS IS A NUN'S JOB!
RATTLE
RATTLE
SHE'S SUCH A GOOD GIRL!!

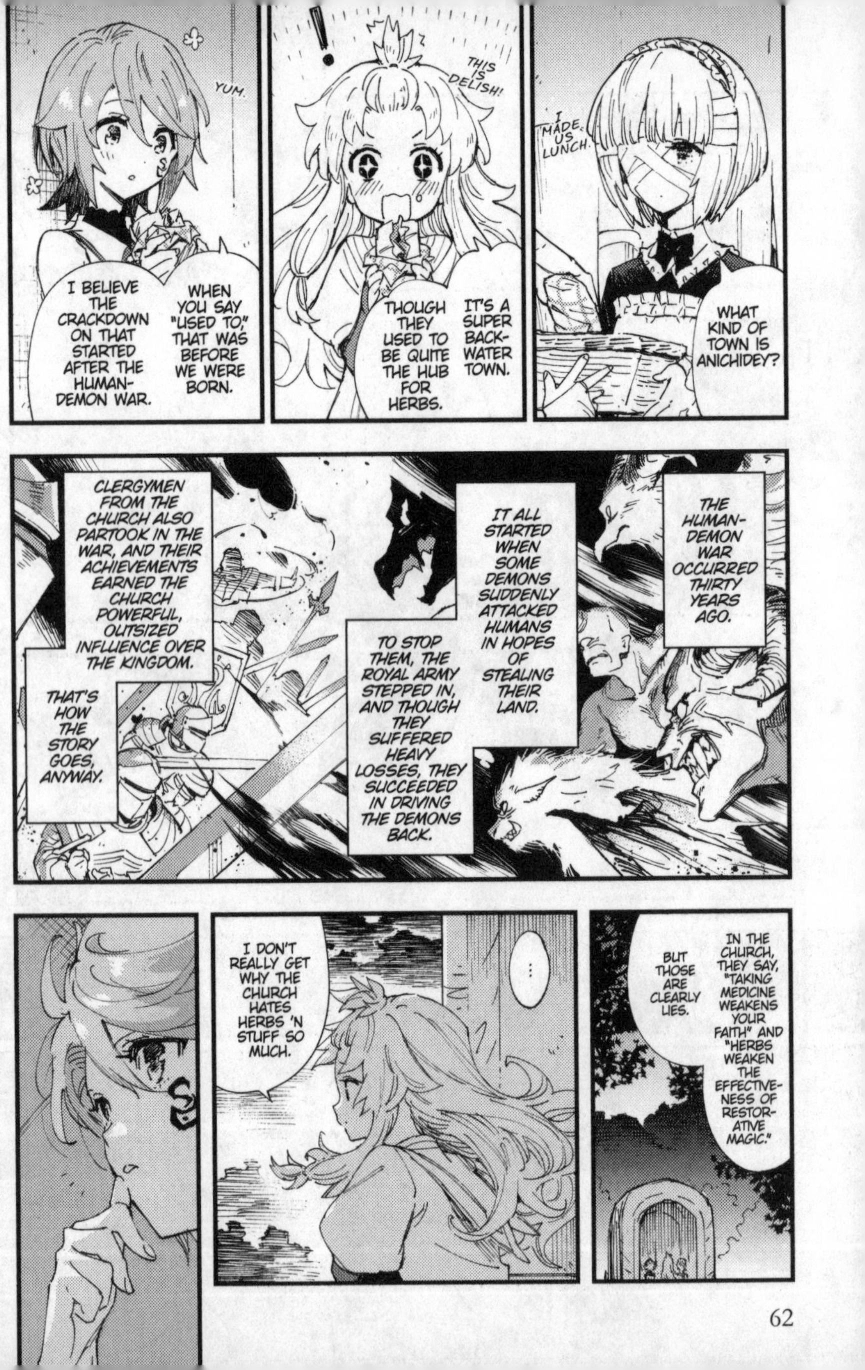
I MADE US LUNCH.
WHAT KIND OF TOWN IS ANICHIDEY?
THIS IS DELISH!
IT'S A SUPER BACKWATER TOWN.
THOUGH THEY USED TO BE QUITE THE HUB FOR HERBS.
YUM.
WHEN YOU SAY "USED TO," THAT WAS BEFORE WE WERE BORN.
I BELIEVE THE CRACKDOWN ON THAT STARTED AFTER THE HUMAN-DEMON WAR.
THE HUMAN-DEMON WAR OCCURRED THIRTY YEARS AGO.
IT ALL STARTED WHEN SOME DEMONS SUDDENLY ATTACKED HUMANS IN HOPES OF STEALING THEIR LAND.
TO STOP THEM, THE ROYAL ARMY STEPPED IN, AND THOUGH THEY SUFFERED HEAVY LOSSES, THEY SUCCEEDED IN DRIVING THE DEMONS BACK.
CLERGYMEN FROM THE CHURCH ALSO PARTOOK IN THE WAR, AND THEIR ACHIEVEMENTS EARNED THE CHURCH POWERFUL, OUTSIZED INFLUENCE OVER THE KINGDOM.
THAT'S HOW THE STORY GOES, ANYWAY.
IN THE CHURCH, THEY SAY, "TAKING MEDICINE WEAKENS YOUR FAITH" AND "HERBS WEAKEN THE EFFECTIVENESS OF RESTORATIVE MAGIC."
BUT THOSE ARE CLEARLY LIES.
...
I DON'T REALLY GET WHY THE CHURCH HATES HERBS 'N STUFF SO MUCH.

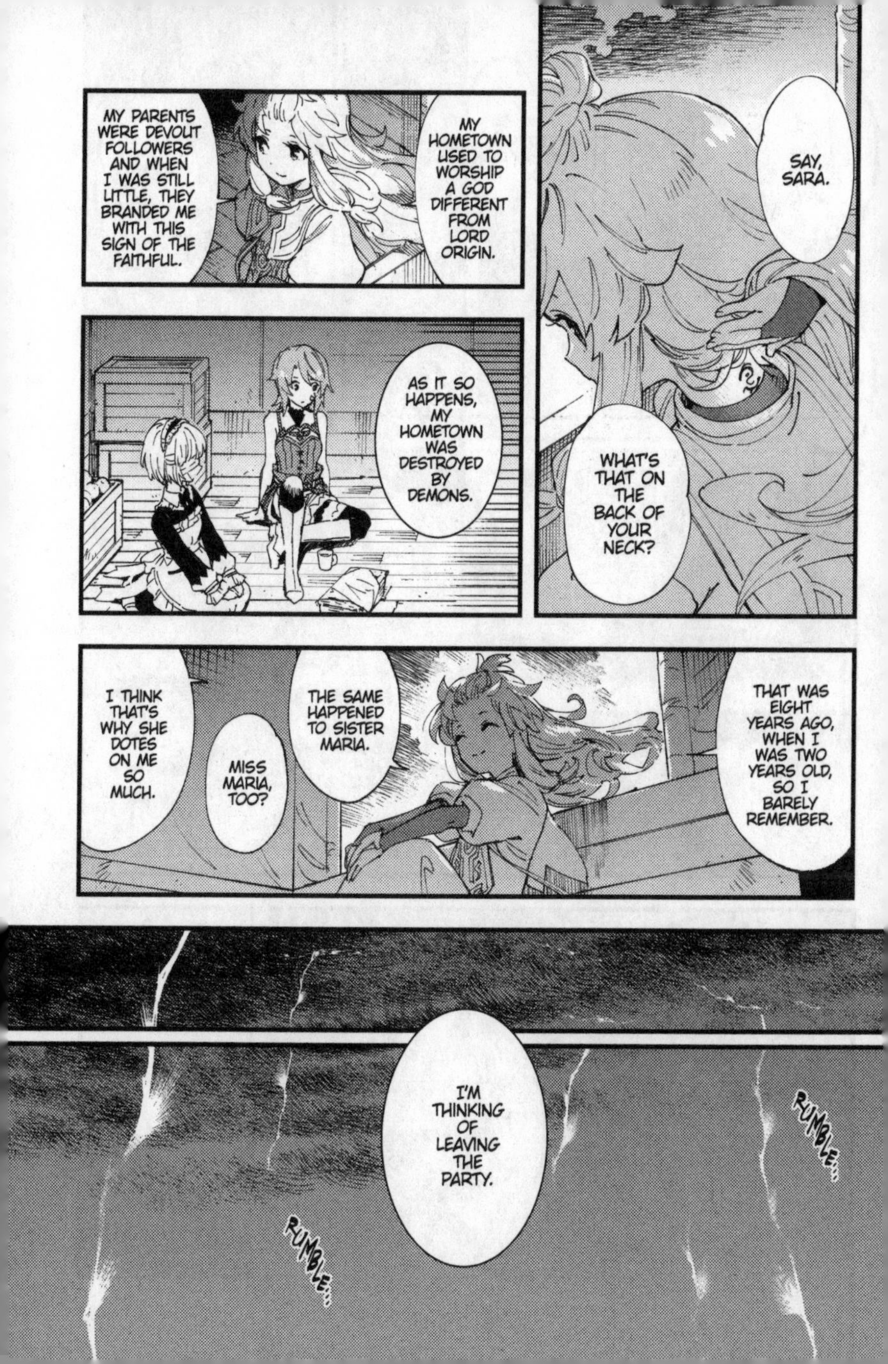
SAY, SARA.
WHAT'S THAT ON THE BACK OF YOUR NECK?
MY HOMETOWN USED TO WORSHIP A GOD DIFFERENT FROM LORD ORIGIN.
MY PARENTS WERE DEVOUT FOLLOWERS AND WHEN I WAS STILL LITTLE, THEY BRANDED ME WITH THIS SIGN OF THE FAITHFUL.
AS IT SO HAPPENS, MY HOMETOWN WAS DESTROYED BY DEMONS.
THAT WAS EIGHT YEARS AGO, WHEN I WAS TWO YEARS OLD, SO I BARELY REMEMBER.
THE SAME HAPPENED TO SISTER MARIA.
MISS MARIA, TOO?
I THINK THAT'S WHY SHE DOTES ON ME SO MUCH.
RUMBLE...
I'M THINKING OF LEAVING THE PARTY.
RUMBLE...

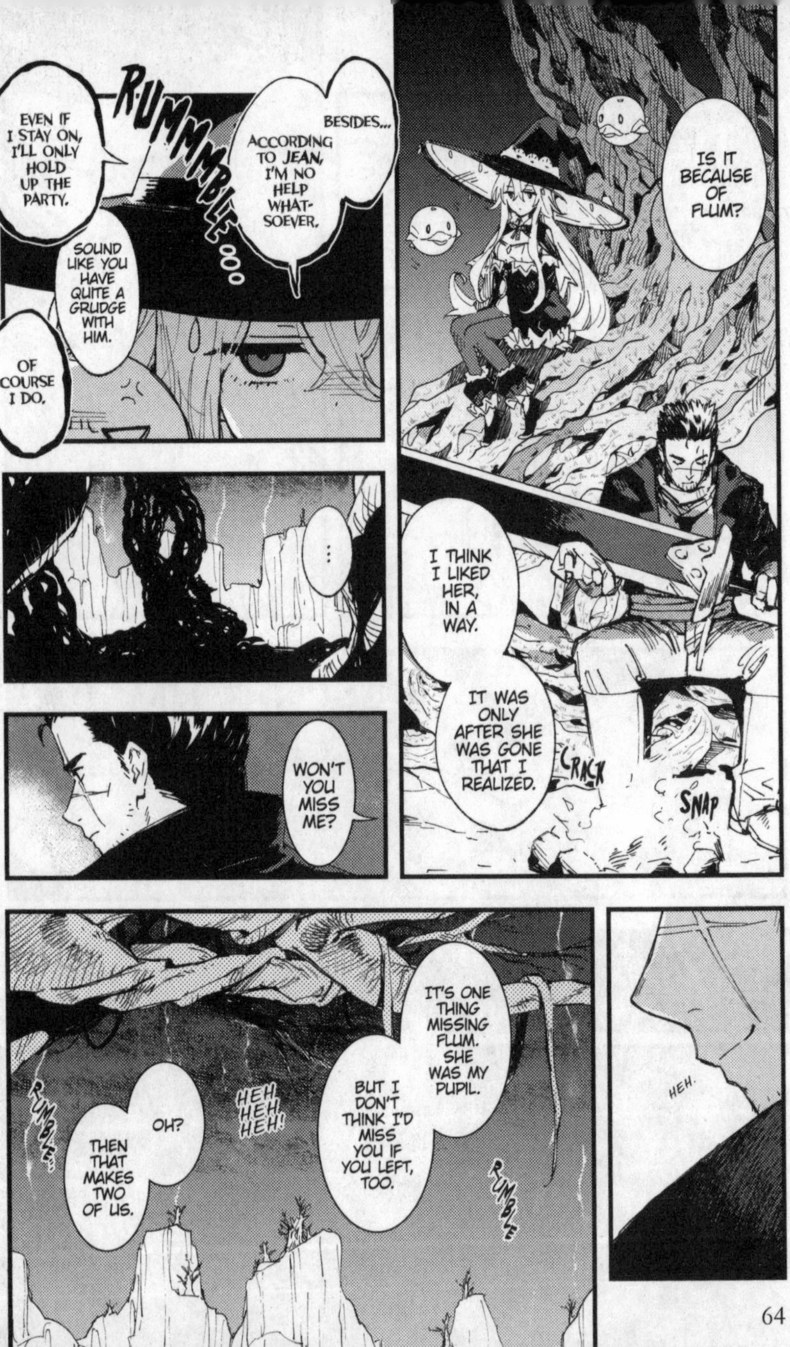

IS IT BECAUSE OF FLUM?
I THINK I LIKED HER, IN A WAY.
IT WAS ONLY AFTER SHE WAS GONE THAT I REALIZED.
CRACK
SNAP
BESIDES... ACCORDING TO JEAN, I'M NO HELP WHATSOEVER.
RUMMMBLE ooo
EVEN IF I STAY ON, I'LL ONLY HOLD UP THE PARTY.
SOUND LIKE YOU HAVE QUITE A GRUDGE WITH HIM.
OF COURSE I DO.
...
WON'T YOU MISS ME?
HEH.
IT'S ONE THING MISSING FLUM. SHE WAS MY PUPIL.
BUT I DON'T THINK I'D MISS YOU IF YOU LEFT, TOO.
RUMBLE
HEH HEH HEH!
OH?
THEN THAT MAKES TWO OF US.
RUMBLE

Chapter 7: The Entrance to Despair

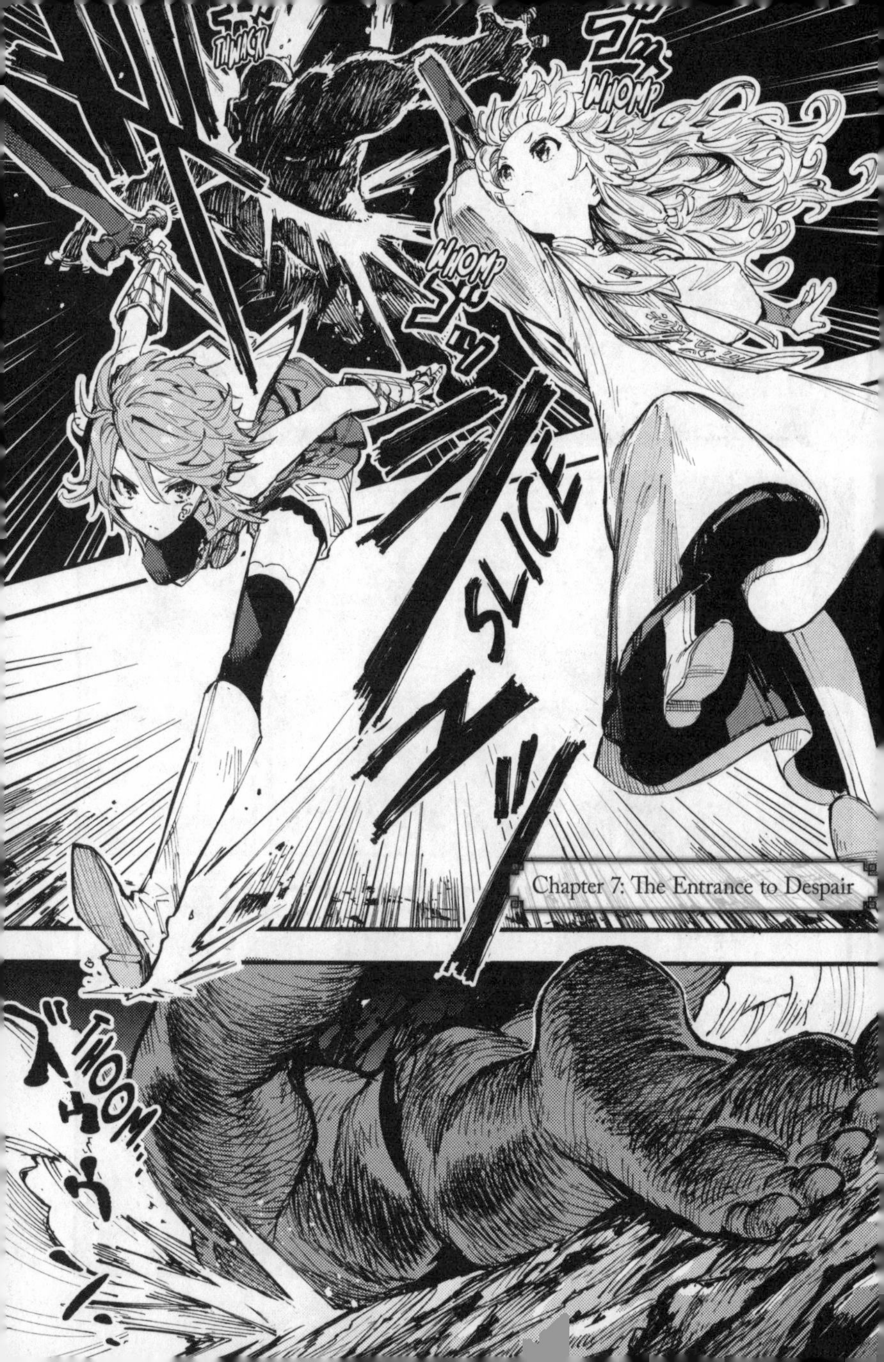
WHOMP
THWACK
WHOMP
SLICE
THOOM

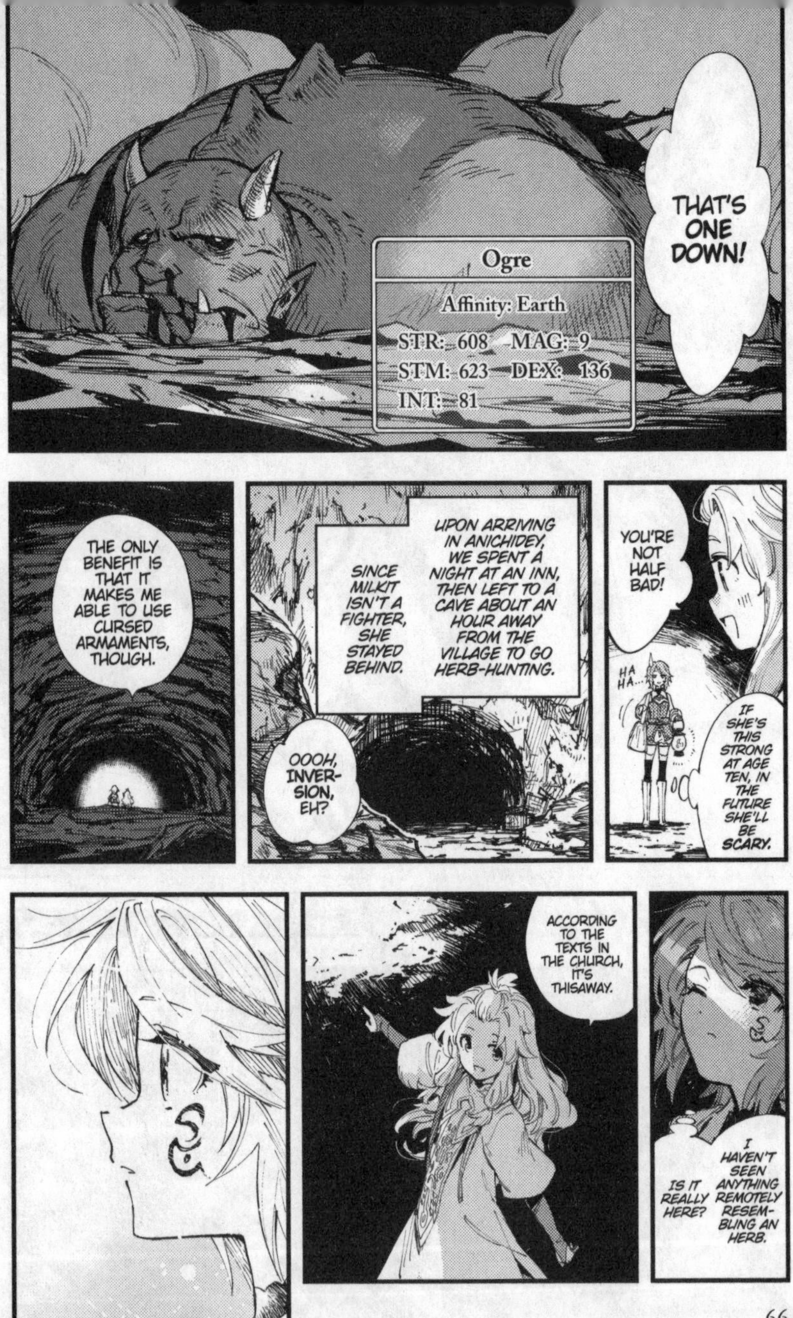
THAT'S ONE DOWN!
Ogre
Affinity: Earth
STR: 608 MAG: 9
STM: 623 DEX: 136
INT: 81
YOU'RE NOT HALF BAD!
HA HA...
IF SHE'S THIS STRONG AT AGE TEN, IN THE FUTURE SHE'LL BE SCARY.
UPON ARRIVING IN ANICHIDEY, WE SPENT A NIGHT AT AN INN, THEN LEFT TO A CAVE ABOUT AN HOUR AWAY FROM THE VILLAGE TO GO HERB-HUNTING.
SINCE MILKIT ISN'T A FIGHTER, SHE STAYED BEHIND.
OOOH, INVERSION, EH?
THE ONLY BENEFIT IS THAT IT MAKES ME ABLE TO USE CURSED ARMAMENTS, THOUGH.
I HAVEN'T SEEN ANYTHING REMOTELY RESEMBLING AN HERB.
IS IT REALLY HERE?
ACCORDING TO THE TEXTS IN THE CHURCH, IT'S THISAWAY.

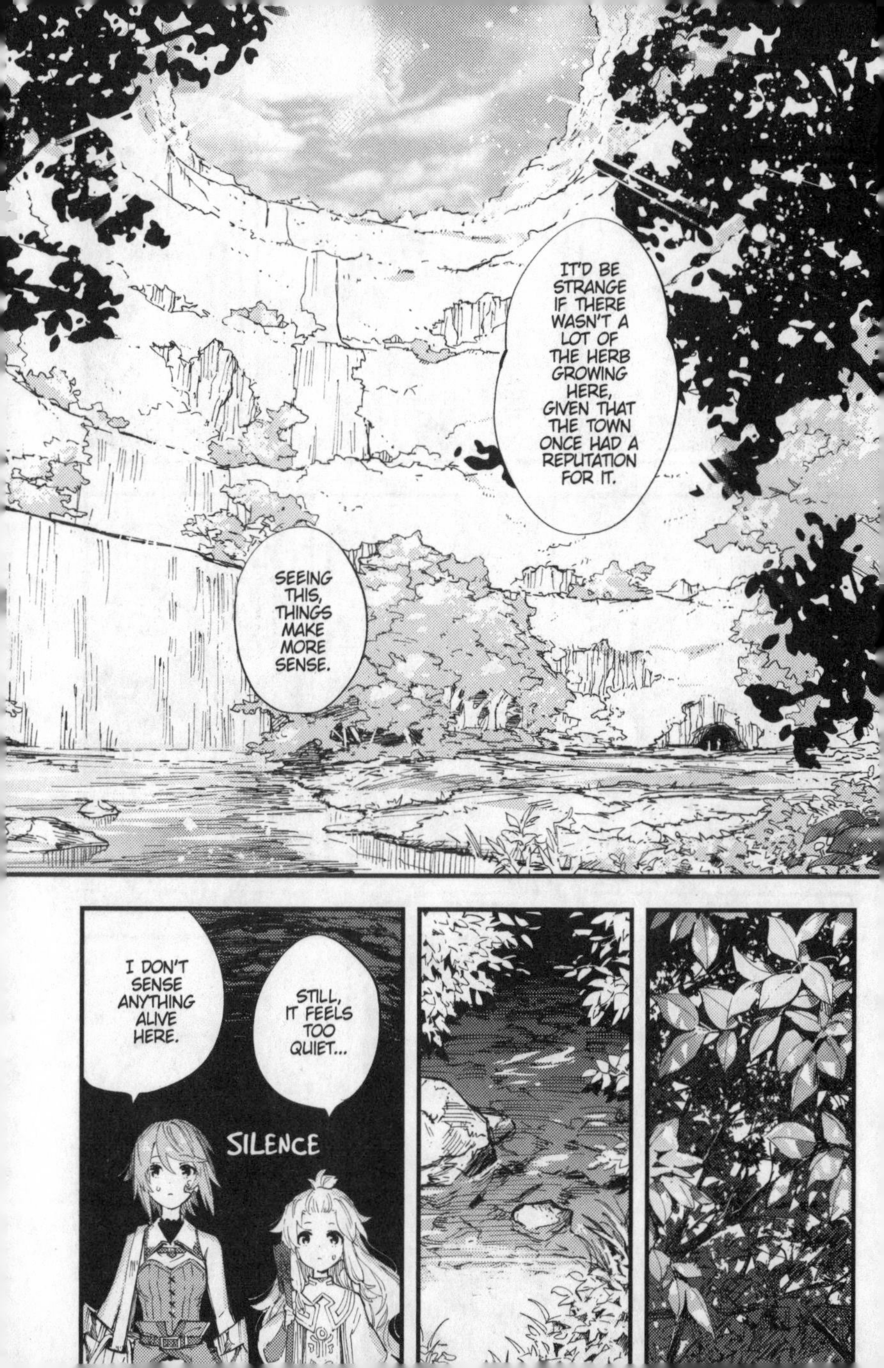
IT'D BE STRANGE IF THERE WASN'T A LOT OF THE HERB GROWING HERE, GIVEN THAT THE TOWN ONCE HAD A REPUTATION FOR IT.
SEEING THIS, THINGS MAKE MORE SENSE.
STILL, IT FEELS TOO QUIET...
I DON'T SENSE ANYTHING ALIVE HERE.
SILENCE

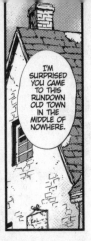

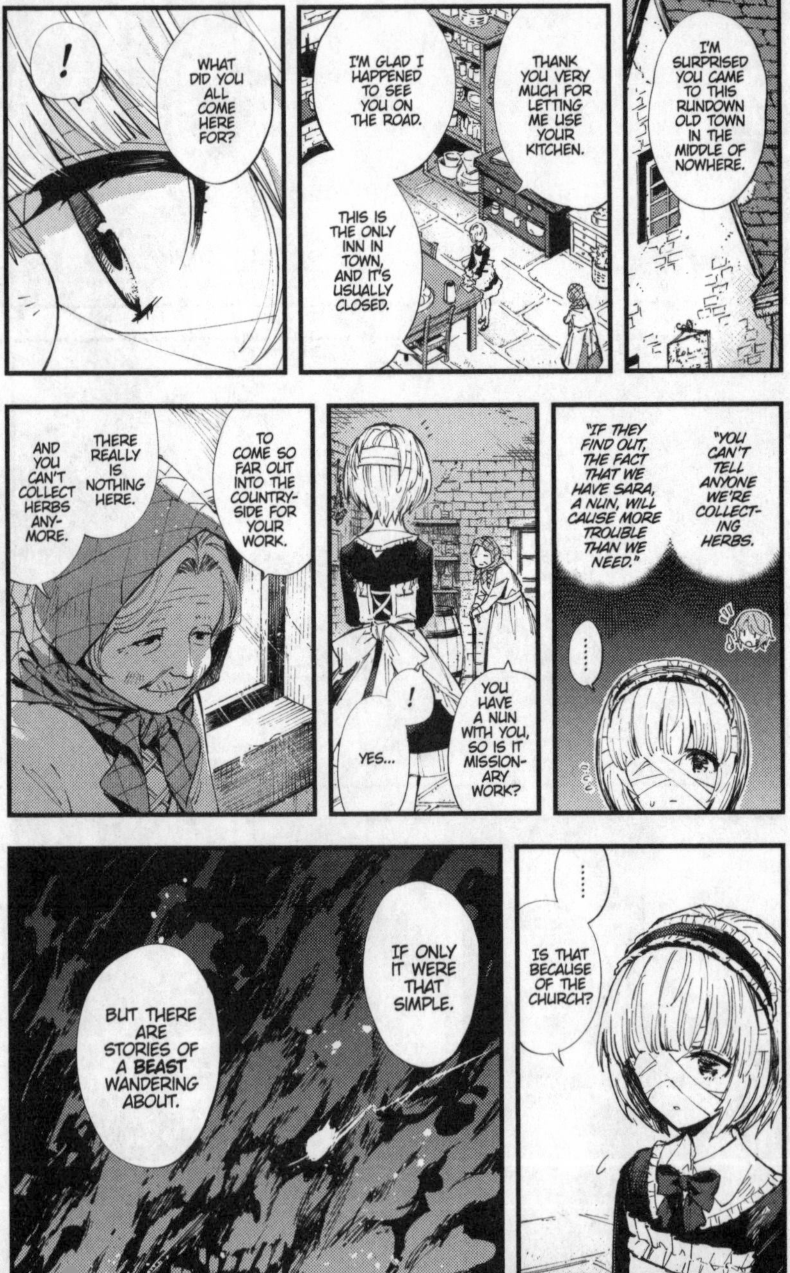
I'M SURPRISED YOU CAME TO THIS RUNDOWN OLD TOWN IN THE MIDDLE OF NOWHERE.
THANK YOU VERY MUCH FOR LETTING ME USE YOUR KITCHEN.
I'M GLAD I HAPPENED TO SEE YOU ON THE ROAD.
THIS IS THE ONLY INN IN TOWN, AND IT'S USUALLY CLOSED.
WHAT DID YOU ALL COME HERE FOR?
!
"YOU CAN'T TELL ANYONE WE'RE COLLECTING HERBS.
"IF THEY FIND OUT, THE FACT THAT WE HAVE SARA, A NUN, WILL CAUSE MORE TROUBLE THAN WE NEED."
......
YOU HAVE A NUN WITH YOU, SO IS IT MISSIONARY WORK?
!
YES...
TO COME SO FAR OUT INTO THE COUNTRYSIDE FOR YOUR WORK.
THERE REALLY IS NOTHING HERE.
AND YOU CAN'T COLLECT HERBS ANYMORE.
......
IS THAT BECAUSE OF THE CHURCH?
IF ONLY IT WERE THAT SIMPLE.
BUT THERE ARE STORIES OF A BEAST WANDERING ABOUT.

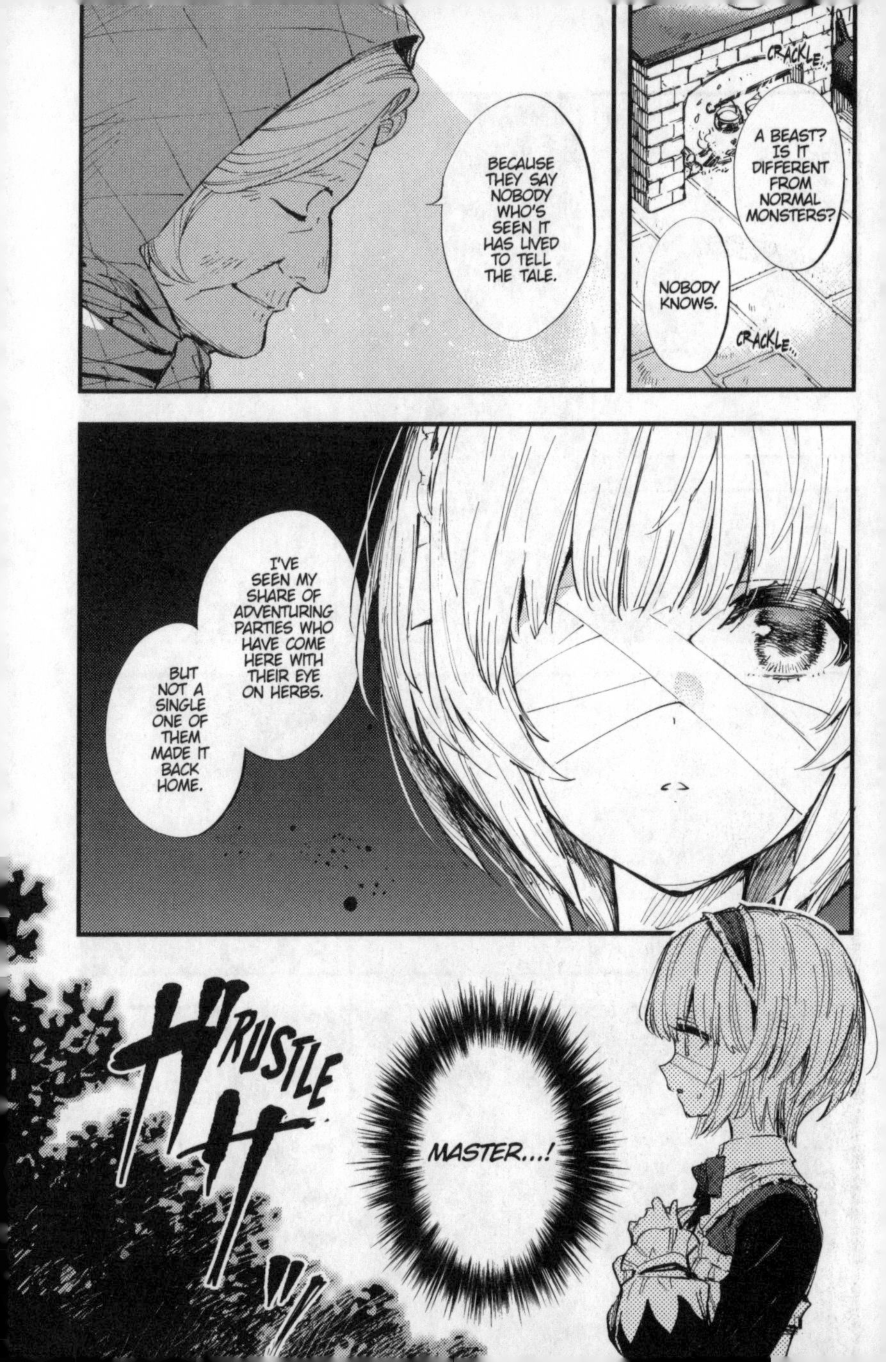
CRACKLE...
A BEAST? IS IT DIFFERENT FROM NORMAL MONSTERS?
NOBODY KNOWS.
CRACKLE...
BECAUSE THEY SAY NOBODY WHO'S SEEN IT HAS LIVED TO TELL THE TALE.
I'VE SEEN MY SHARE OF ADVENTURING PARTIES WHO HAVE COME HERE WITH THEIR EYE ON HERBS.
BUT NOT A SINGLE ONE OF THEM MADE IT BACK HOME.
MASTER...!
RUSTLE

LOOKS LIKE AN OGRE. LET'S TAKE IT DOWN QUICK-LIKE.

CLANK

RUSTLE   RUSTLE

HOLD ON A SECOND.

......

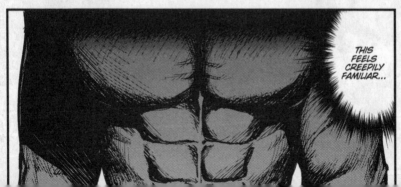

THIS FEELS CREEPILY FAMILIAR...

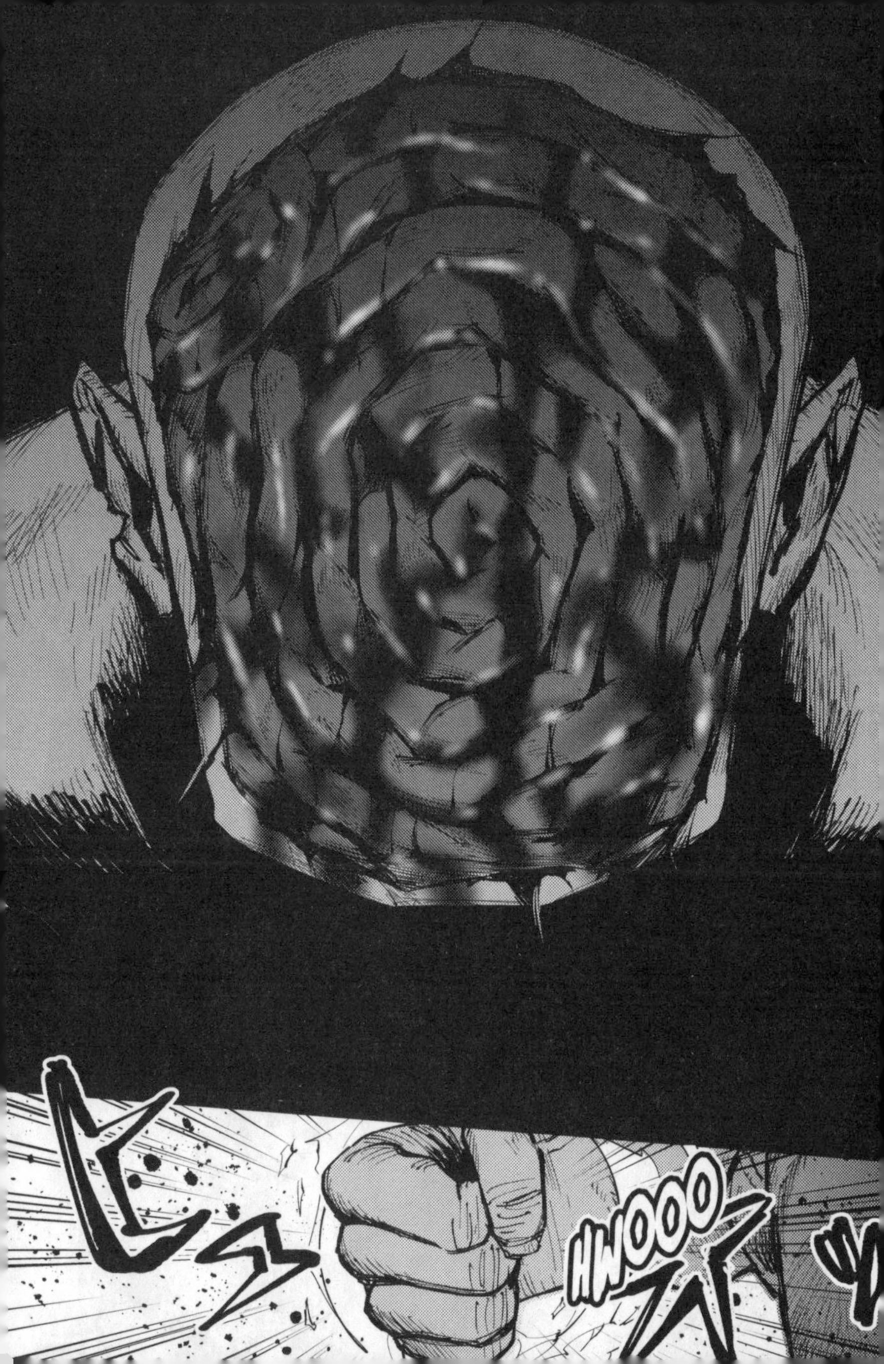
HWOOO

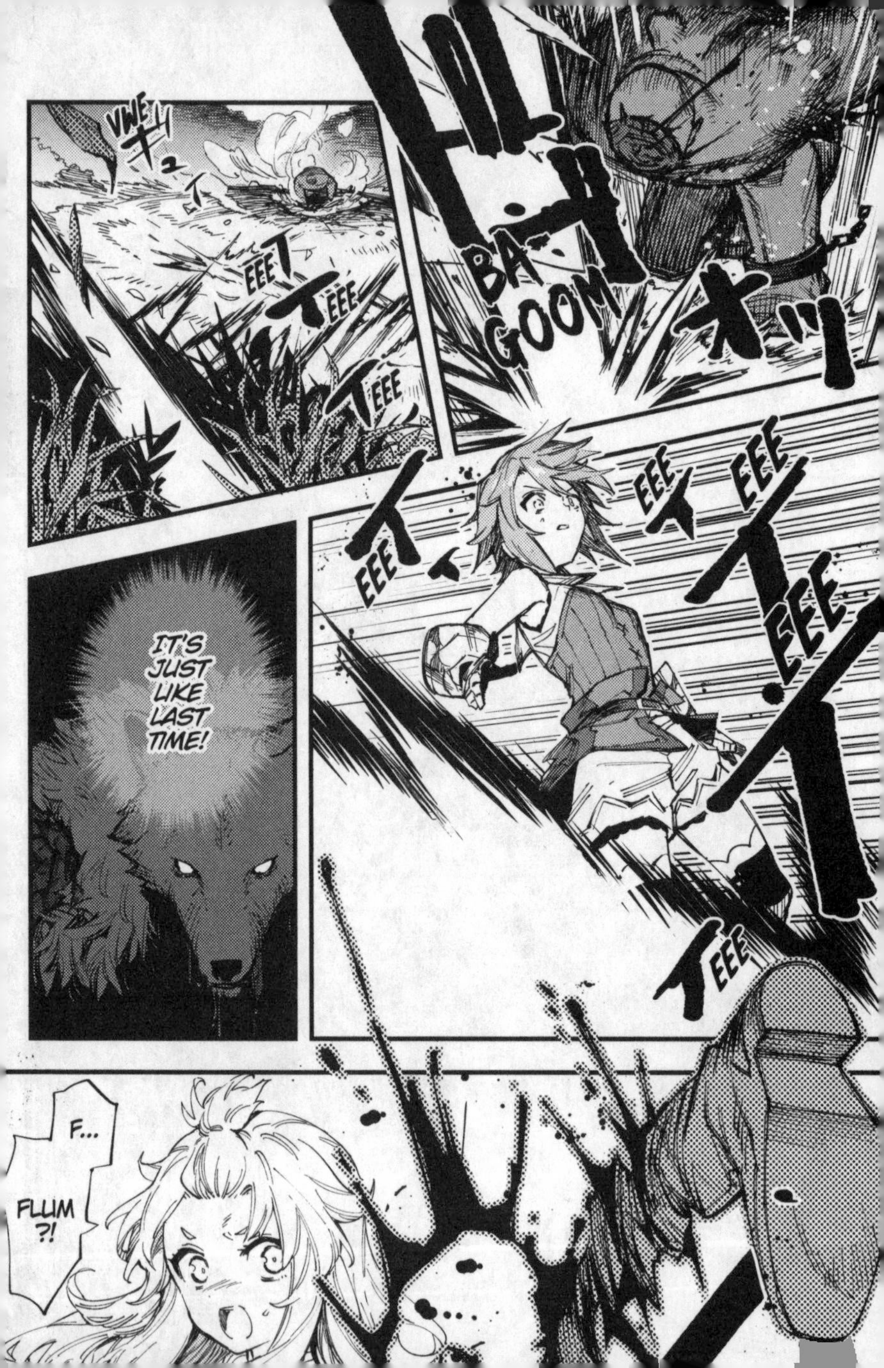
BA-GOOM
VWEE
EEET
TEEE
TEEE
EEE
EEE
EEE
EEE
TEEE
IT'S JUST LIKE LAST TIME!
F...
FLUUM?!

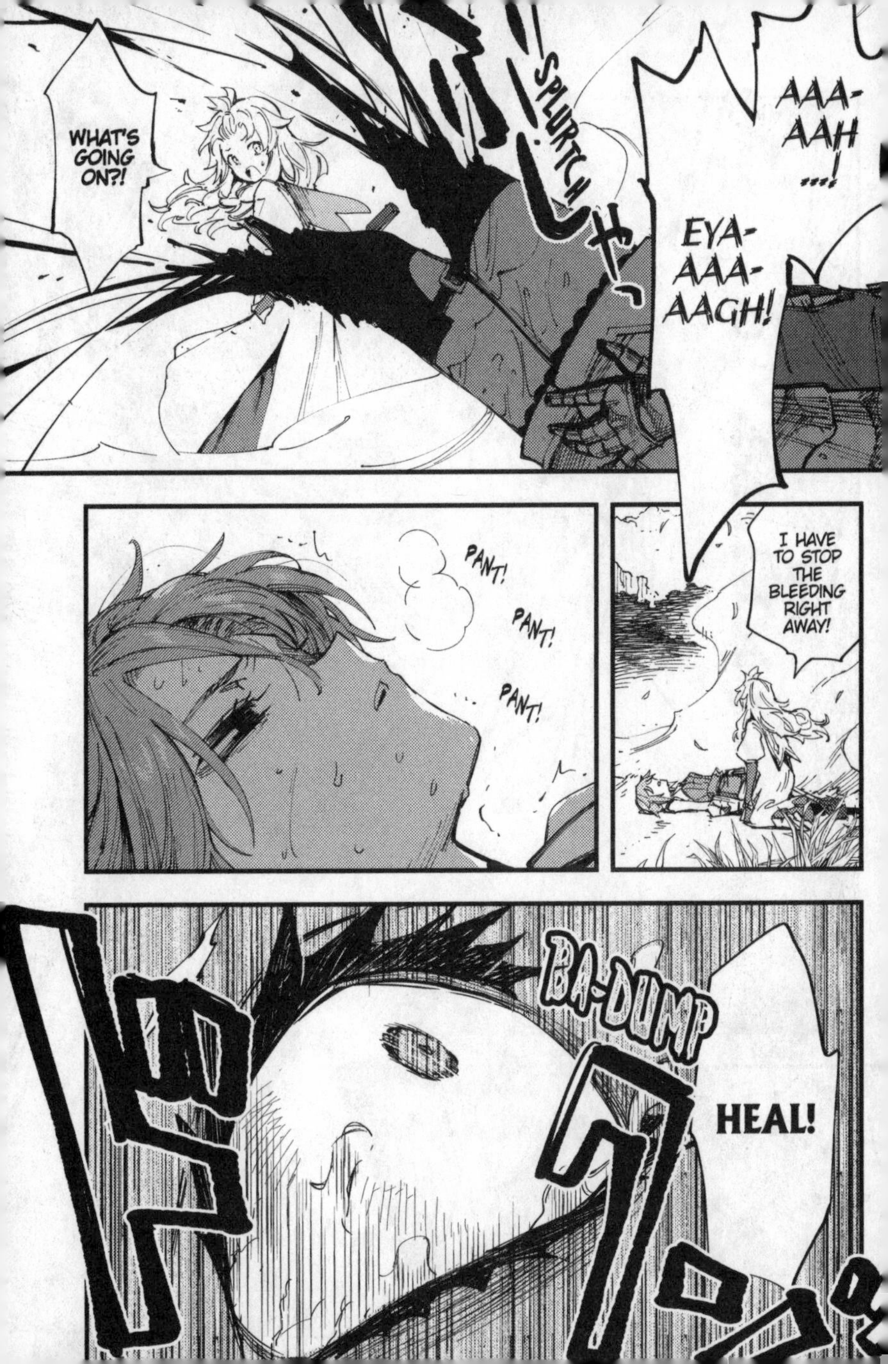
AAA-AAH ...!
EYA-AAA-AAGH!
SPLURTCH!!
WHAT'S GOING ON?!
I HAVE TO STOP THE BLEEDING RIGHT AWAY!
PANT!
PANT!
PANT!
BA-DUMP
HEAL!

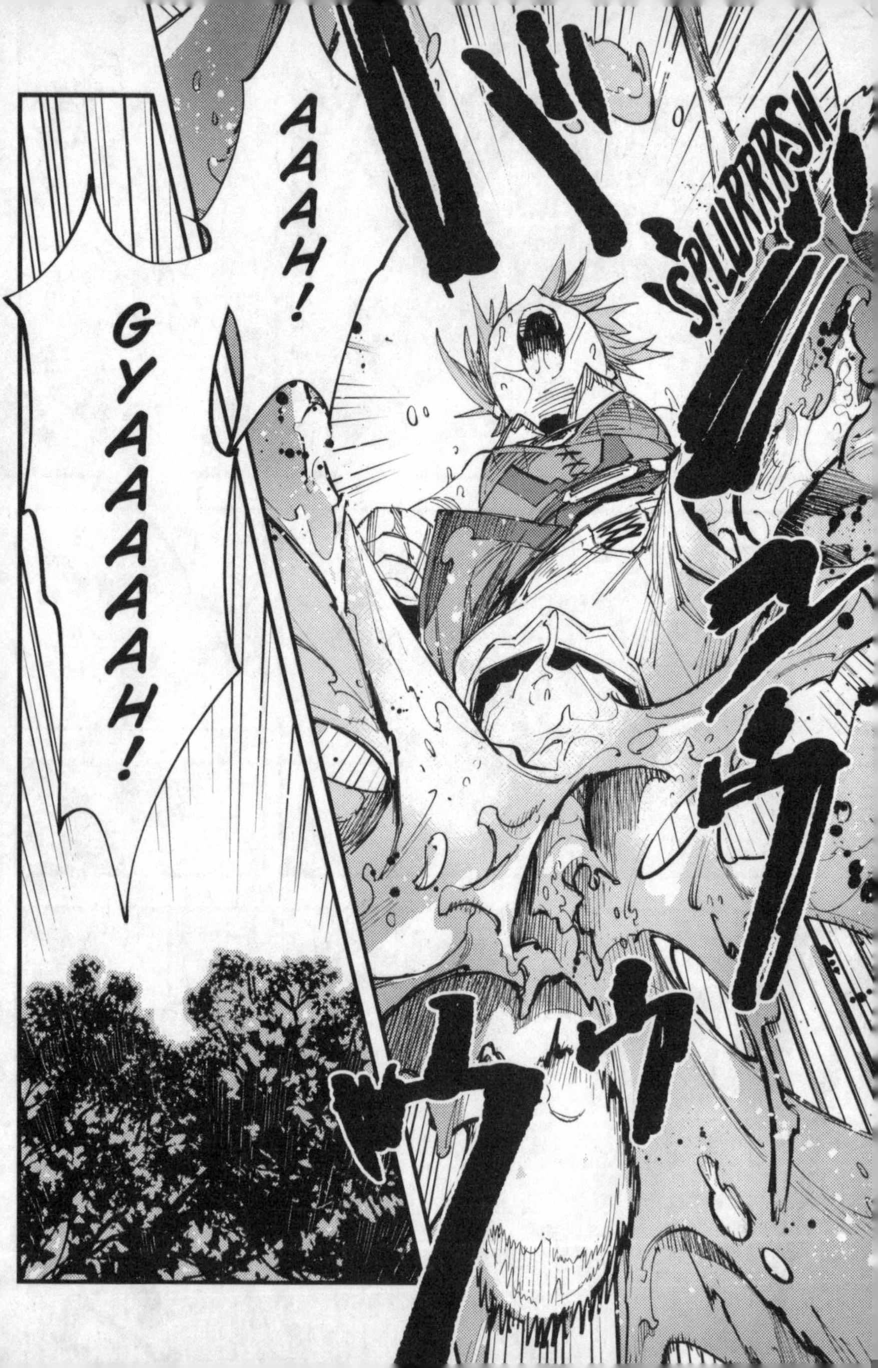
SPLURRRSH
AAAH!
GYAAAAAH!

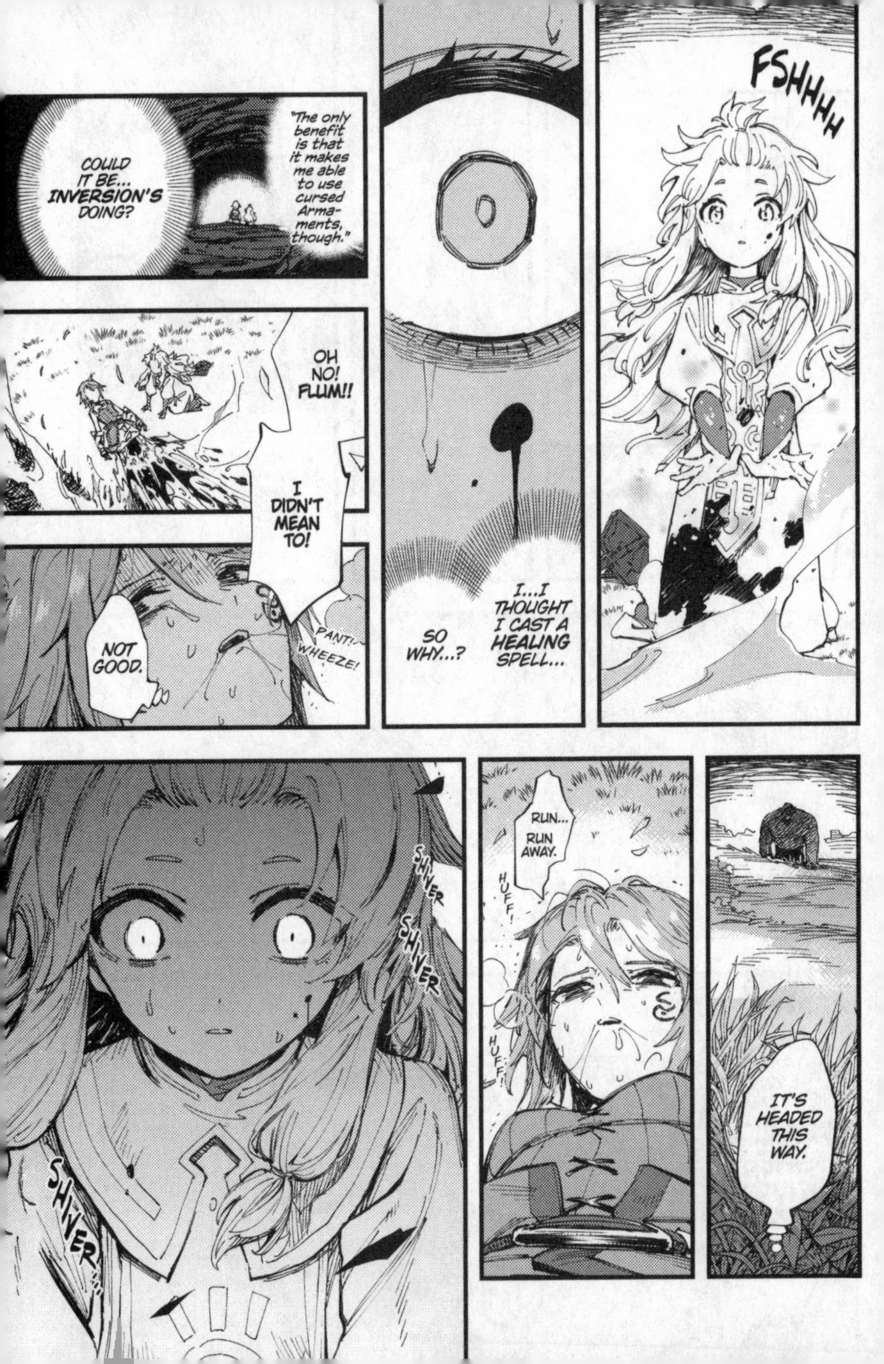
FSHHHH
I...I THOUGHT I CAST A HEALING SPELL...
SO WHY...?
"The only benefit is that it makes me able to use cursed Armaments, though."
COULD IT BE... INVERSION'S DOING?
OH NO! FLUM!!
I DIDN'T MEAN TO!
PANT! WHEEZE!
NOT GOOD.
IT'S HEADED THIS WAY.
RUN... RUN AWAY.
HUFF! HUFF!
SHIVER SHIVER
SHIVER...

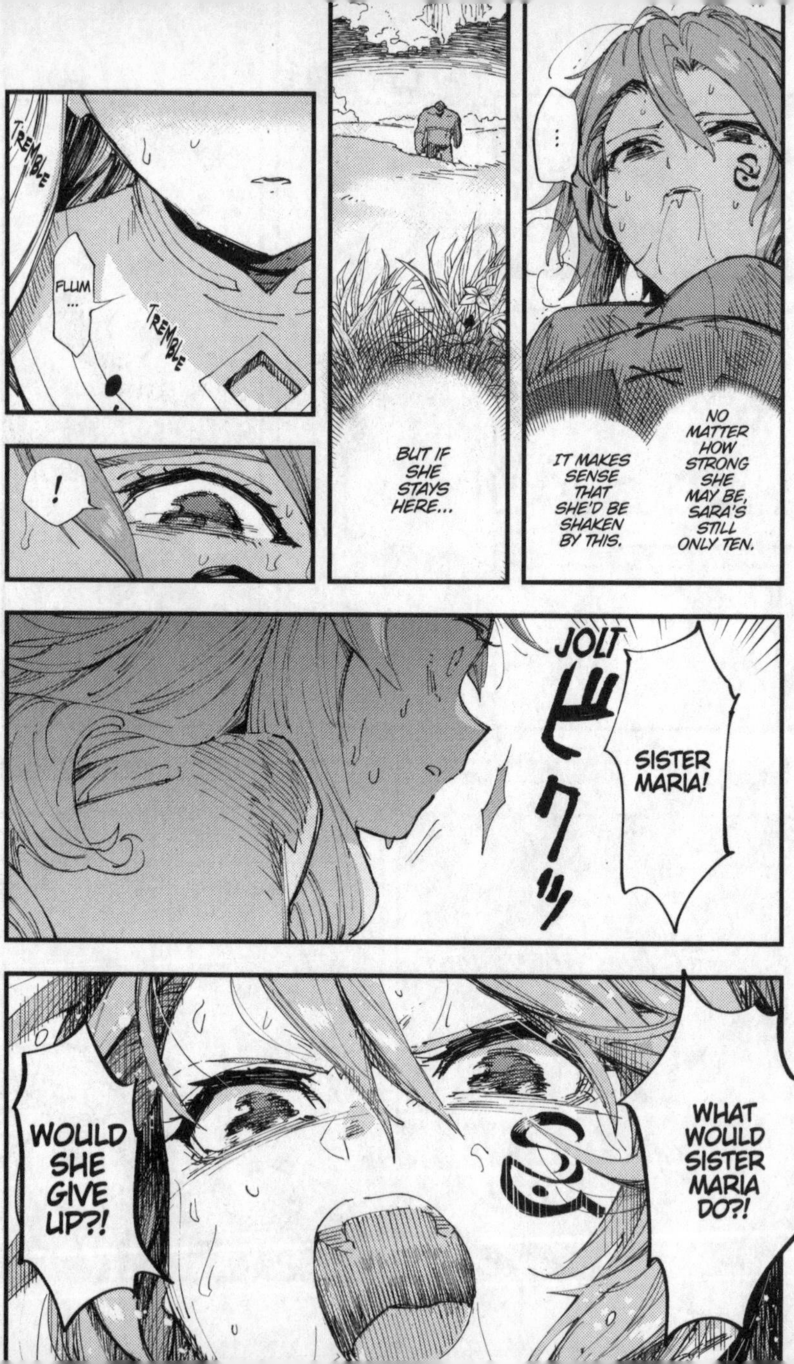
...
NO MATTER HOW STRONG SHE MAY BE, SARA'S STILL ONLY TEN.
IT MAKES SENSE THAT SHE'D BE SHAKEN BY THIS.
BUT IF SHE STAYS HERE...
TREMBLE
FLUM...
TREMBLE
!
JOLT
ビクッ
SISTER MARIA!
WHAT WOULD SISTER MARIA DO?!
WOULD SHE GIVE UP?!

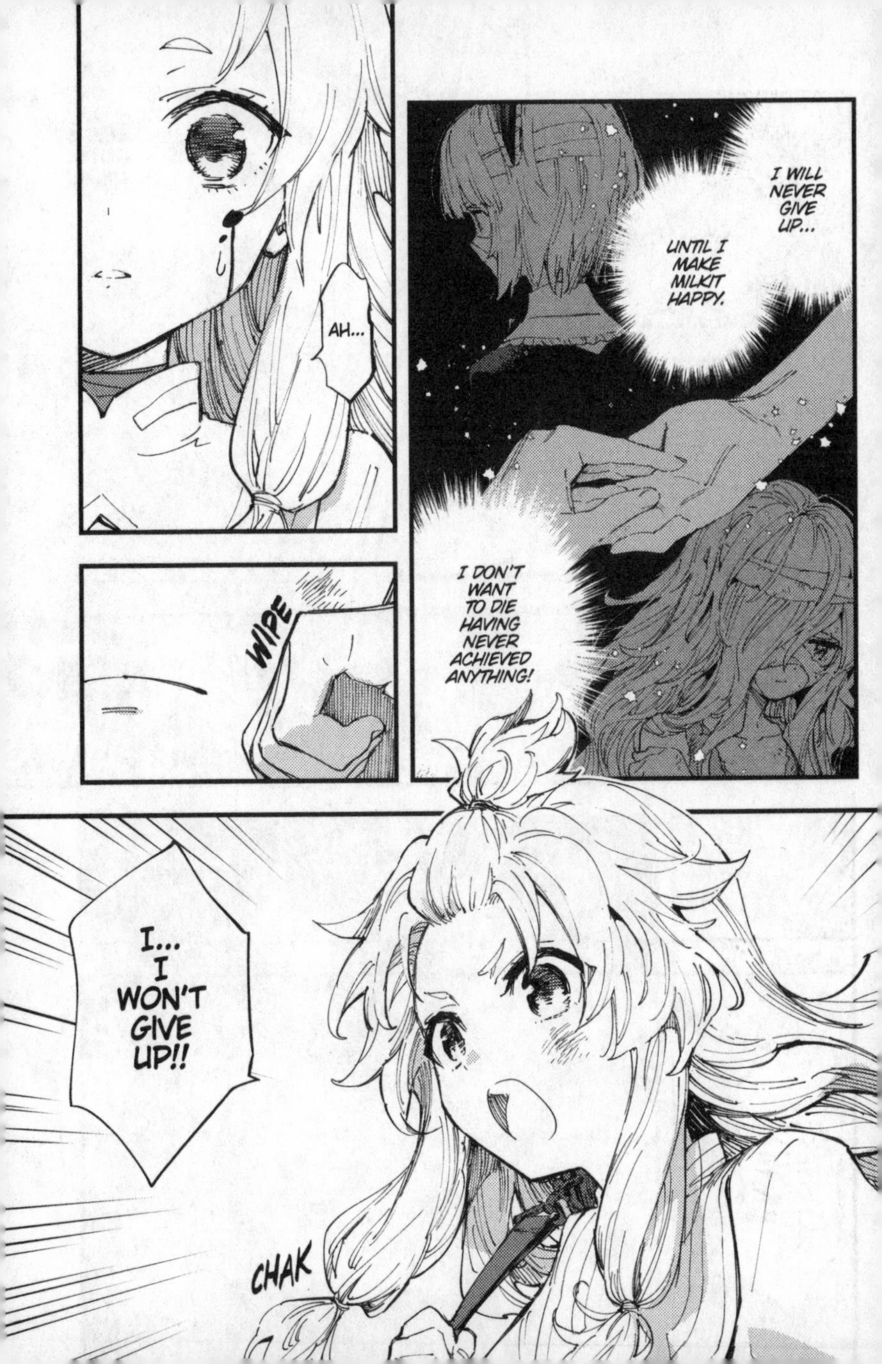
I WILL NEVER GIVE UP...
UNTIL I MAKE MILKIT HAPPY.
I DON'T WANT TO DIE HAVING NEVER ACHIEVED ANYTHING!
AH...
WIPE
I... I WON'T GIVE UP!!
CHAK

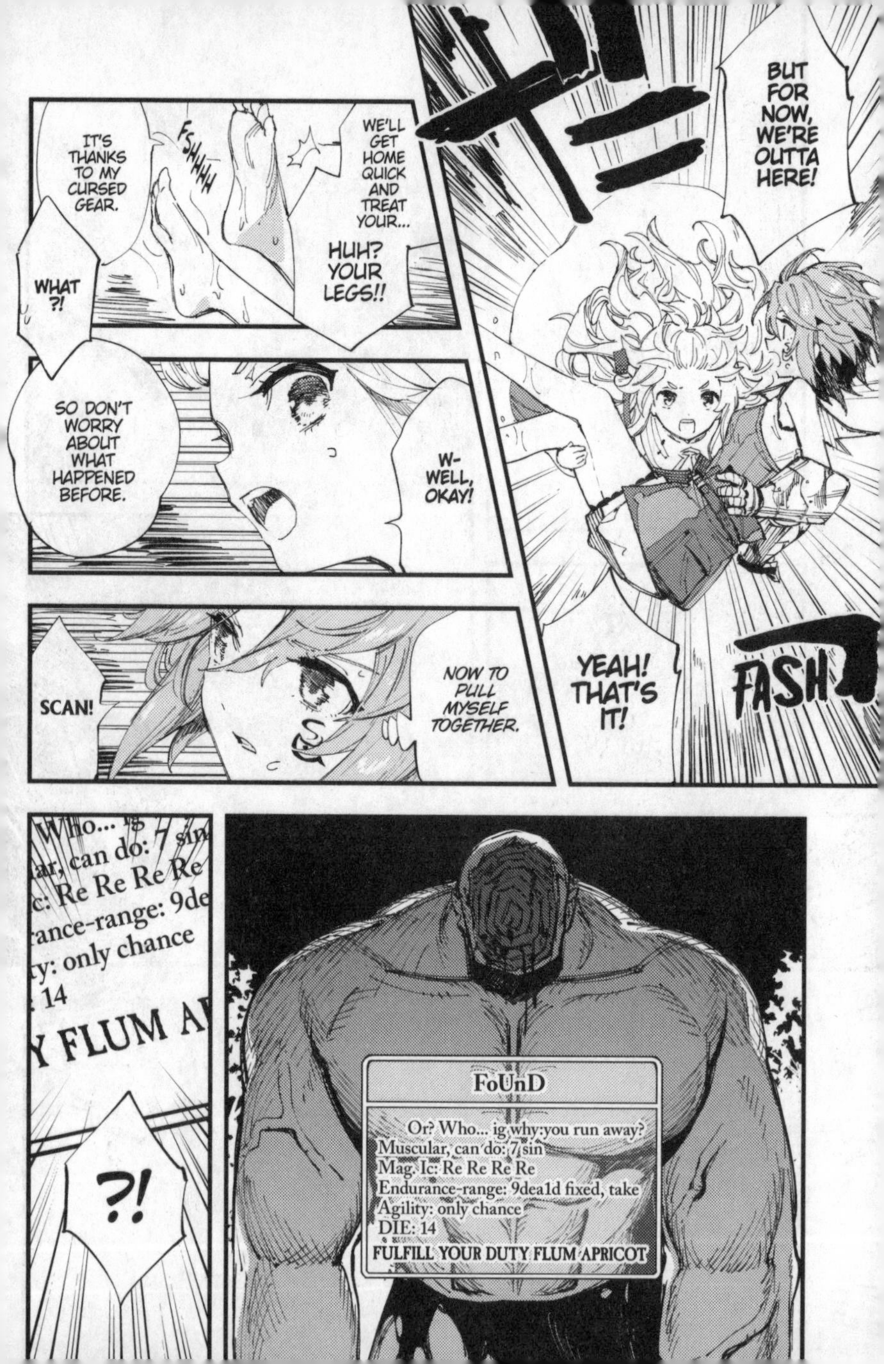
BUT FOR NOW, WE'RE OUTTA HERE!
YEAH! THAT'S IT!
FASH
WE'LL GET HOME QUICK AND TREAT YOUR...
HUH? YOUR LEGS!!
FSHHHH
IT'S THANKS TO MY CURSED GEAR.
WHAT?!
W-WELL, OKAY!
SO DON'T WORRY ABOUT WHAT HAPPENED BEFORE.
NOW TO PULL MYSELF TOGETHER.
SCAN!
FoUnD
Or? Who... ig why:you run away?
Muscular, can do: 7 sin
Mag. Ic: Re Re Re Re
Endurance-range: 9dea1d fixed, take
Agility: only chance
DIE: 14
FULFILL YOUR DUTY FLUM APRICOT
Who... 18
ar, can do: 7 sin
c: Re Re Re Re
ance-range: 9de
ty: only chance
14
Y FLUM AI
?!

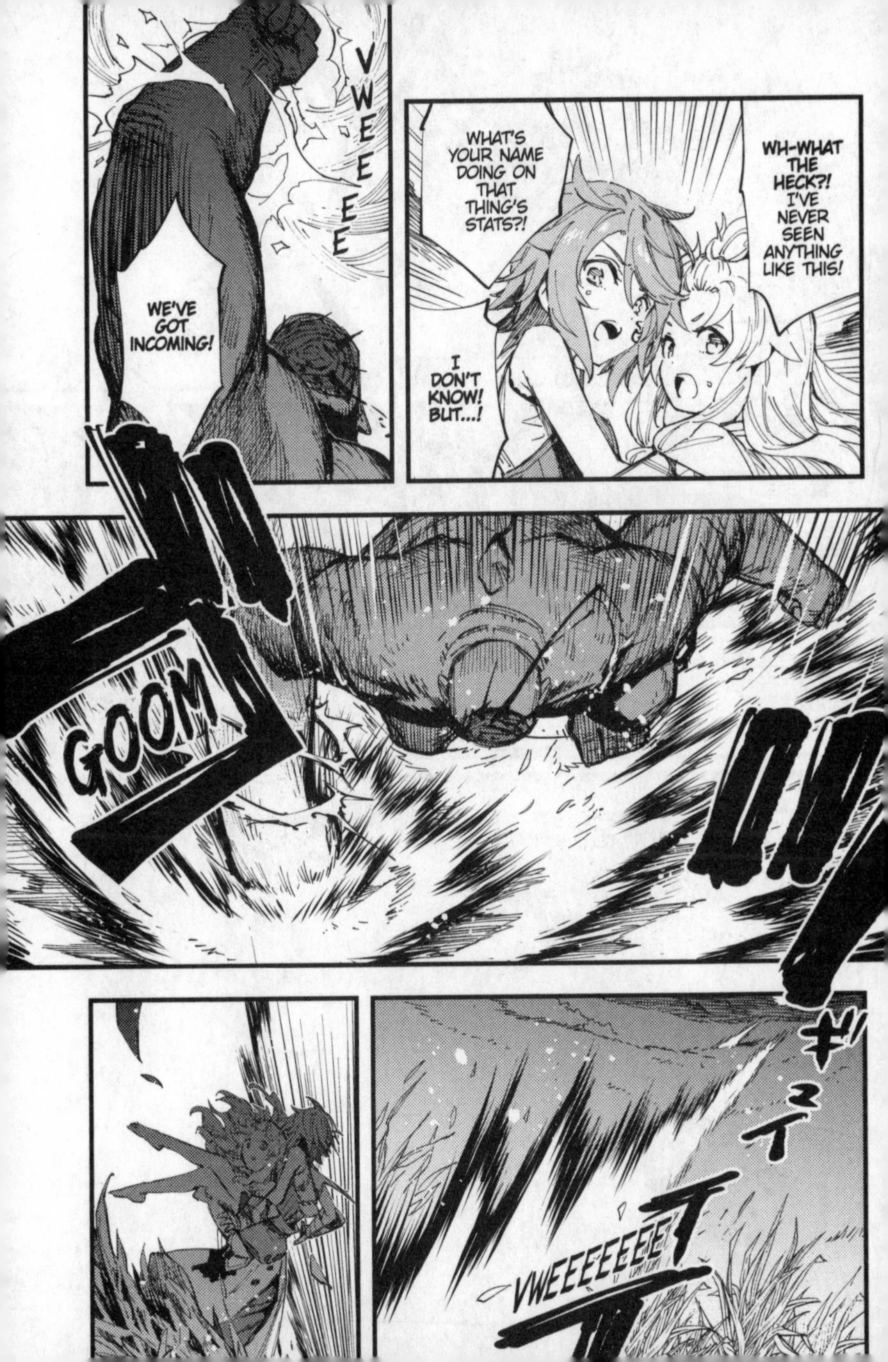
WH-WHAT THE HECK?! I'VE NEVER SEEN ANYTHING LIKE THIS!
WHAT'S YOUR NAME DOING ON THAT THING'S STATS?!
I DON'T KNOW! BUT...!
VWEEEE
WE'VE GOT INCOMING!
GOOM
ギュイ
VWEEEEEEEE

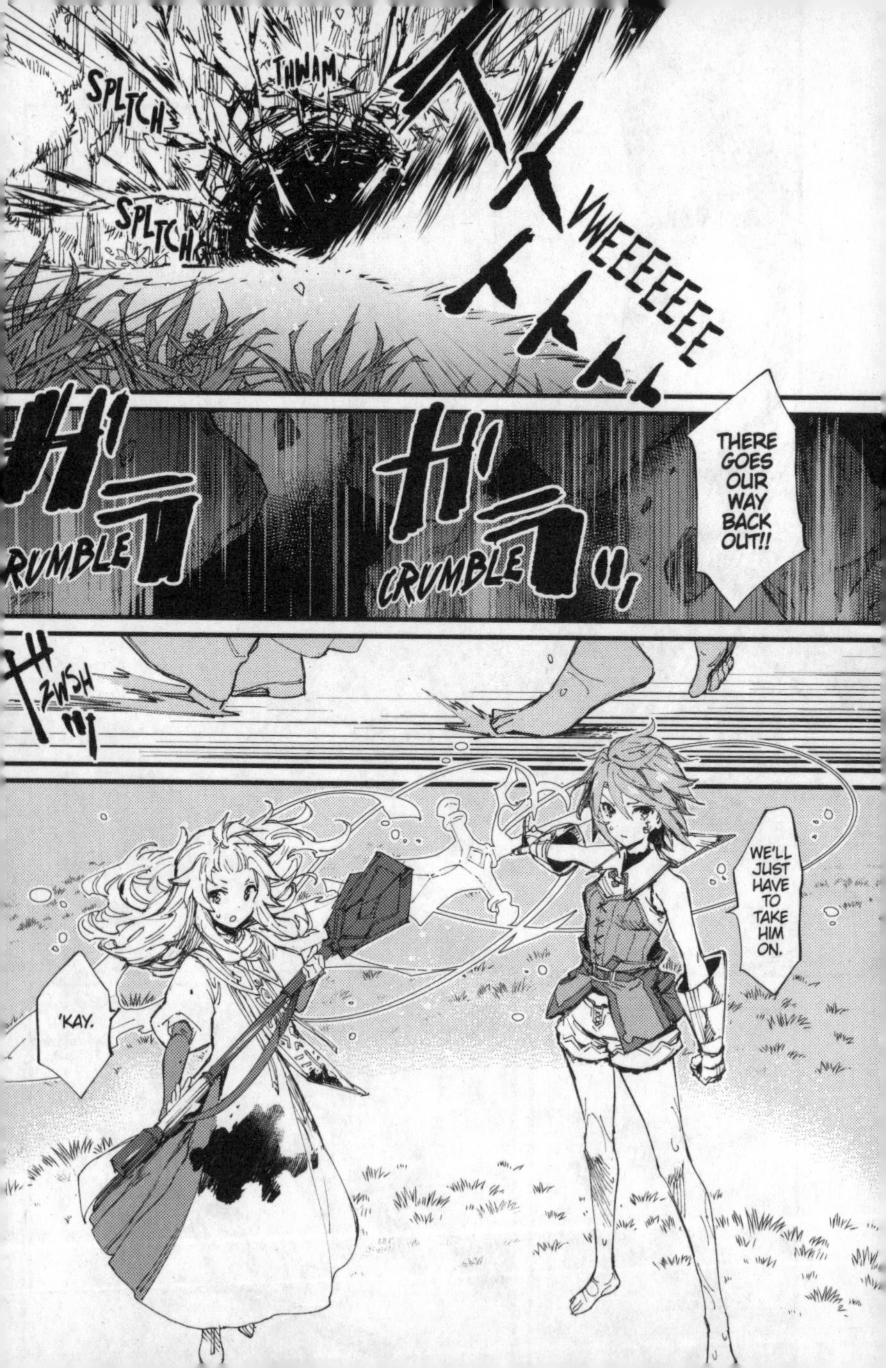

VWEEEEEEE
THWAM
SPLTCH
SPLTCH
THERE GOES OUR WAY BACK OUT!!
ガラ
CRUMBLE
ガラ
RUMBLE
ZWSH
WE'LL JUST HAVE TO TAKE HIM ON.
'KAY.

TAKE THIS!

C'MON, YOU FREAK!

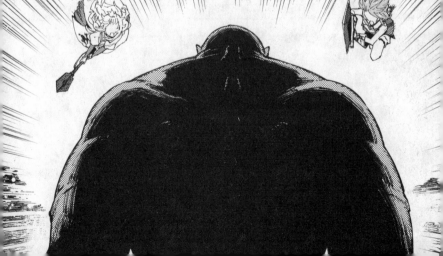

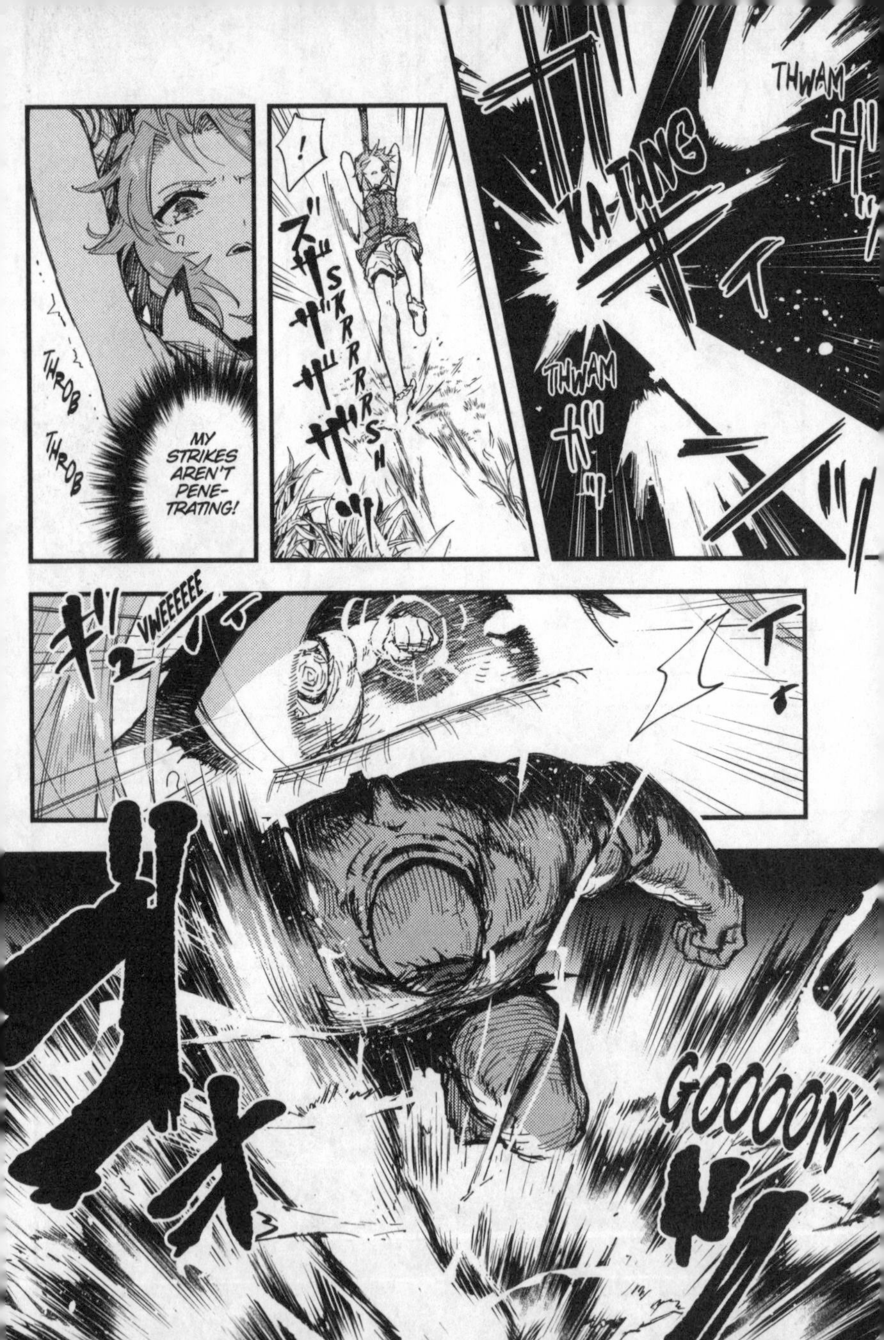
THWAM
KA-TANG
THWAM
!
SKRRRRRSH
THROB
THROB
MY STRIKES AREN'T PENE-TRATING!
VWEEEEEE
GOOOOM

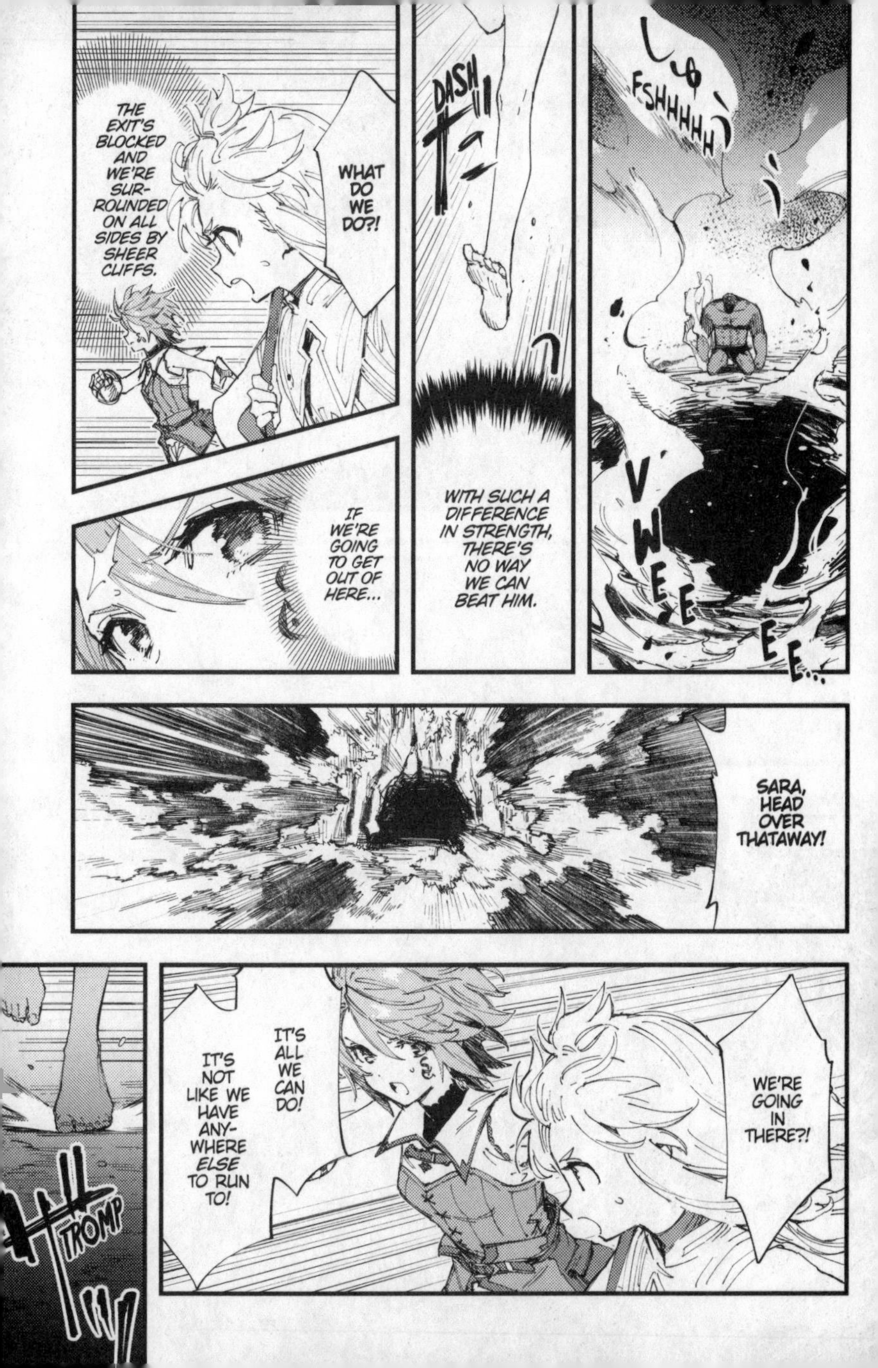
FSHHHHH
VWEEEEE...
DASH
WITH SUCH A DIFFERENCE IN STRENGTH, THERE'S NO WAY WE CAN BEAT HIM.
WHAT DO WE DO?!
THE EXIT'S BLOCKED AND WE'RE SUR-ROUNDED ON ALL SIDES BY SHEER CLIFFS.
IF WE'RE GOING TO GET OUT OF HERE...
SARA, HEAD OVER THATAWAY!
WE'RE GOING IN THERE?!
IT'S ALL WE CAN DO!
IT'S NOT LIKE WE HAVE ANY-WHERE ELSE TO RUN TO!
TROMP

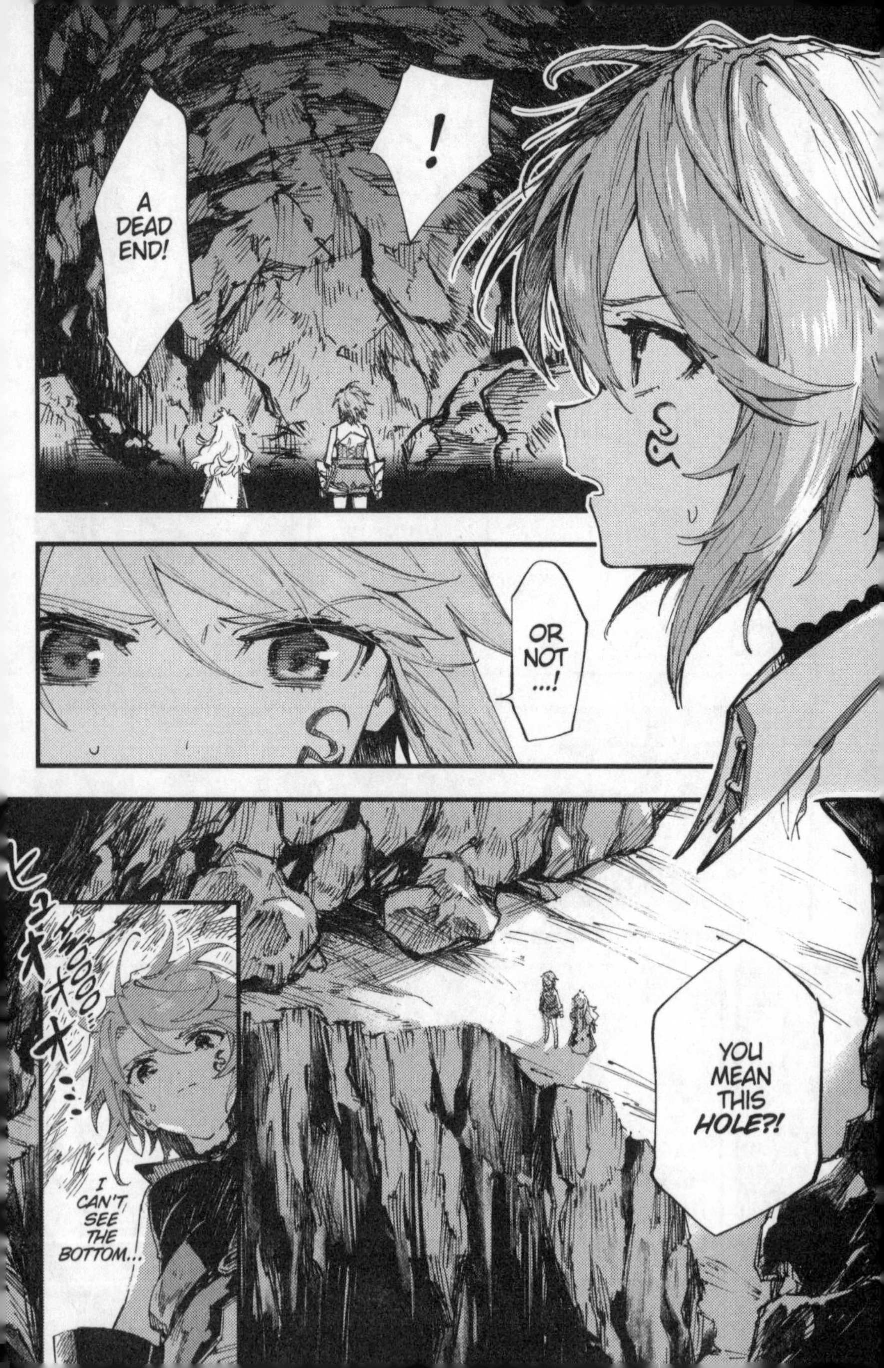
!
A DEAD END!
OR NOT ...!
YOU MEAN THIS HOLE?!
HWOOOO...
...
I CAN'T SEE THE BOTTOM...

CLASP

!

FLUM, YOU CAN'T MEAN...

RUSTLE

HE'S COMING!

I'M SORRY FOR ALWAYS BEING SO RECKLESS.

......

OKIE-DOKE.

I'M READY WHENEVER YOU ARE!

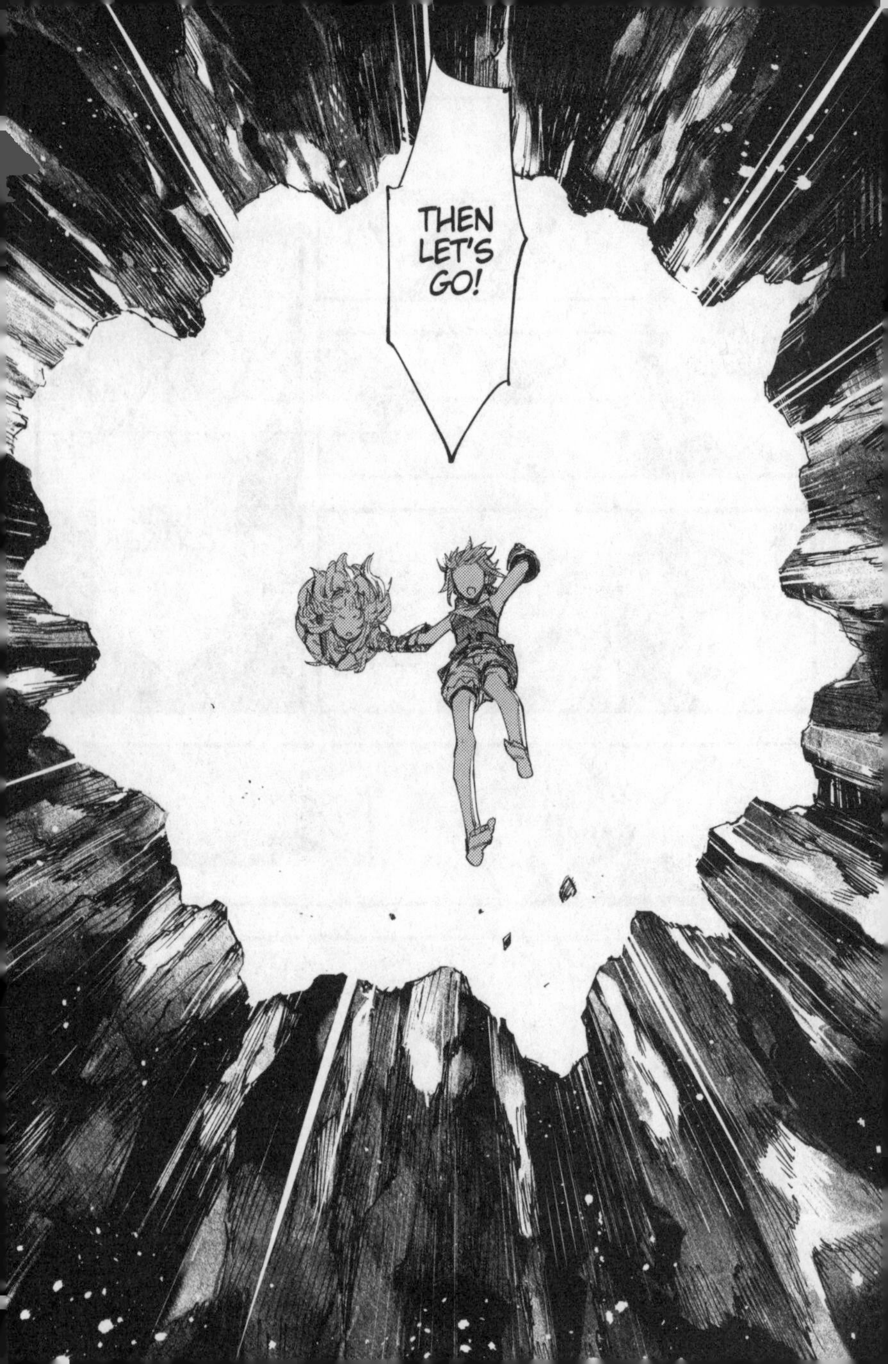
THEN LET'S GO!

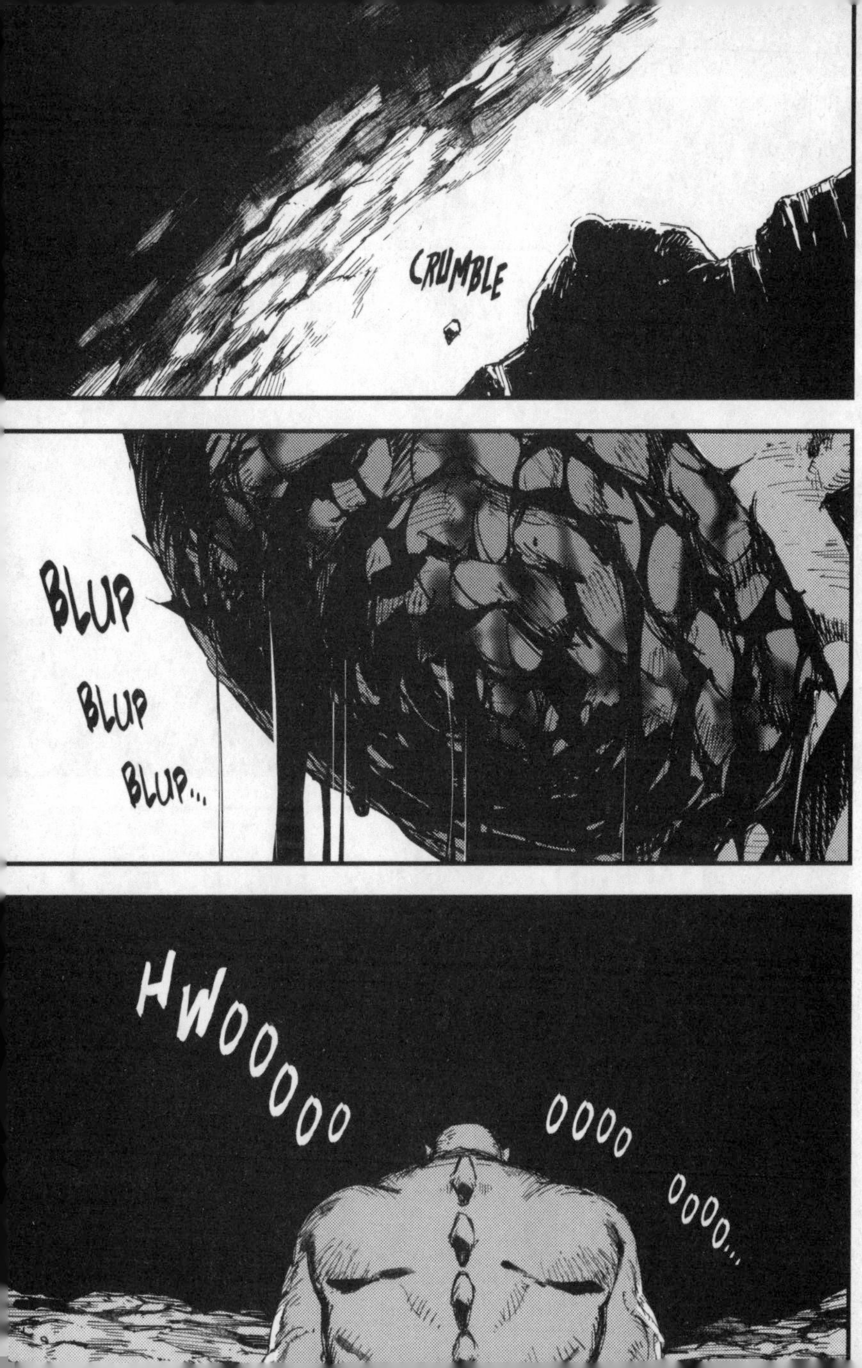
CRUMBLE
BLUP
BLUP
BLUP...
HWOOOOOO
OOOO
OOOO...

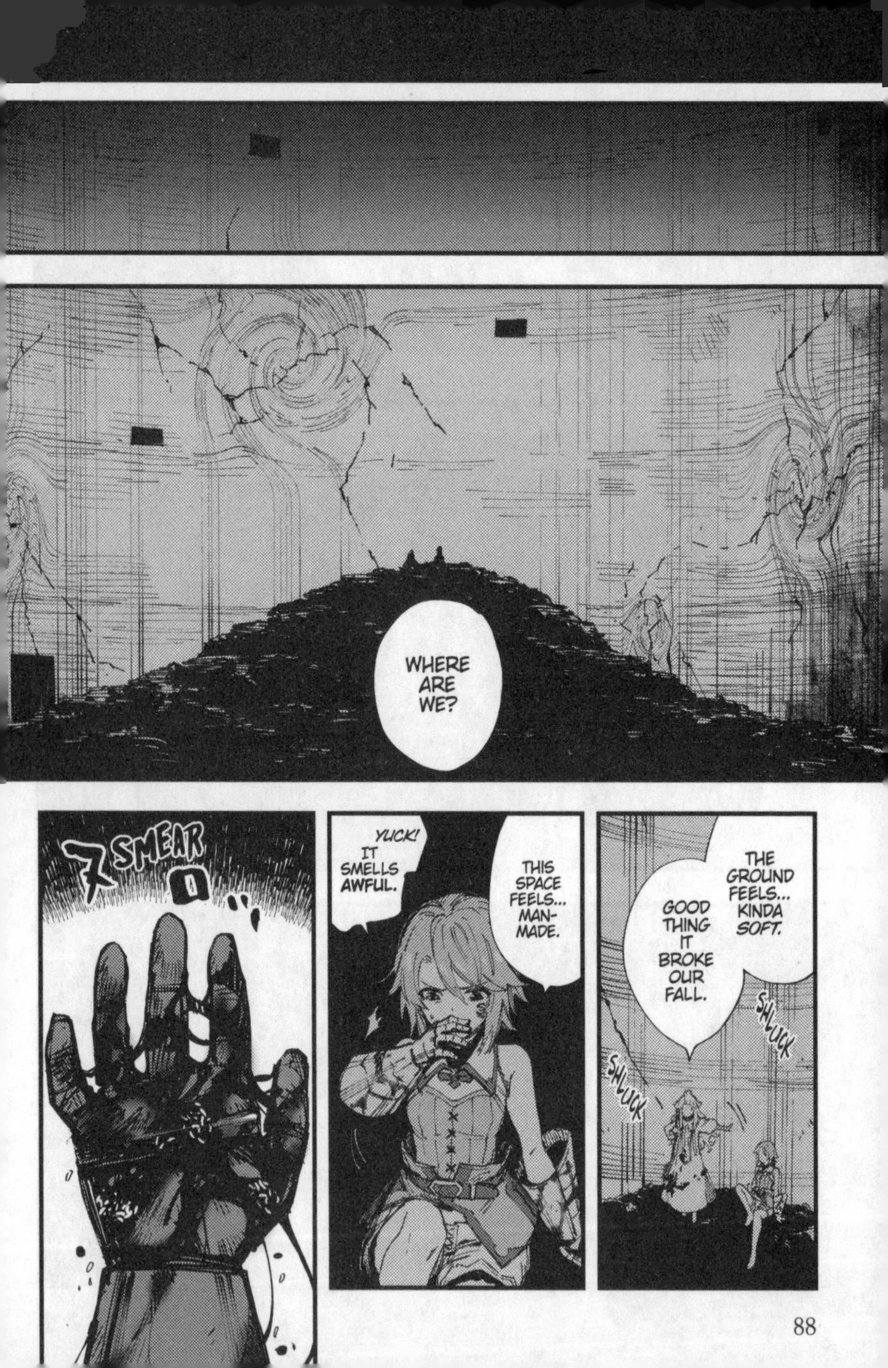
WHERE ARE WE?
THE GROUND FEELS... KINDA SOFT.
GOOD THING IT BROKE OUR FALL.
SHLUCK
SHLUCK
THIS SPACE FEELS... MAN-MADE.
YUCK! IT SMELLS AWFUL.
SMEAR

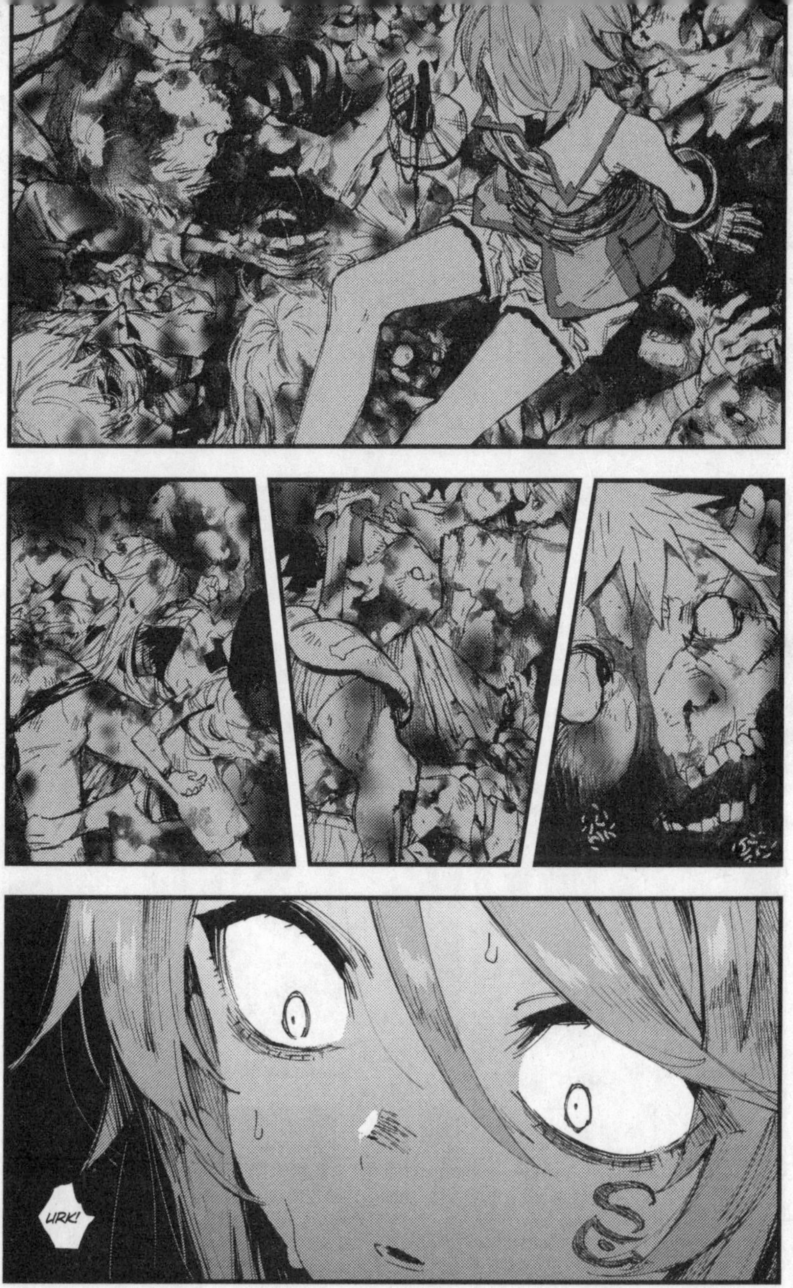
URK!

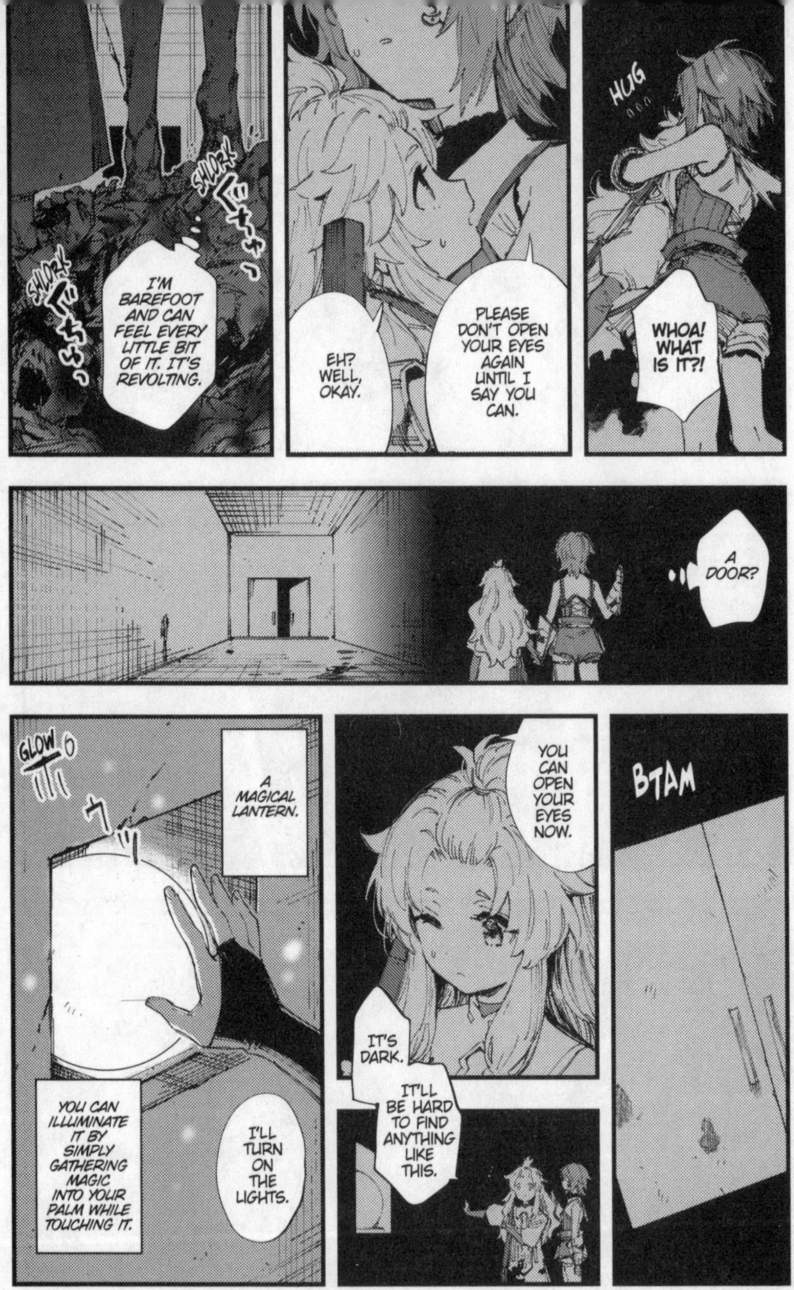
HUG
WHOA! WHAT IS IT?!
PLEASE DON'T OPEN YOUR EYES AGAIN UNTIL I SAY YOU CAN.
EH? WELL, OKAY.
SHLORK
SHLORK
I'M BAREFOOT AND CAN FEEL EVERY LITTLE BIT OF IT. IT'S REVOLTING.
A DOOR?
BTAM
YOU CAN OPEN YOUR EYES NOW.
IT'S DARK.
IT'LL BE HARD TO FIND ANYTHING LIKE THIS.
GLOW
A MAGICAL LANTERN.
I'LL TURN ON THE LIGHTS.
YOU CAN ILLUMINATE IT BY SIMPLY GATHERING MAGIC INTO YOUR PALM WHILE TOUCHING IT.

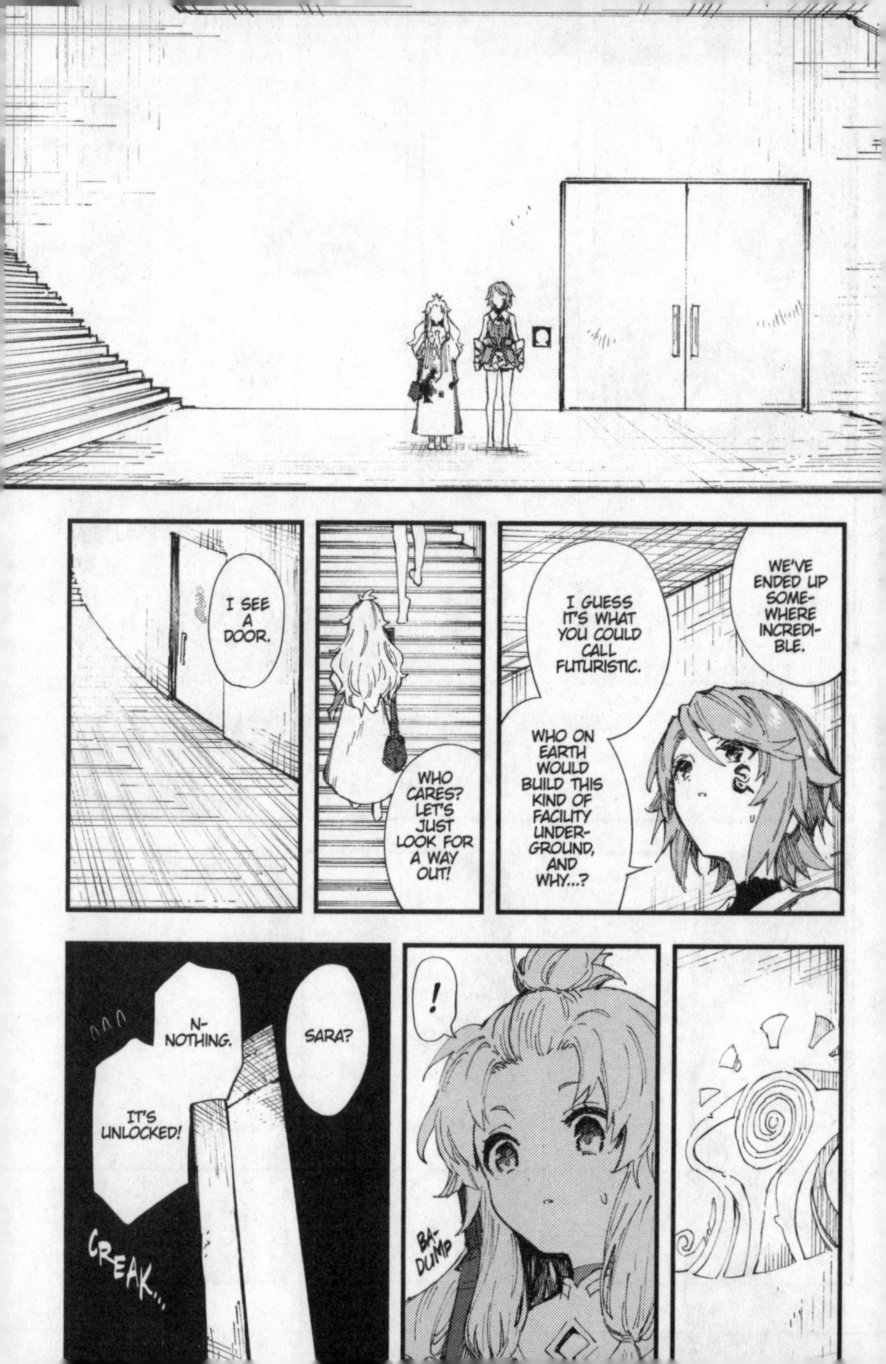

WE'VE ENDED UP SOME-WHERE INCREDI-BLE.
I GUESS IT'S WHAT YOU COULD CALL FUTURISTIC.
WHO ON EARTH WOULD BUILD THIS KIND OF FACILITY UNDER-GROUND, AND WHY...?
WHO CARES? LET'S JUST LOOK FOR A WAY OUT!
I SEE A DOOR.
!
BA-DUMP
SARA?
N-NOTHING.
IT'S UNLOCKED!
CREAK...

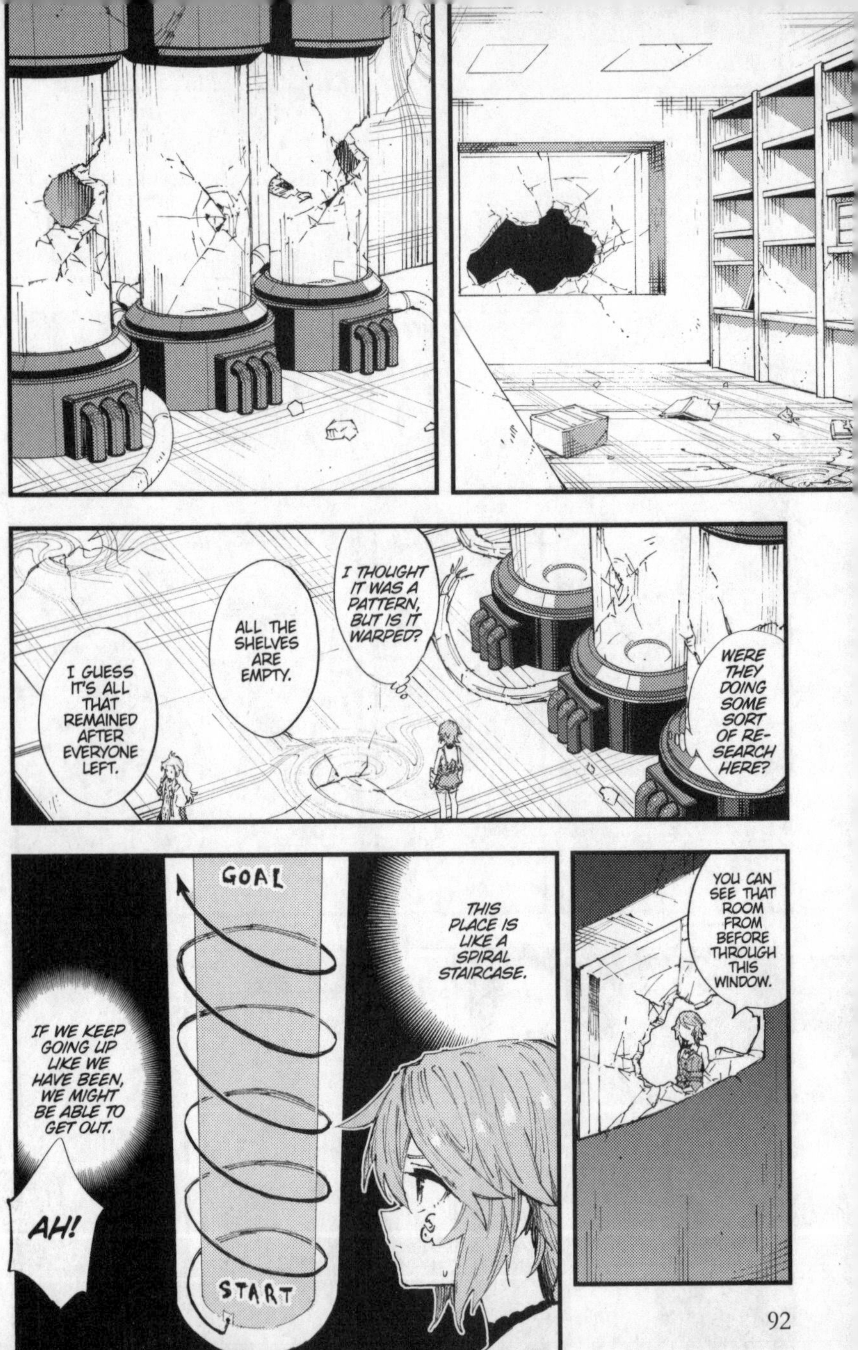
WERE THEY DOING SOME SORT OF RE-SEARCH HERE?
I THOUGHT IT WAS A PATTERN, BUT IS IT WARPED?
ALL THE SHELVES ARE EMPTY.
I GUESS IT'S ALL THAT REMAINED AFTER EVERYONE LEFT.
YOU CAN SEE THAT ROOM FROM BEFORE THROUGH THIS WINDOW.
THIS PLACE IS LIKE A SPIRAL STAIRCASE.
GOAL
START
IF WE KEEP GOING UP LIKE WE HAVE BEEN, WE MIGHT BE ABLE TO GET OUT.
AH!

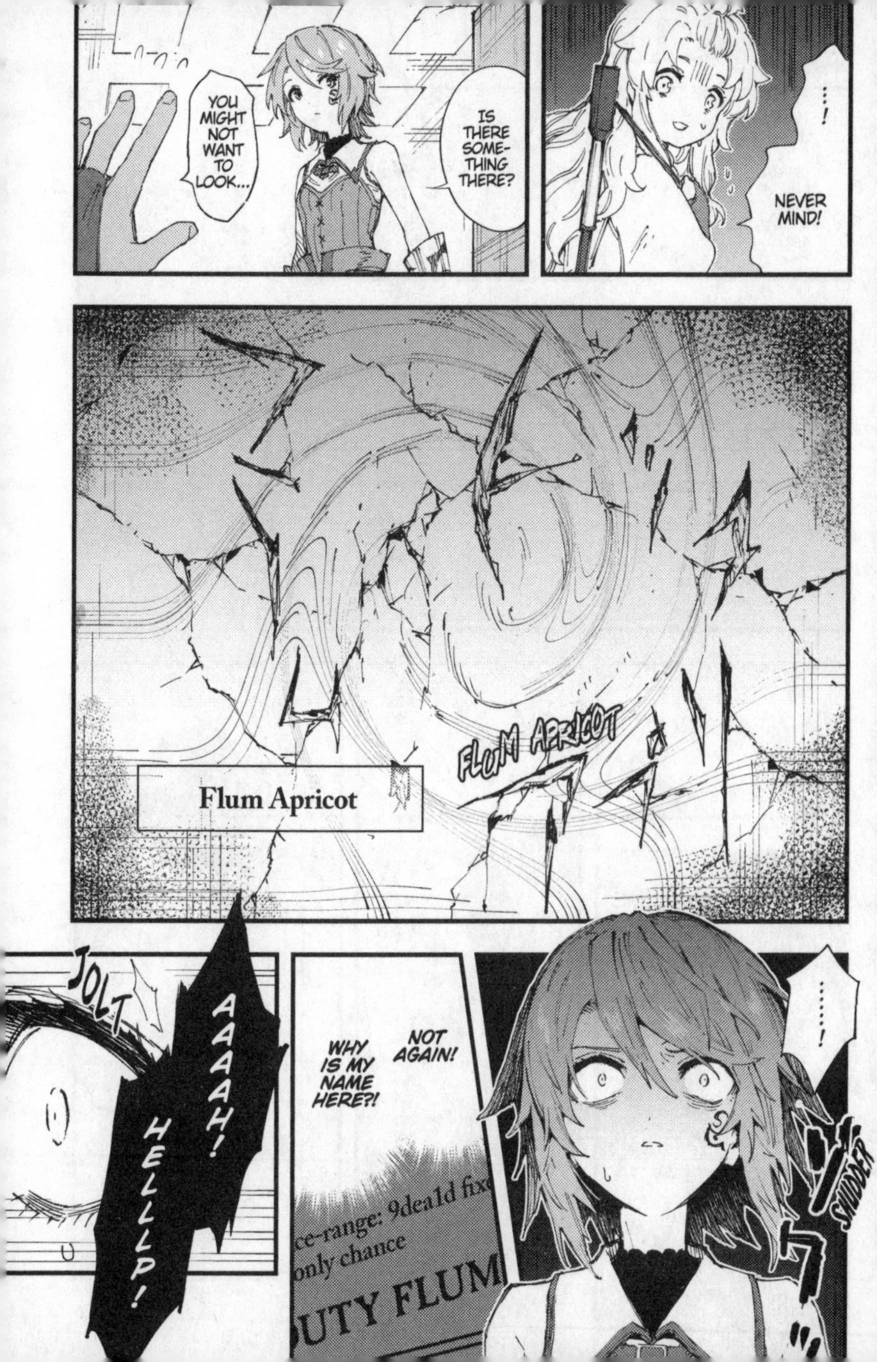
...!
NEVER MIND!
IS THERE SOMETHING THERE?
YOU MIGHT NOT WANT TO LOOK...
FLUM APRICOT
Flum Apricot
......!
SHUDDER
NOT AGAIN!
WHY IS MY NAME HERE?!
ce-range: 9dea1d fixe
only chance
UTY FLUM
JOLT
AAAAAH!
HELLLP!

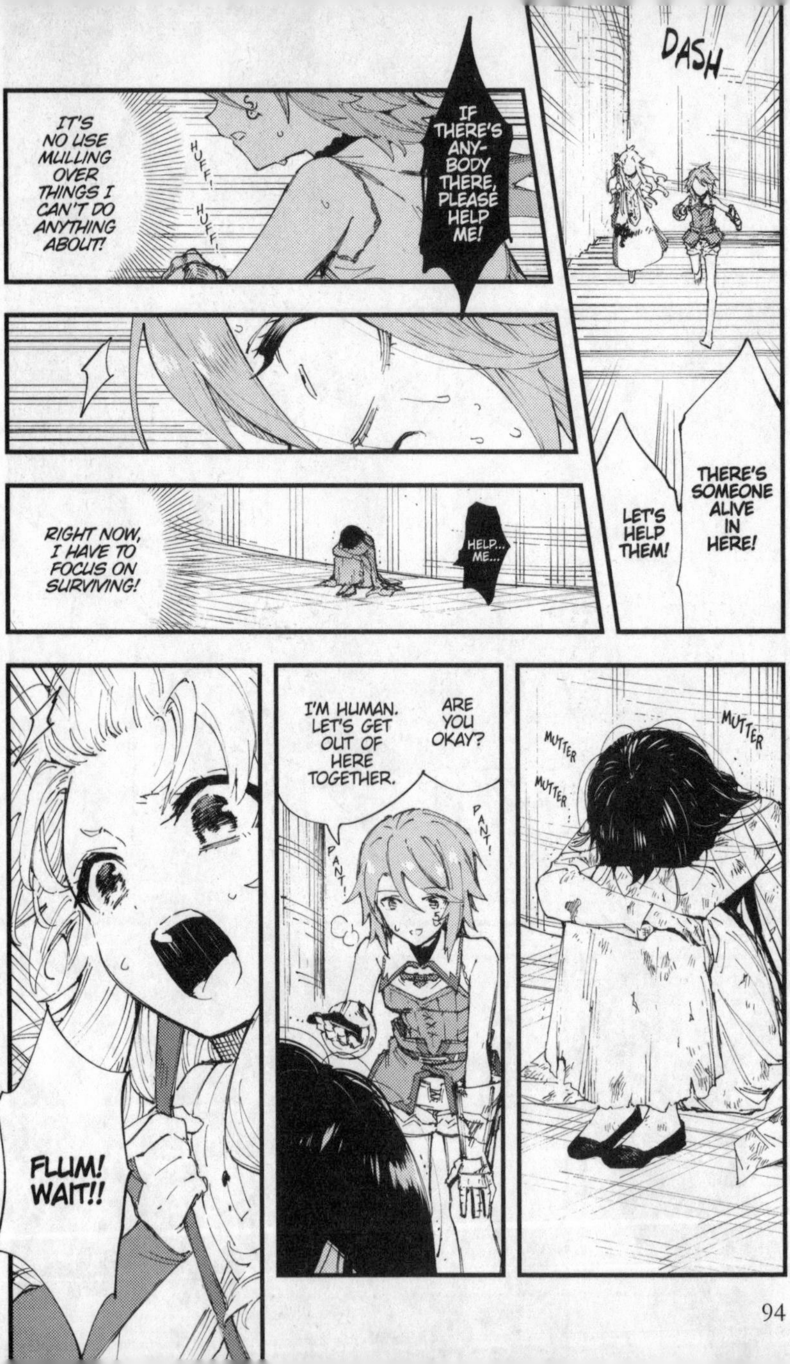
DASH
THERE'S SOMEONE ALIVE IN HERE!
LET'S HELP THEM!
IF THERE'S ANYBODY THERE, PLEASE HELP ME!
IT'S NO USE MULLING OVER THINGS I CAN'T DO ANYTHING ABOUT!
HUFF! HUFF!
...HELP... ME...
RIGHT NOW, I HAVE TO FOCUS ON SURVIVING!
MUTTER
MUTTER
MUTTER
ARE YOU OKAY?
I'M HUMAN. LET'S GET OUT OF HERE TOGETHER.
PANT! PANT!
FLUM! WAIT!!

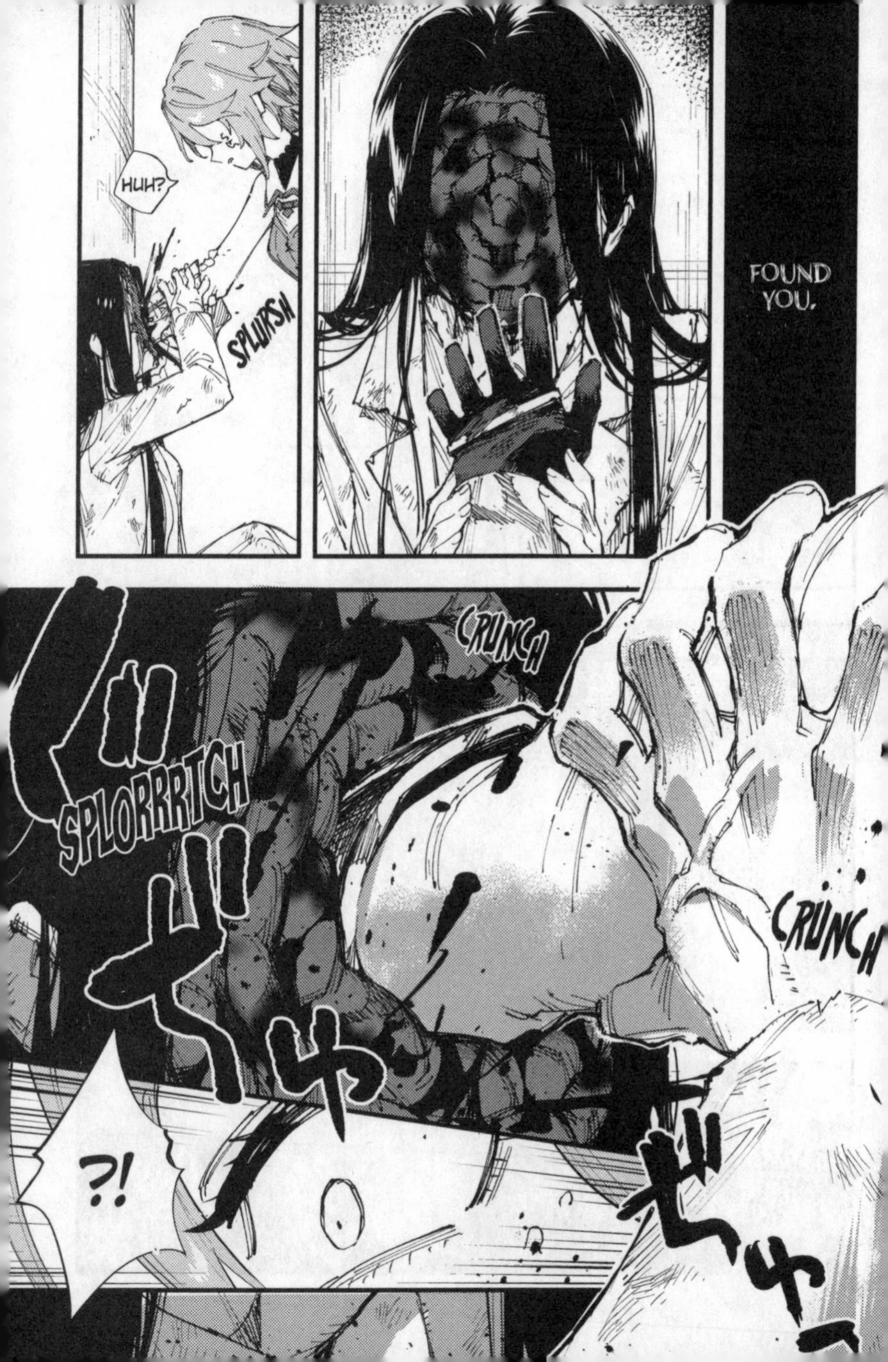
FOUND YOU.
HUH?
SPLURSH
CRUNCH
CRUNCH
SPLORRRTCH
?!

AH!

AGH!

THUMP

THUMP

SHE WON'T BUDGE!

SHLUCK

SHLUCK

SHLUCK

EEGH--

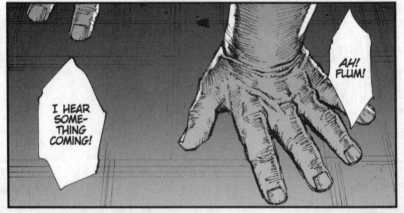

I HEAR SOME-THING COMING!

AH! FLUM!

PLURP

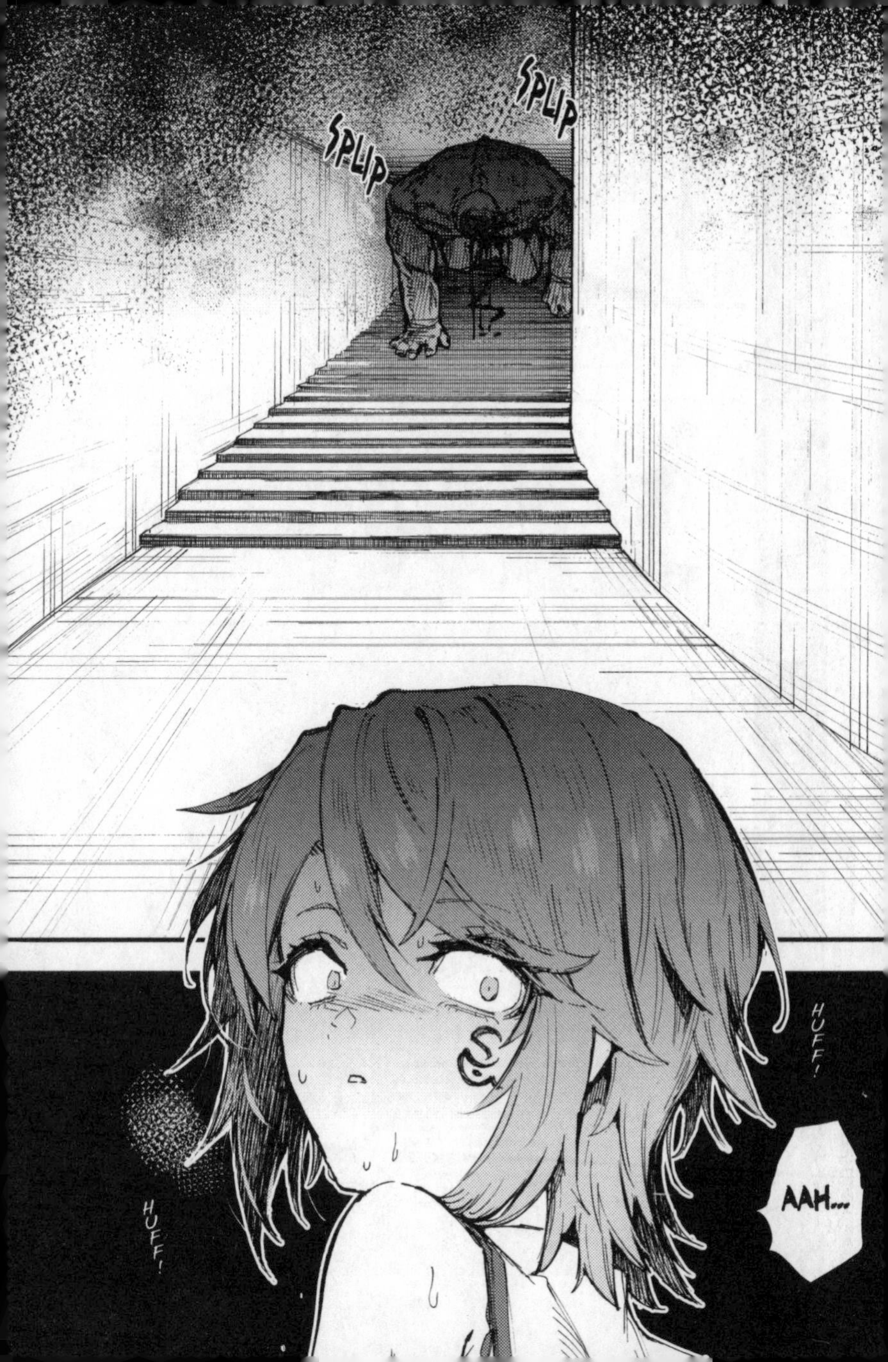
SPLIP
SPLIP
HUFF!
AAH...
HUFF!

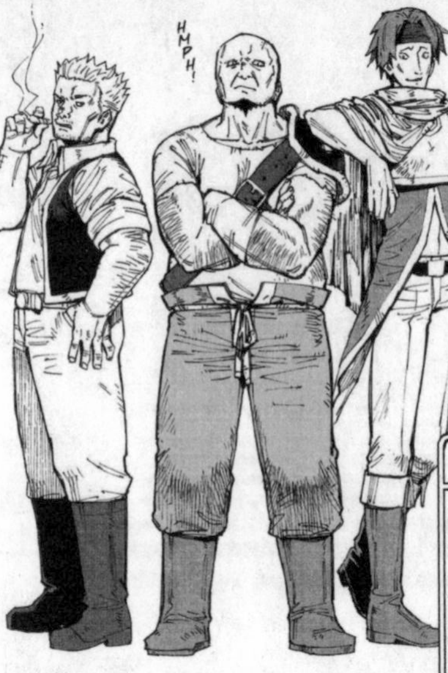
HMPH!

Dein's Lackeys

Bad Guy Level: ★★★★★★

From left to right, there's "Grimmie," "Budras," and "Quarante." Their adventurer ranking is C~D. These ill-bred hooligans will steal, blackmail, and sometimes even murder. Since Dein basically rules the West District of the capital, not even the guards can mess with them.
Those who can oppose them are only either fearless adventurers or members of the church with immense authority.

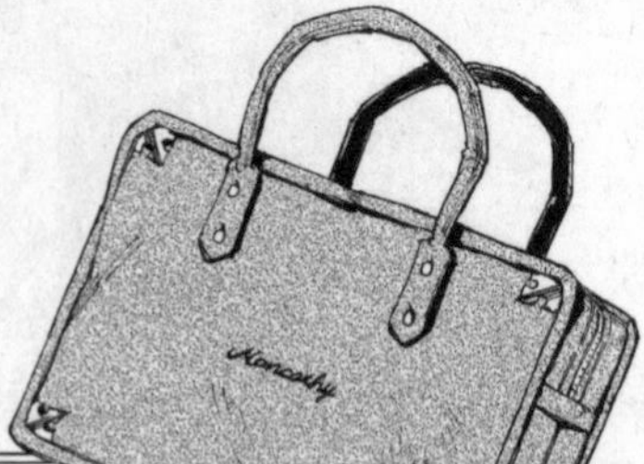
Mancathy

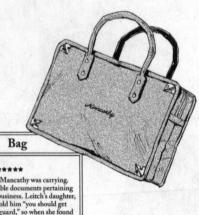

Bag

Value: ★★★★★★★★★★

The bag Leitch Mancathy was carrying. Inside are valuable documents pertaining to Mancathy's business. Leitch's daughter, Welcy, always told him "you should get yourself a bodyguard," so when she found out it was almost stolen, she and his wife scolded him something fierce. Lately he's taken to going out with a bodyguard.

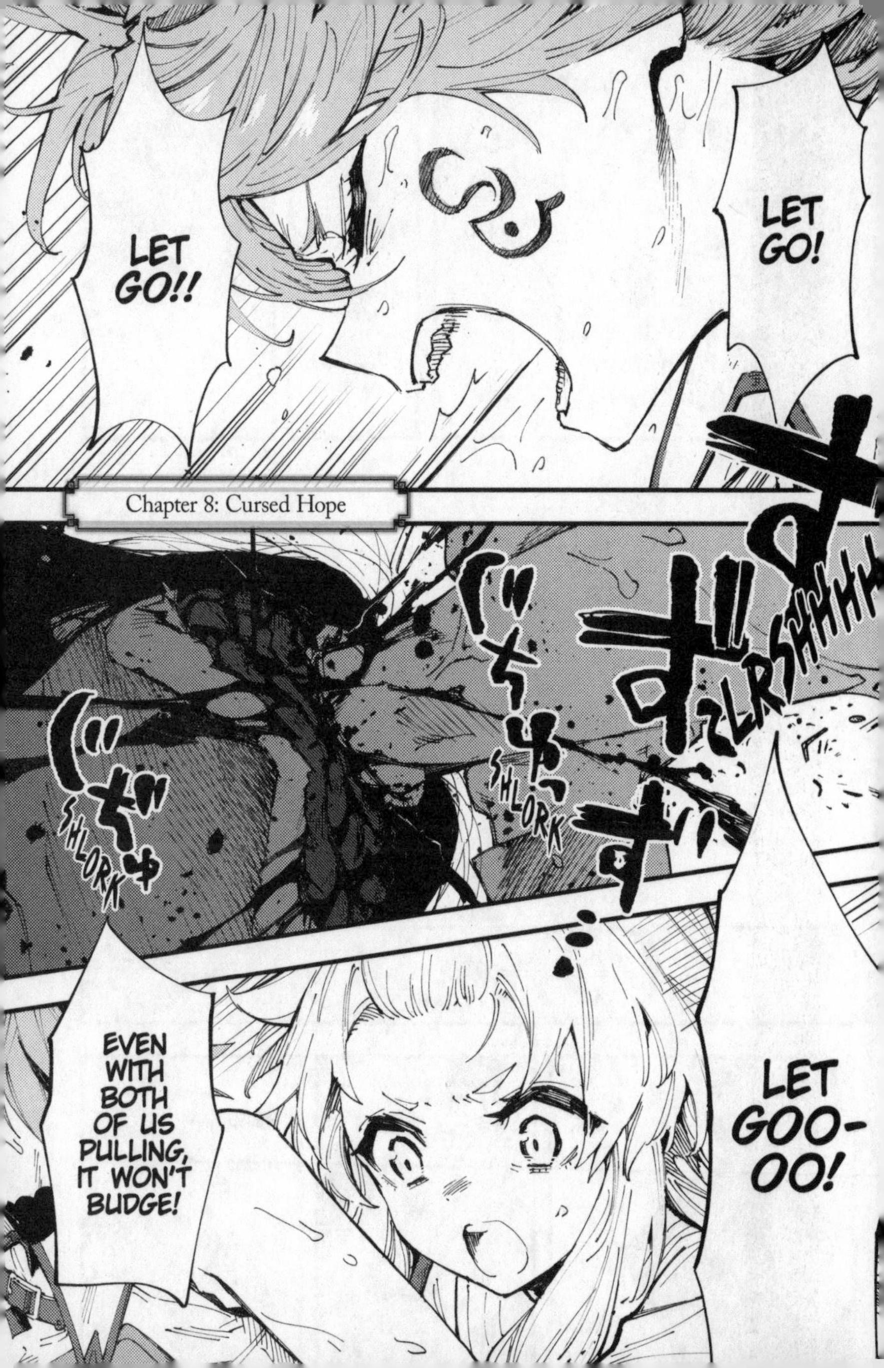
LET GO!
LET GO!!
Chapter 8: Cursed Hope
ZLRSHHHH
SHLORK
SHLORK
LET GOO-OO!
EVEN WITH BOTH OF US PULLING, IT WON'T BUDGE!

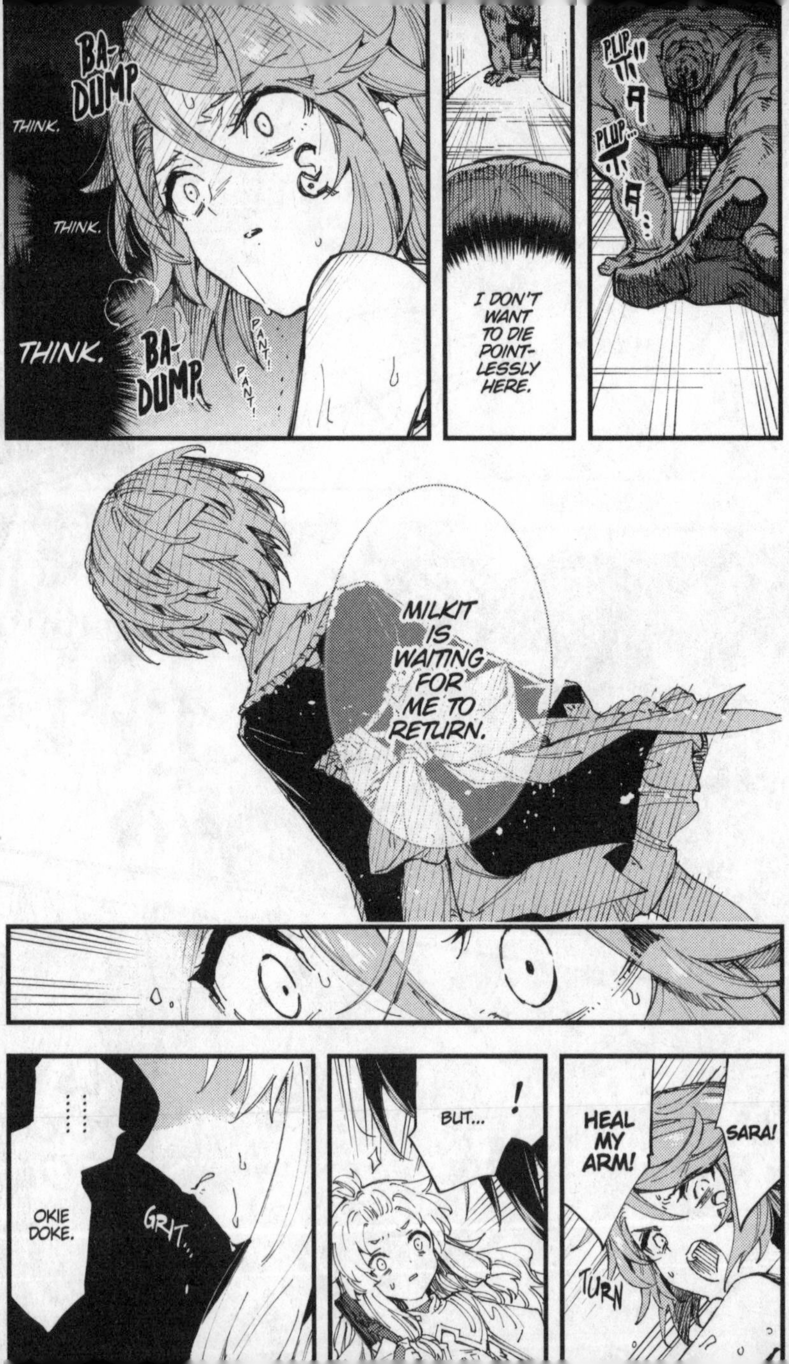
PLIP
PLIP...
I DON'T WANT TO DIE POINTLESSLY HERE.
BA-DUMP
THINK.
THINK.
THINK.
BA-DUMP
PANT!
PANT!
MILKIT IS WAITING FOR ME TO RETURN.
SARA!
HEAL MY ARM!
TURN
!
BUT...
......
OKIE DOKE.
GRIT...

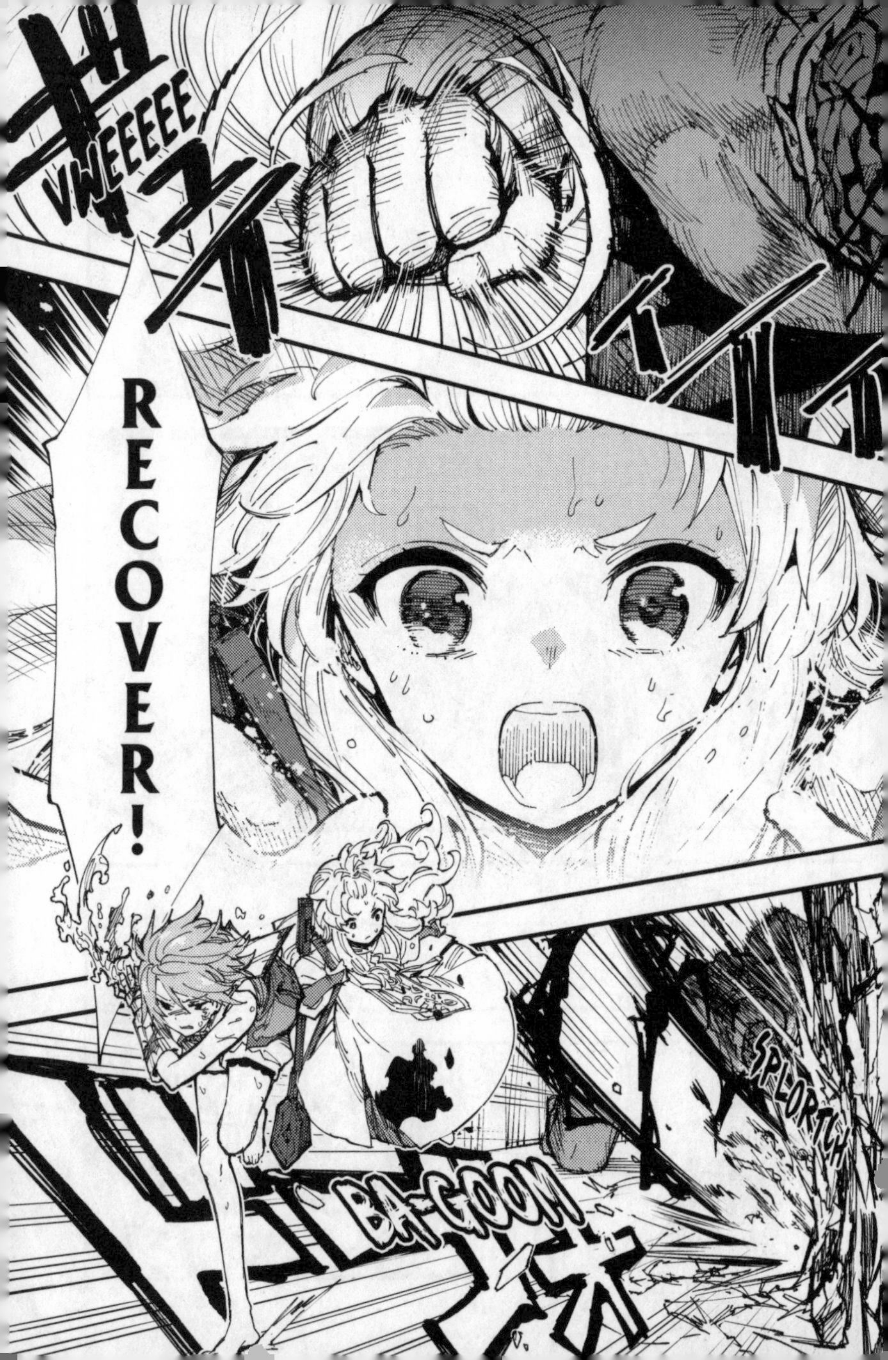
VWEEEEE
RECOVER!
SPLORTCH
BA-GOOM

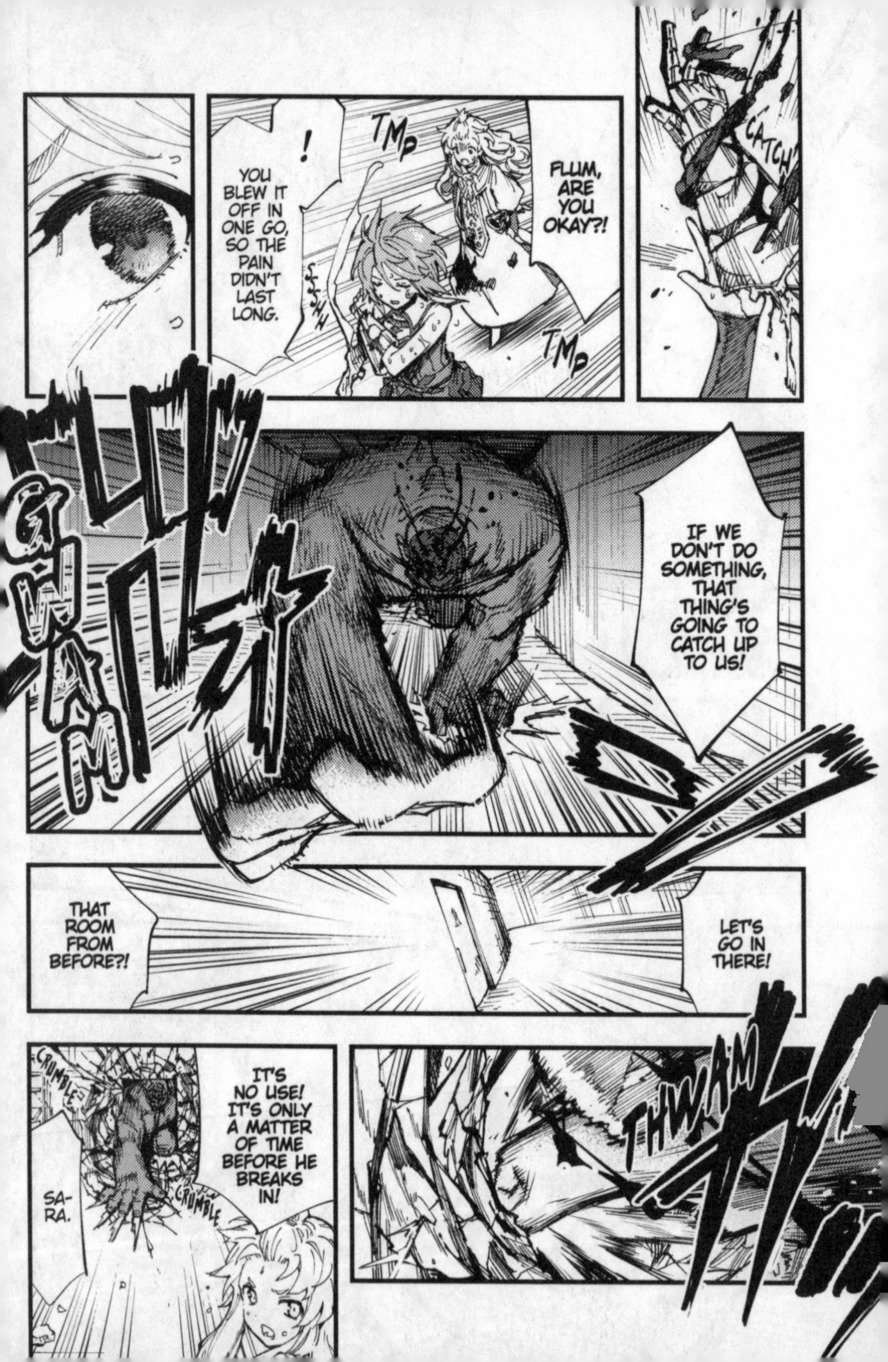
CATCH
FLUM, ARE YOU OKAY?!
TMP
TMP
!
YOU BLEW IT OFF IN ONE GO, SO THE PAIN DIDN'T LAST LONG.
IF WE DON'T DO SOMETHING, THAT THING'S GOING TO CATCH UP TO US!
GWAM
LET'S GO IN THERE!
THAT ROOM FROM BEFORE?!
THWAM
IT'S NO USE! IT'S ONLY A MATTER OF TIME BEFORE HE BREAKS IN!
CRUMBLE
CRUMBLE
SA-RA.

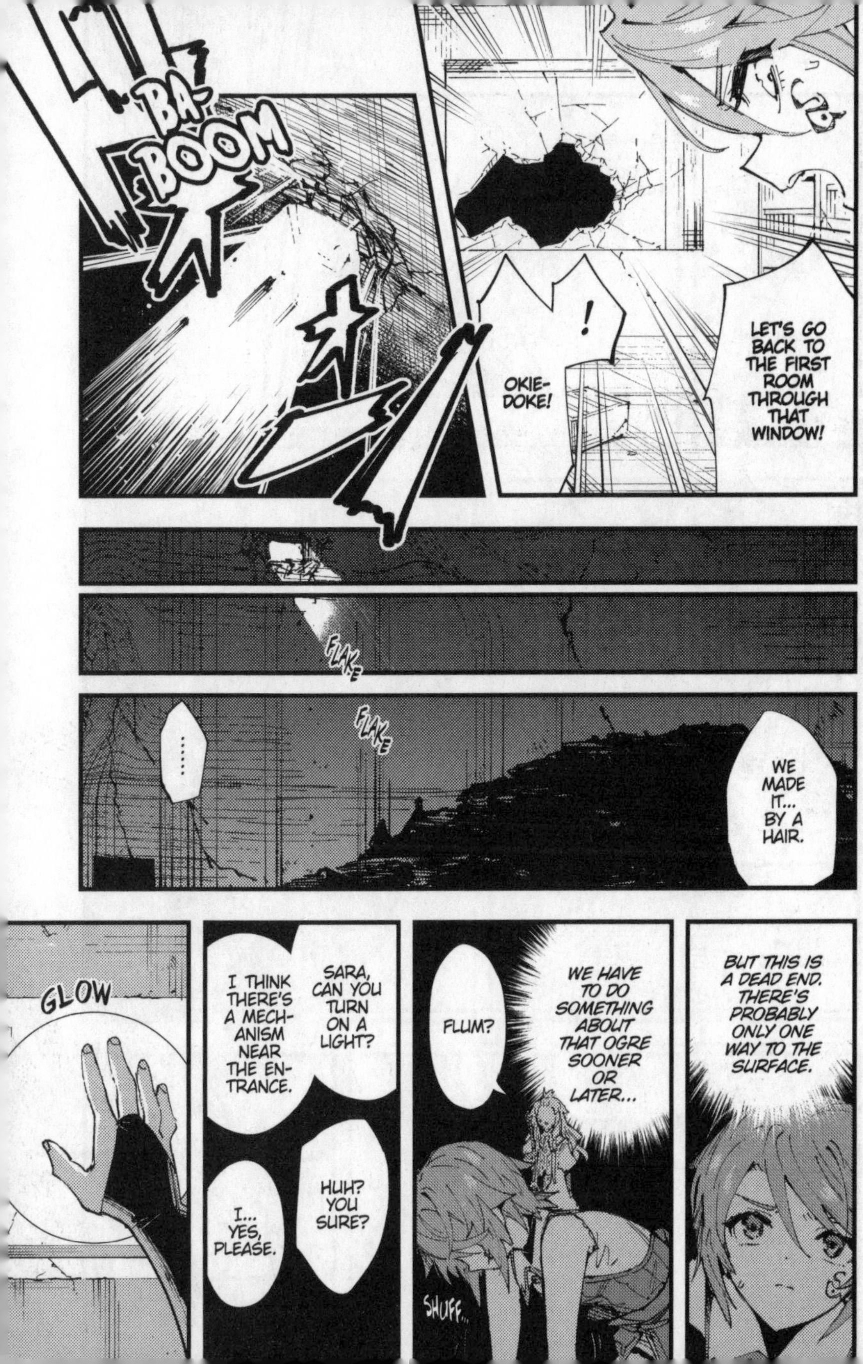
LET'S GO BACK TO THE FIRST ROOM THROUGH THAT WINDOW!
!
OKIE-DOKE!
BA-BOOM
FLAKE
FLAKE
WE MADE IT... BY A HAIR.
......
BUT THIS IS A DEAD END. THERE'S PROBABLY ONLY ONE WAY TO THE SURFACE.
WE HAVE TO DO SOMETHING ABOUT THAT OGRE SOONER OR LATER...
FLUM?
SHUFF...
SARA, CAN YOU TURN ON A LIGHT?
I THINK THERE'S A MECH-ANISM NEAR THE EN-TRANCE.
HUH? YOU SURE?
I... YES, PLEASE.
GLOW

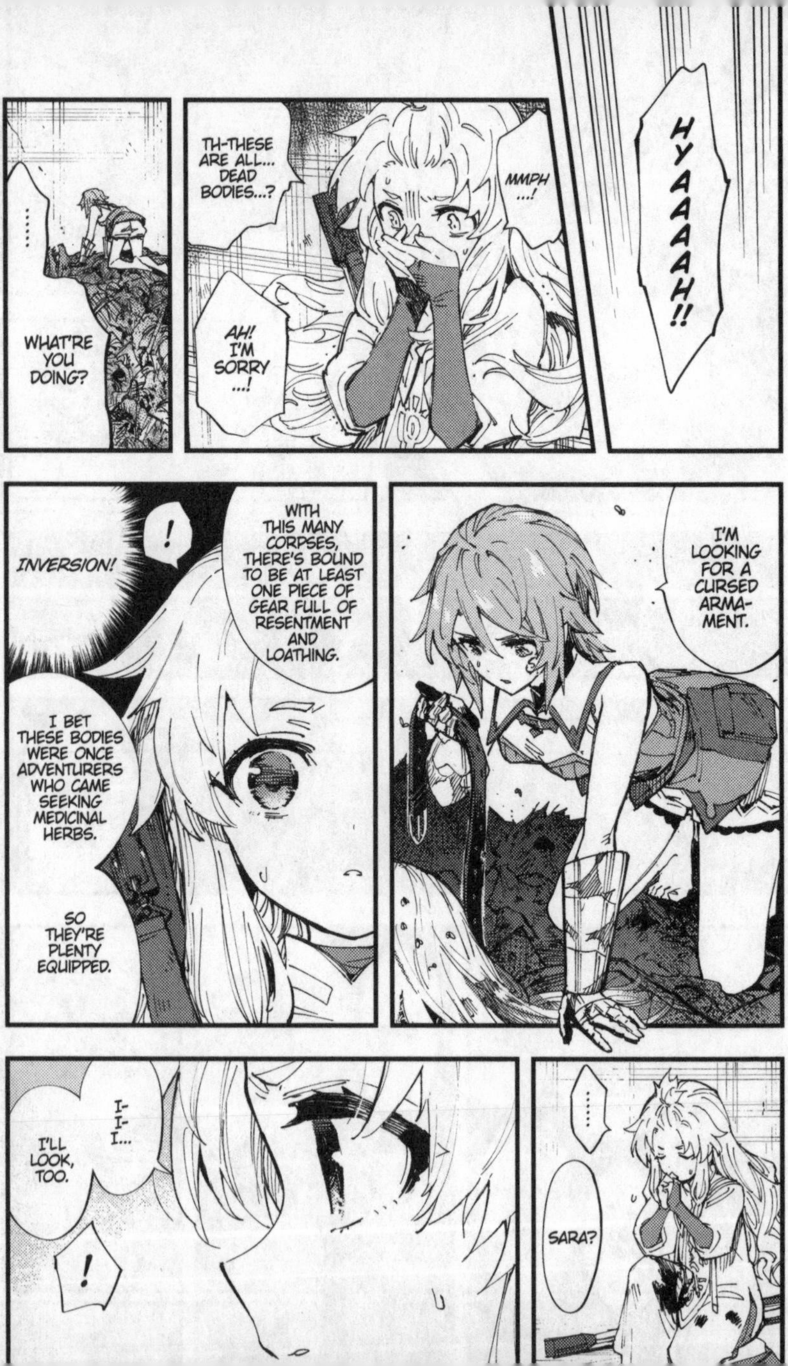
HYAAAAAH!!
MMPH...!
TH-THESE ARE ALL... DEAD BODIES...?
AH! I'M SORRY...!
......
WHAT'RE YOU DOING?
I'M LOOKING FOR A CURSED ARMAMENT.
WITH THIS MANY CORPSES, THERE'S BOUND TO BE AT LEAST ONE PIECE OF GEAR FULL OF RESENTMENT AND LOATHING.
!
INVERSION!
I BET THESE BODIES WERE ONCE ADVENTURERS WHO CAME SEEKING MEDICINAL HERBS.
SO THEY'RE PLENTY EQUIPPED.
......
SARA?
I-I-I...
I'LL LOOK, TOO.
!

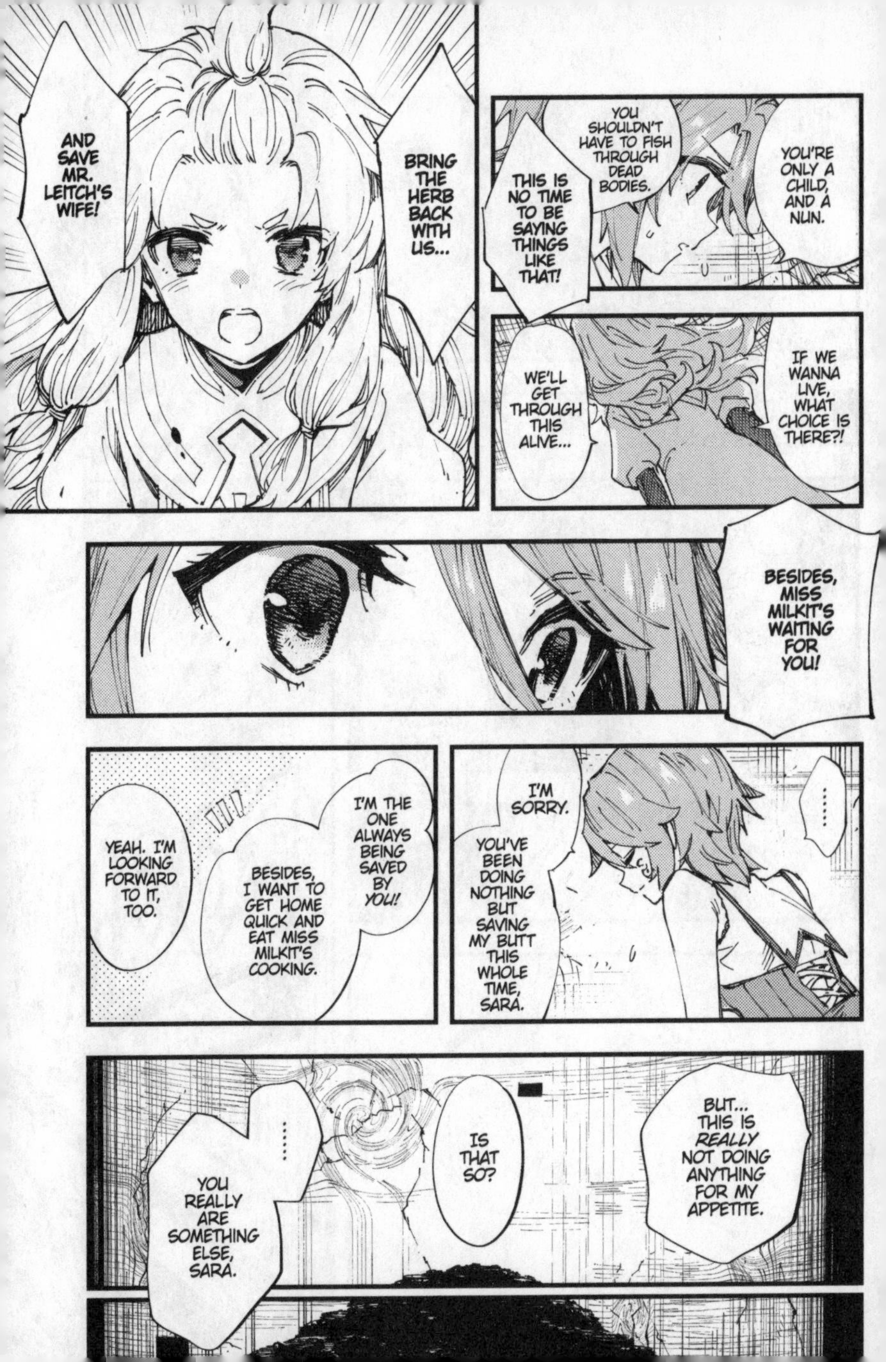
YOU'RE ONLY A CHILD, AND A NUN.
YOU SHOULDN'T HAVE TO FISH THROUGH DEAD BODIES.
THIS IS NO TIME TO BE SAYING THINGS LIKE THAT!
IF WE WANNA LIVE, WHAT CHOICE IS THERE?!
WE'LL GET THROUGH THIS ALIVE...
BRING THE HERB BACK WITH US...
AND SAVE MR. LEITCH'S WIFE!
BESIDES, MISS MILKIT'S WAITING FOR YOU!
......
I'M SORRY.
YOU'VE BEEN DOING NOTHING BUT SAVING MY BUTT THIS WHOLE TIME, SARA.
I'M THE ONE ALWAYS BEING SAVED BY *YOU!*
BESIDES, I WANT TO GET HOME QUICK AND EAT MISS MILKIT'S COOKING.
YEAH. I'M LOOKING FORWARD TO IT, TOO.
BUT... THIS IS *REALLY* NOT DOING ANYTHING FOR MY APPETITE.
IS THAT SO?
......
YOU REALLY ARE SOMETHING ELSE, SARA.

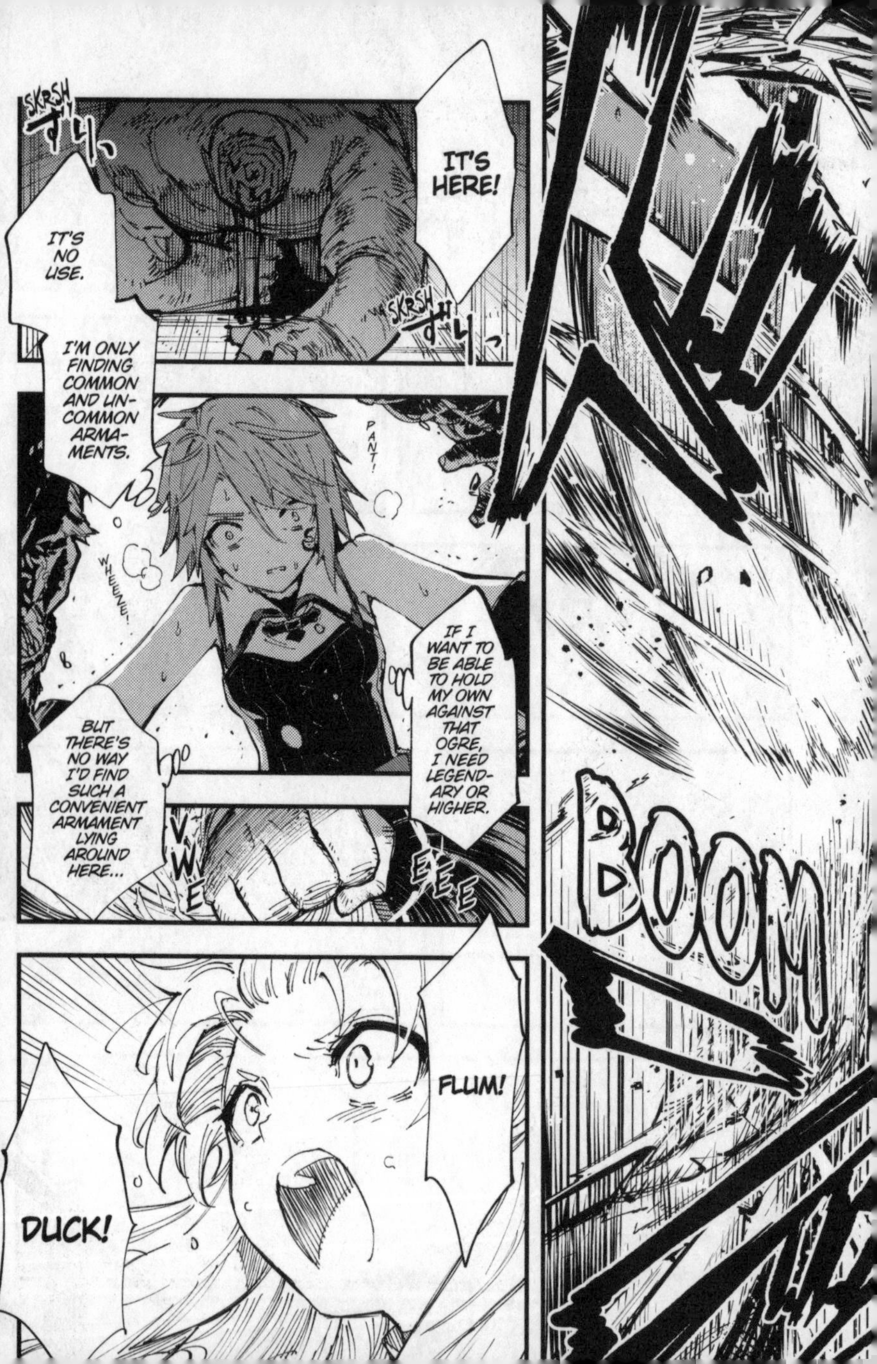
BOOM
IT'S HERE!
SKRSH
IT'S NO USE.
SKRSH
I'M ONLY FINDING COMMON AND UN-COMMON ARMA-MENTS.
PANT!
WHEEZE!
IF I WANT TO BE ABLE TO HOLD MY OWN AGAINST THAT OGRE, I NEED LEGEND-ARY OR HIGHER.
BUT THERE'S NO WAY I'D FIND SUCH A CONVENIENT ARMAMENT LYING AROUND HERE...
VWEEE
FLUM!
DUCK!

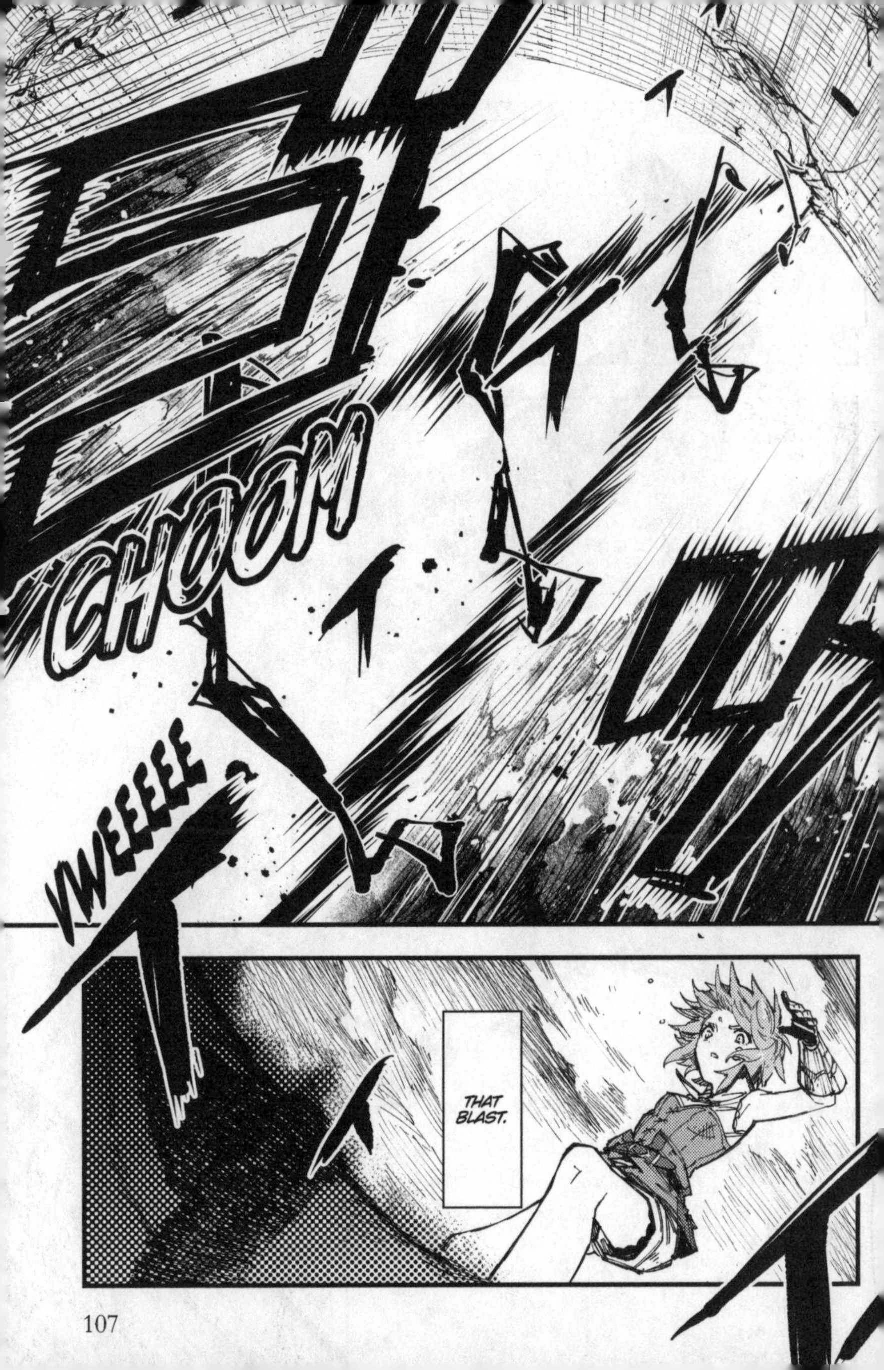
CHOOM
VWEEEEE
THAT BLAST.

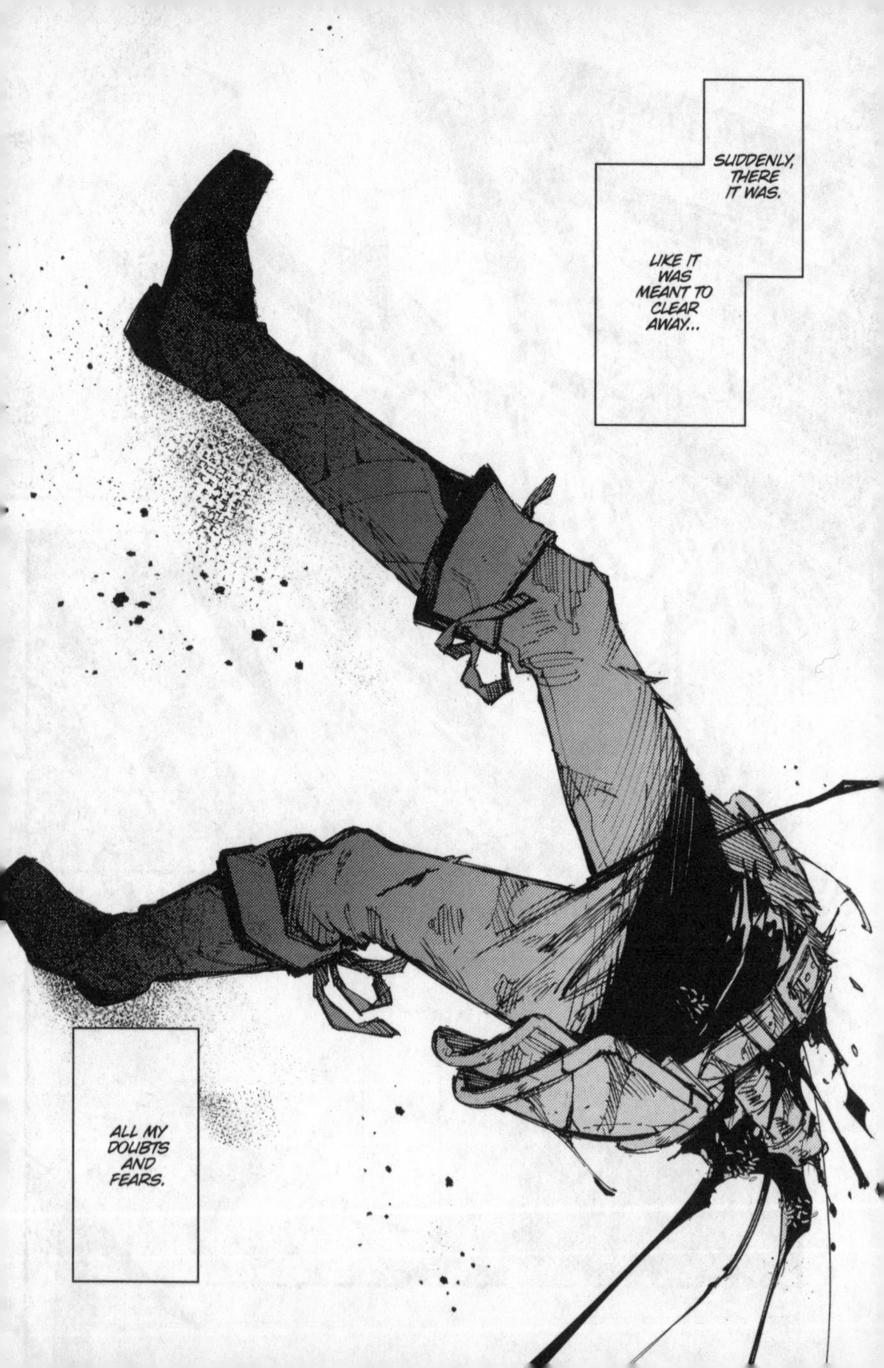
SUDDENLY, THERE IT WAS.
LIKE IT WAS MEANT TO CLEAR AWAY...
ALL MY DOUBTS AND FEARS.

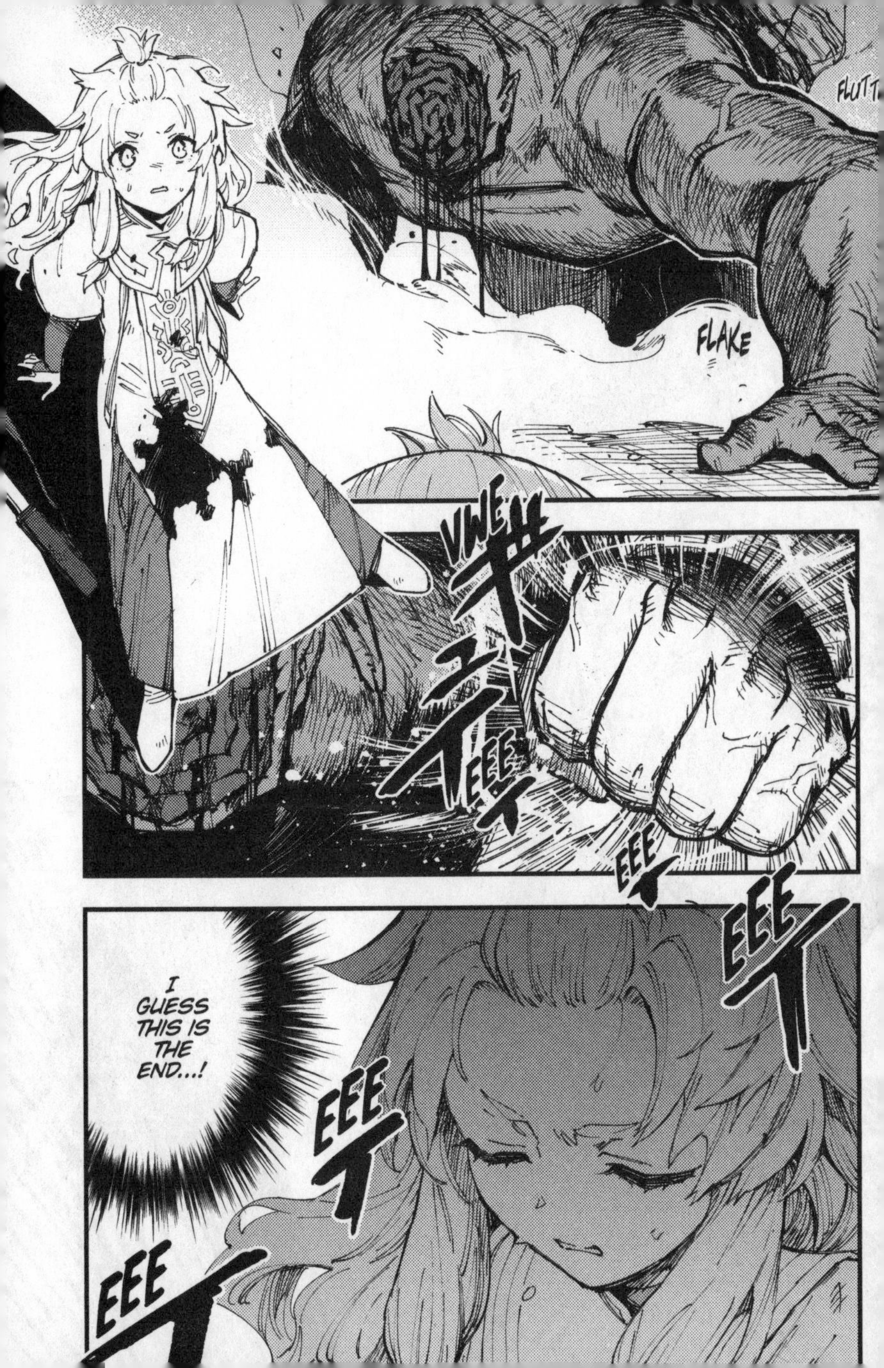
FLUTT
FLAKE
VWEE
EEE
EEE
I GUESS THIS IS THE END...!
EEE
EEE

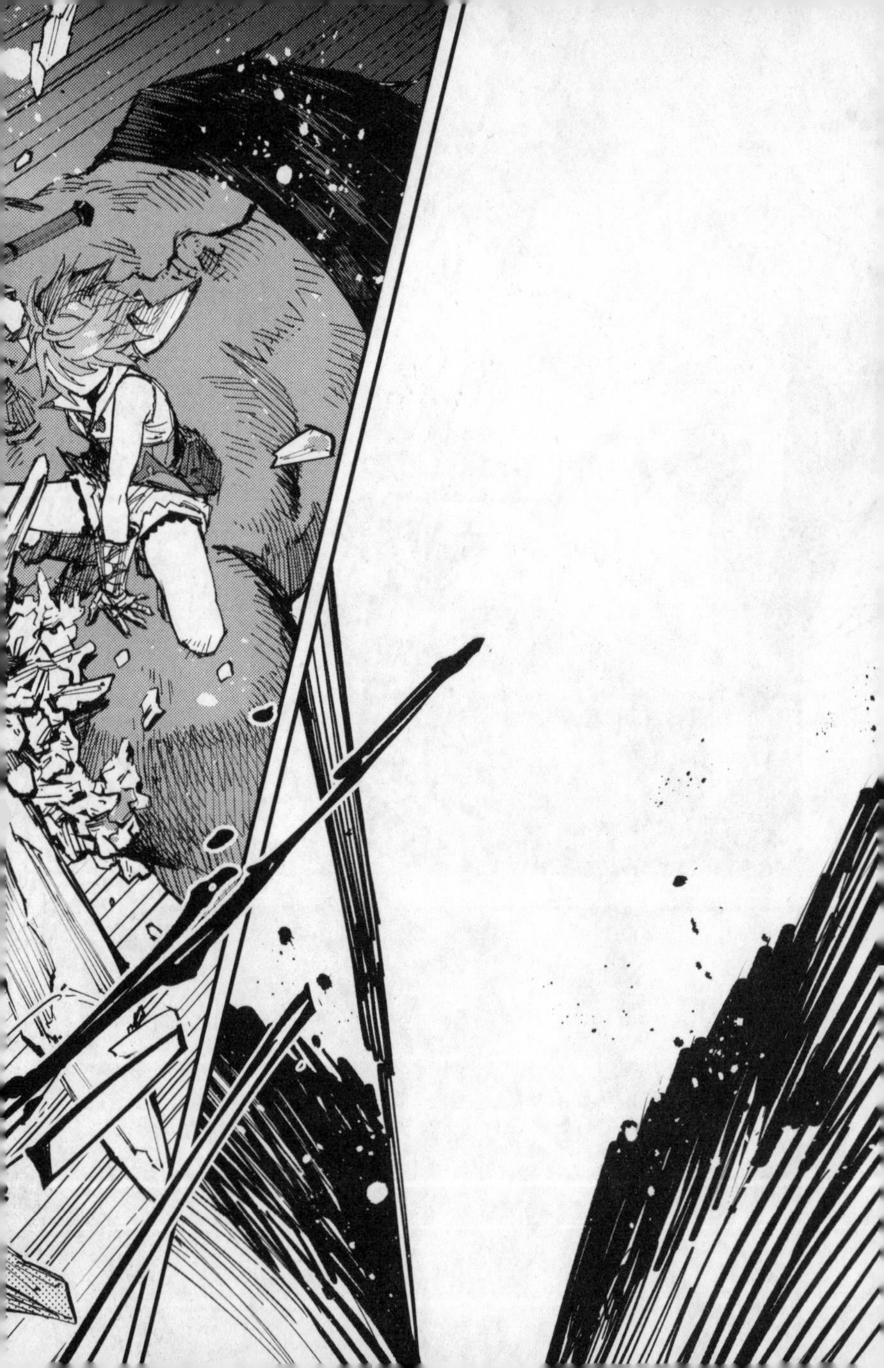

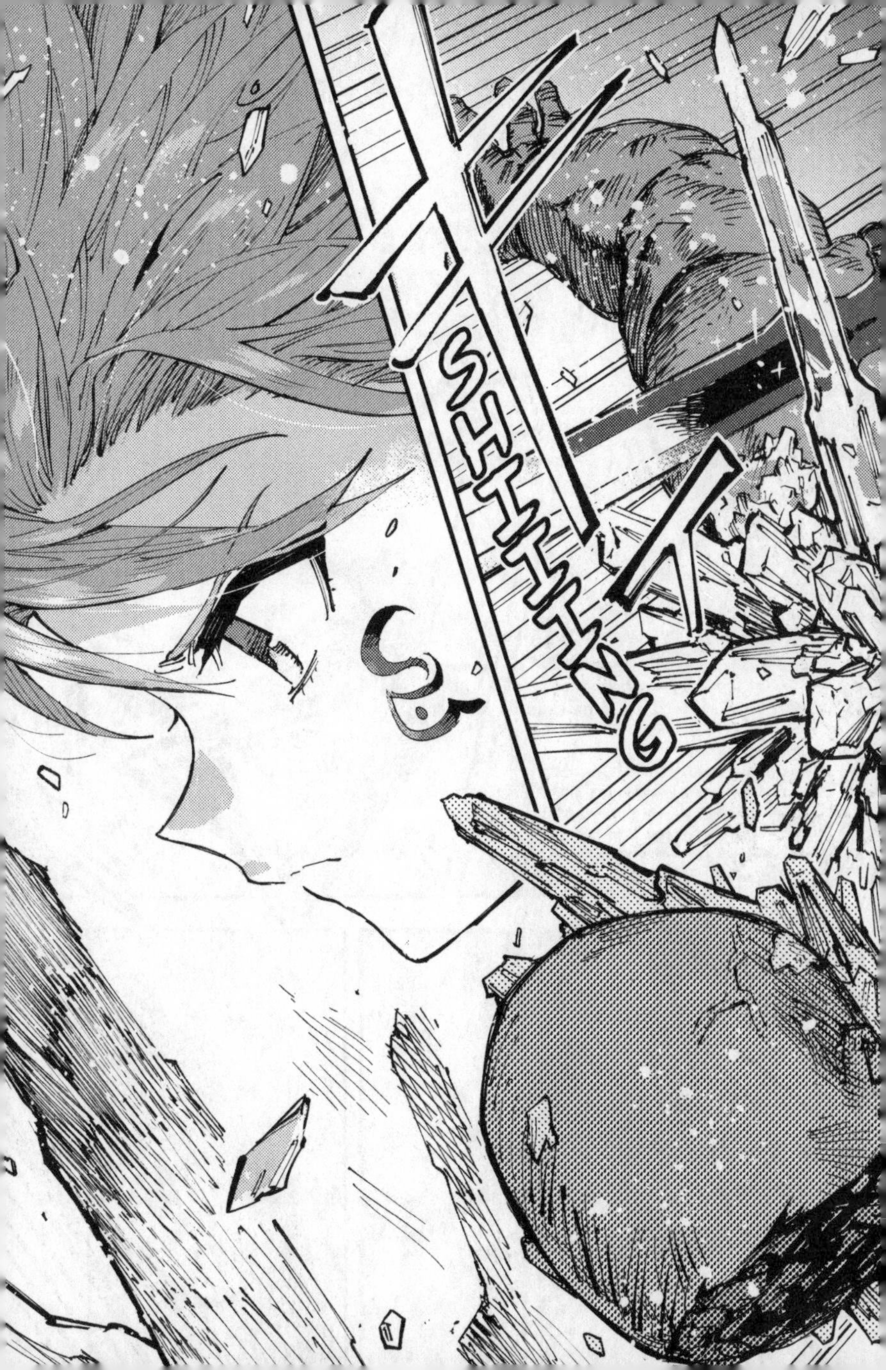
SHIIIING

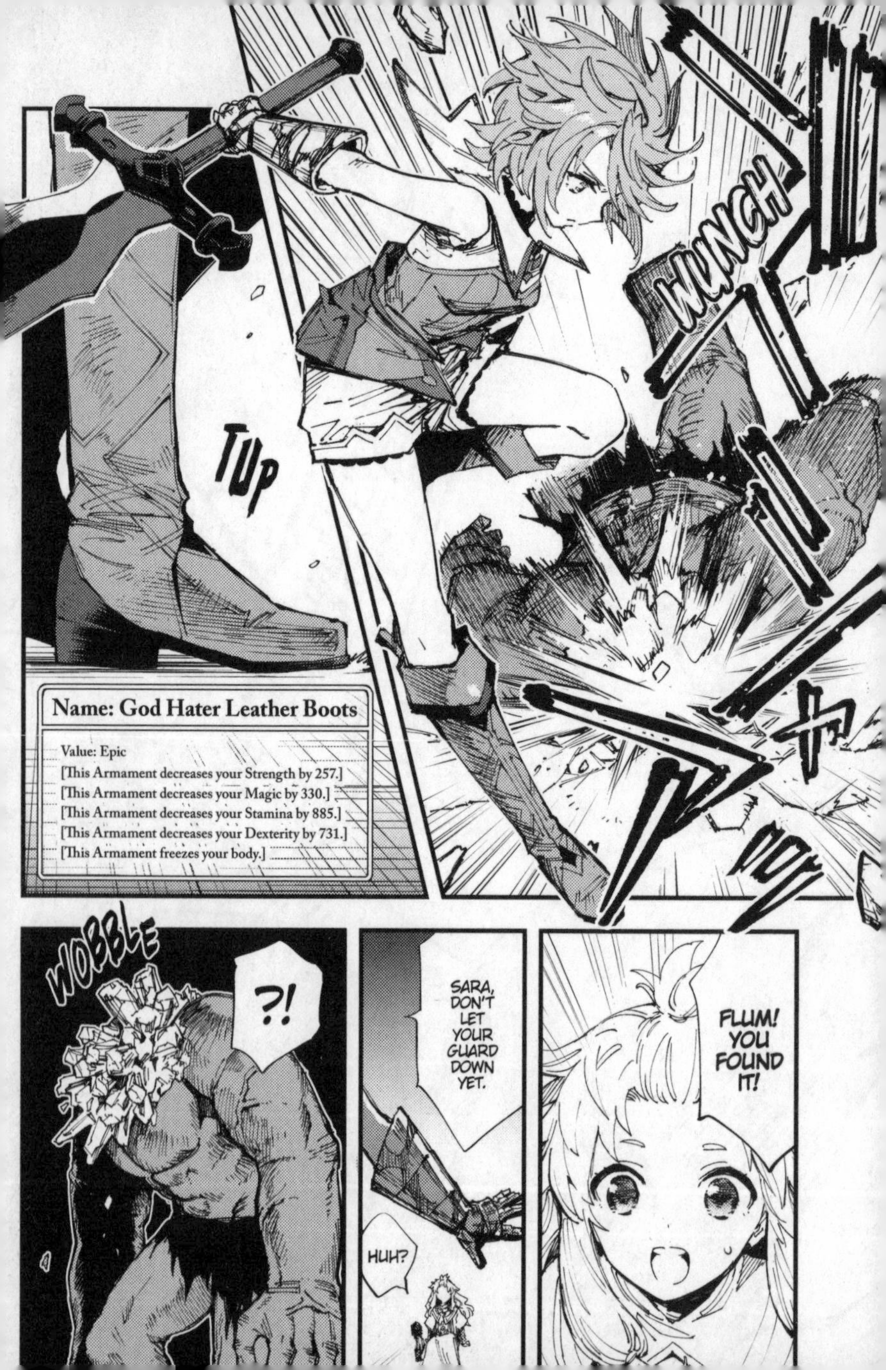
WHUNCH
TUP
Name: God Hater Leather Boots
Value: Epic
[This Armament decreases your Strength by 257.]
[This Armament decreases your Magic by 330.]
[This Armament decreases your Stamina by 885.]
[This Armament decreases your Dexterity by 731.]
[This Armament freezes your body.]
FLUM! YOU FOUND IT!
SARA, DON'T LET YOUR GUARD DOWN YET.
HUH?
WOBBLE
?!

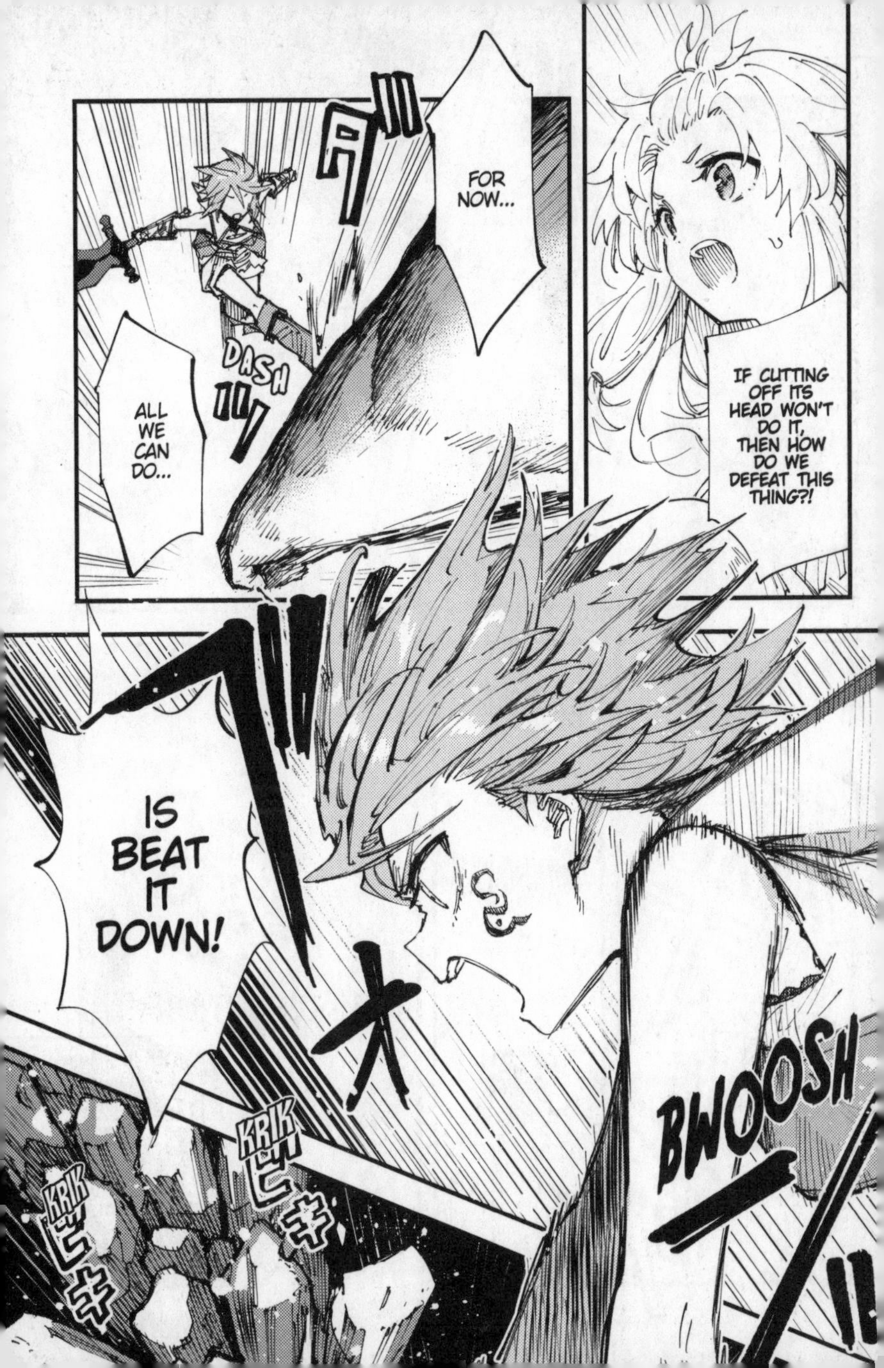
IF CUTTING OFF ITS HEAD WON'T DO IT, THEN HOW DO WE DEFEAT THIS THING?!
FOR NOW...
DASH
ALL WE CAN DO...
IS BEAT IT DOWN!
BWOOSH
KRIK
KRIK

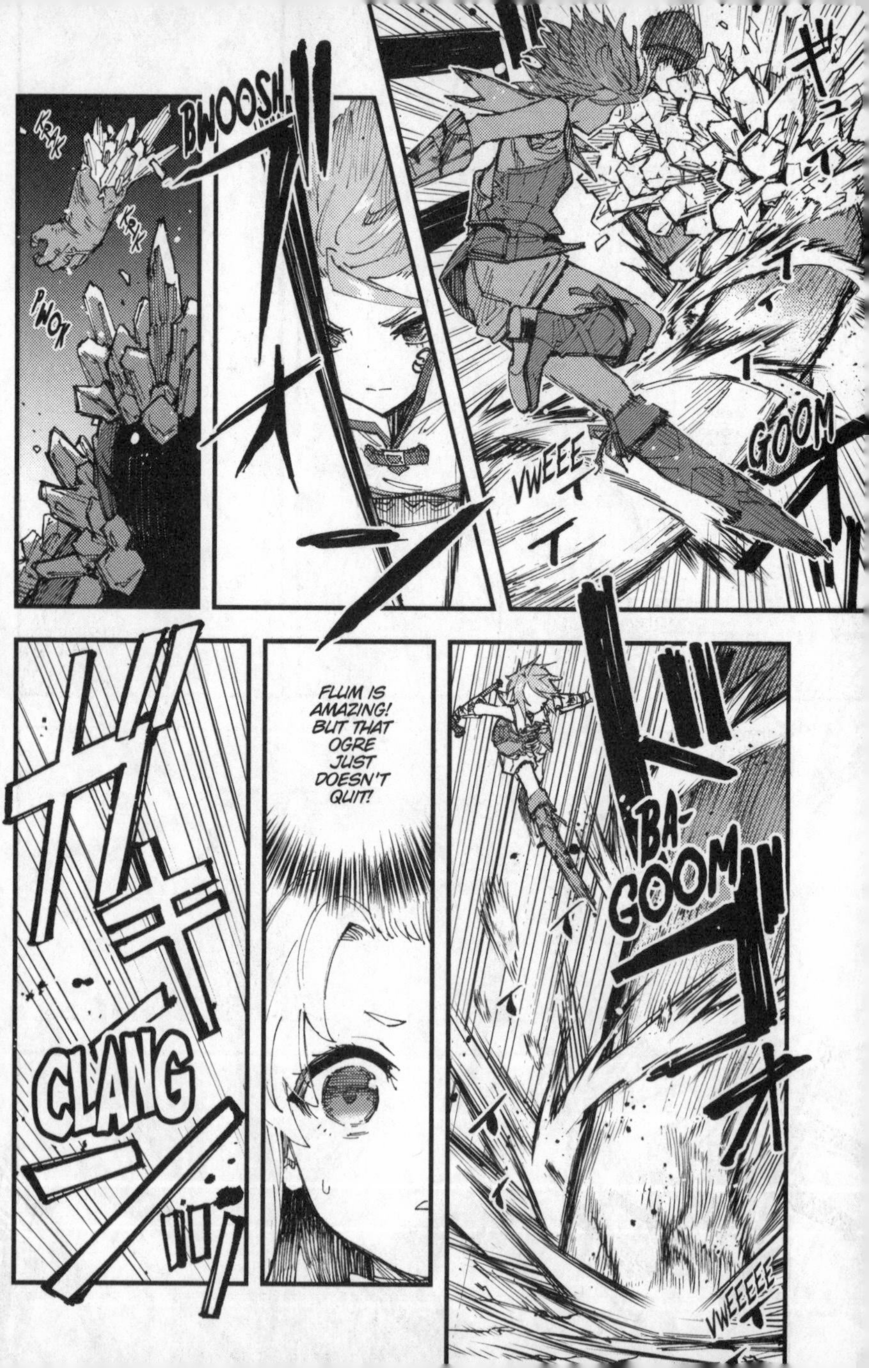

GOOM
VWEEE
BWOOSH
KRAK
KRAK
PWOK
BA-GOOM
VWEEEEE
FLUM IS AMAZING! BUT THAT OGRE JUST DOESN'T QUIT!
CLANG

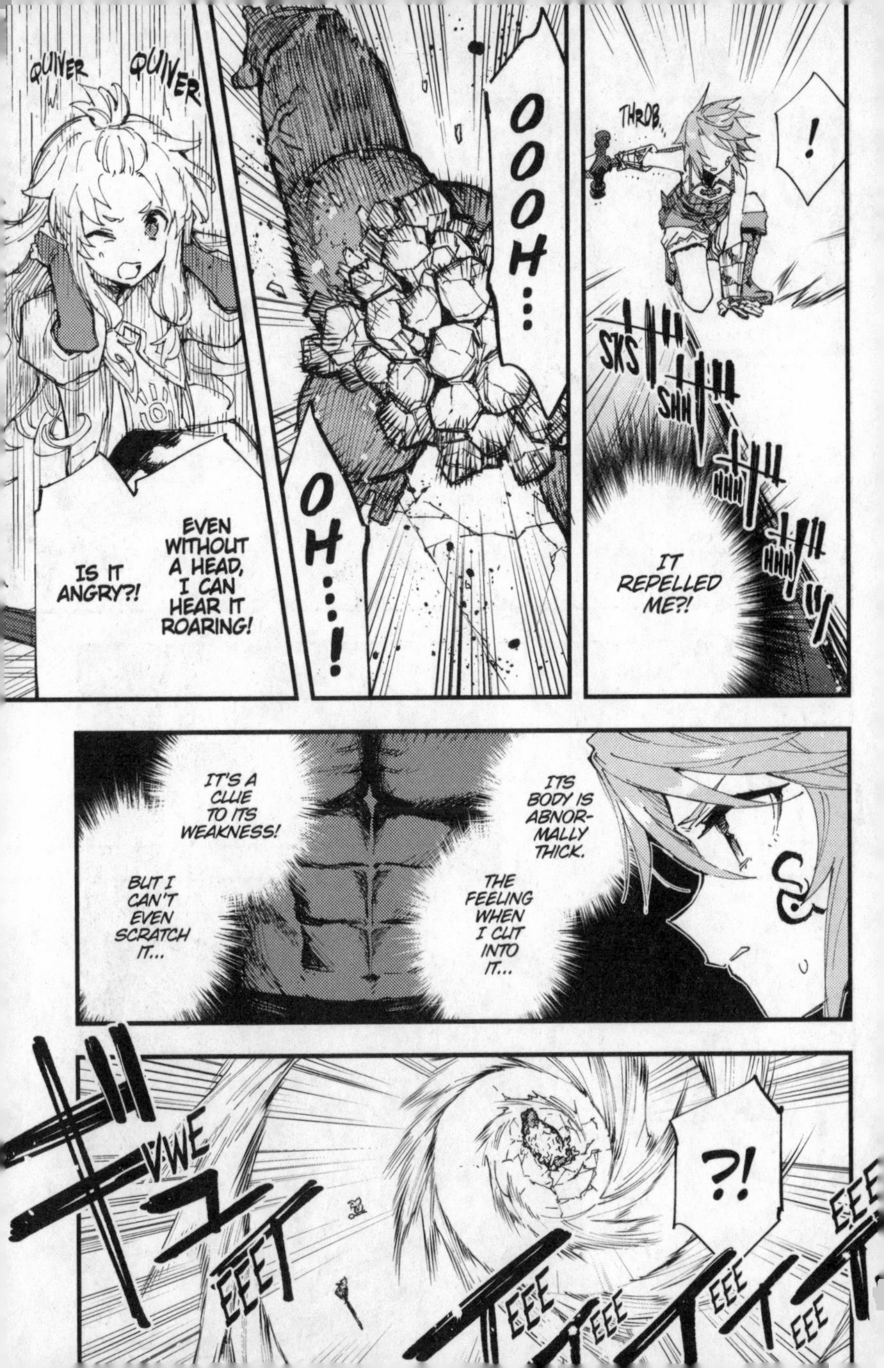
!
THROB...
SKS
SHH
HHH
HHH
IT REPELLED ME?!
OOOOH...
OH...!
QUIVER
QUIVER
EVEN WITHOUT A HEAD, I CAN HEAR IT ROARING!
IS IT ANGRY?!
ITS BODY IS ABNORMALLY THICK.
THE FEELING WHEN I CUT INTO IT...
IT'S A CLUE TO ITS WEAKNESS!
BUT I CAN'T EVEN SCRATCH IT...
?!
EEE
EEE
EEE
EEE
EEE
VWE
EEET

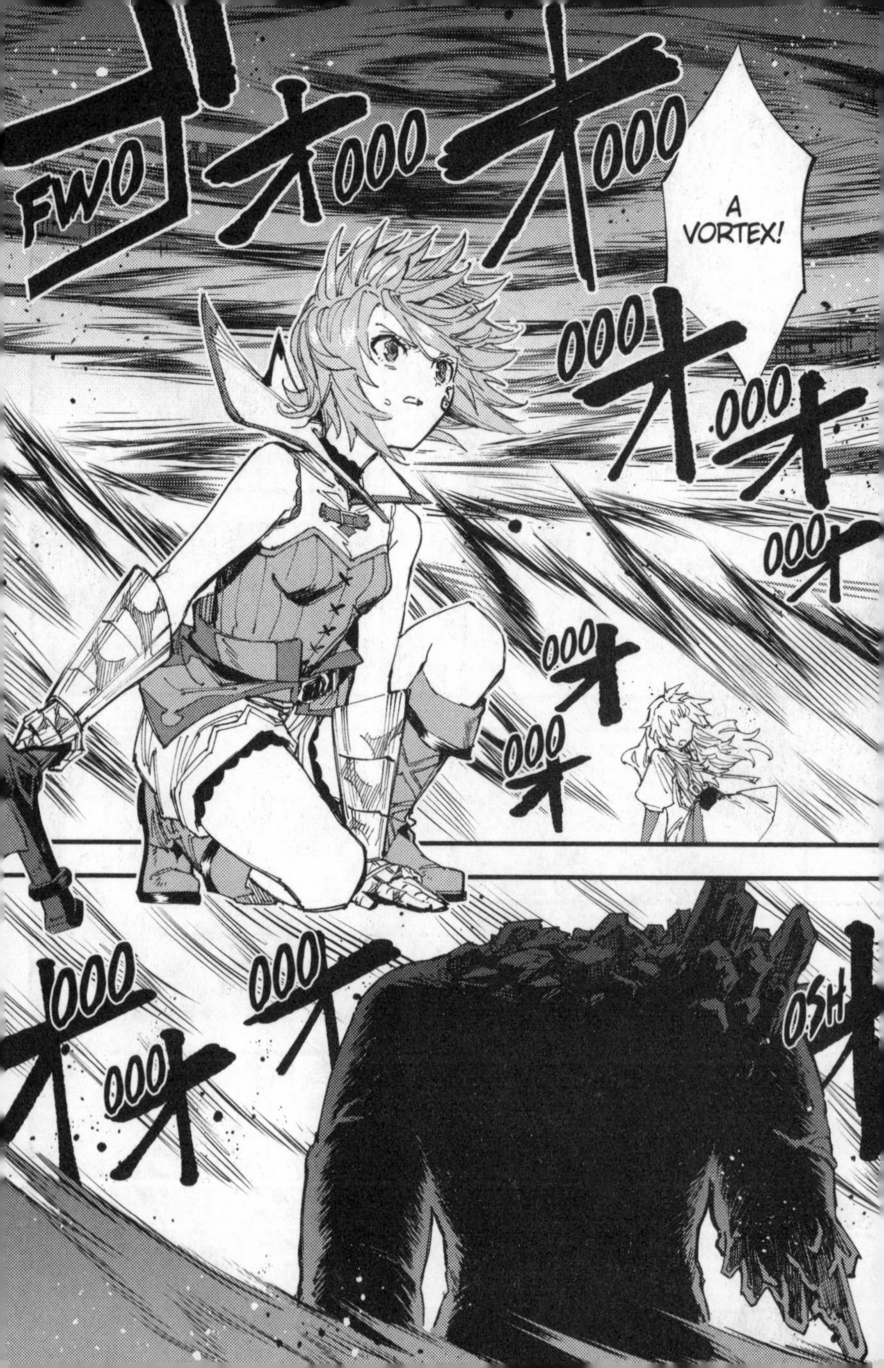

A VORTEX!
FWO OOO OOO
OOO OOO OOO
OOO OOO
OOO OOO OOO
OSH

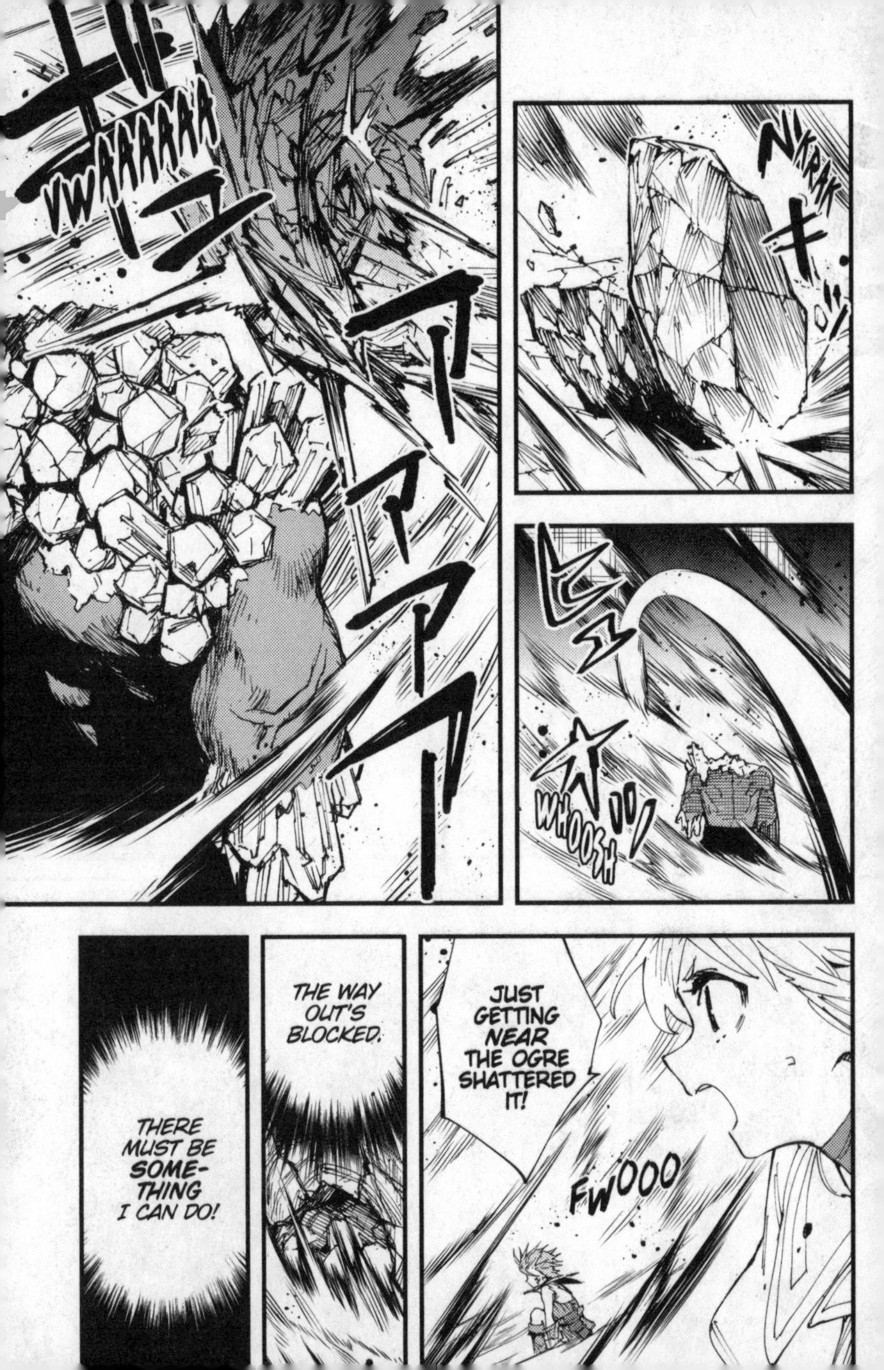
NKRAK
WHOOSH
VWAAAAAR
JUST GETTING NEAR THE OGRE SHATTERED IT!
FWOOO
THE WAY OUT'S BLOCKED.
THERE MUST BE SOME-THING I CAN DO!

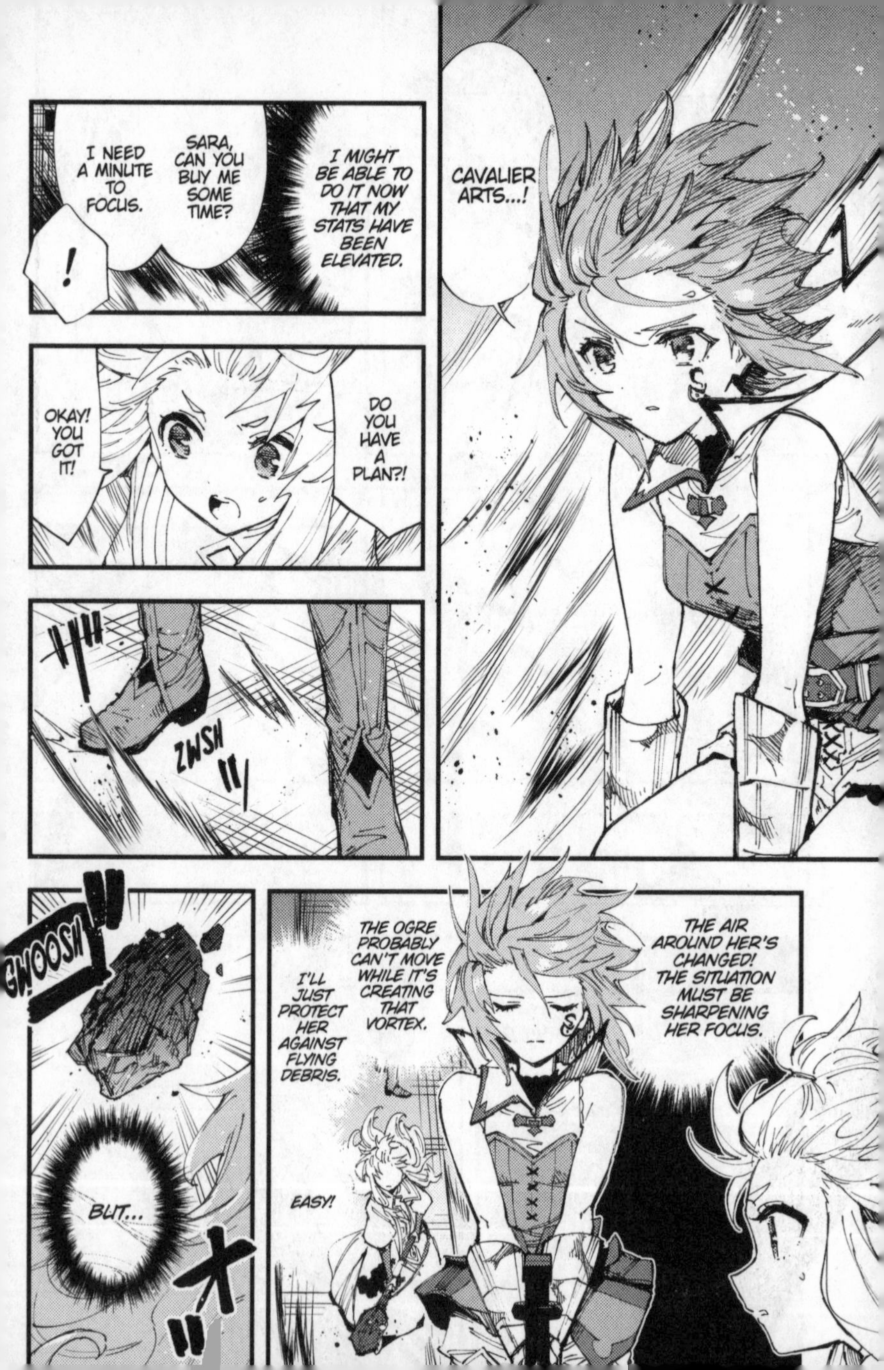
CAVALIER ARTS...!
I MIGHT BE ABLE TO DO IT NOW THAT MY STATS HAVE BEEN ELEVATED.
SARA, CAN YOU BUY ME SOME TIME?
I NEED A MINUTE TO FOCUS.
!
DO YOU HAVE A PLAN?!
OKAY! YOU GOT IT!
ZWSH
THE AIR AROUND HER'S CHANGED! THE SITUATION MUST BE SHARPENING HER FOCUS.
THE OGRE PROBABLY CAN'T MOVE WHILE IT'S CREATING THAT VORTEX.
I'LL JUST PROTECT HER AGAINST FLYING DEBRIS.
EASY!
GWOOSH
BUT...

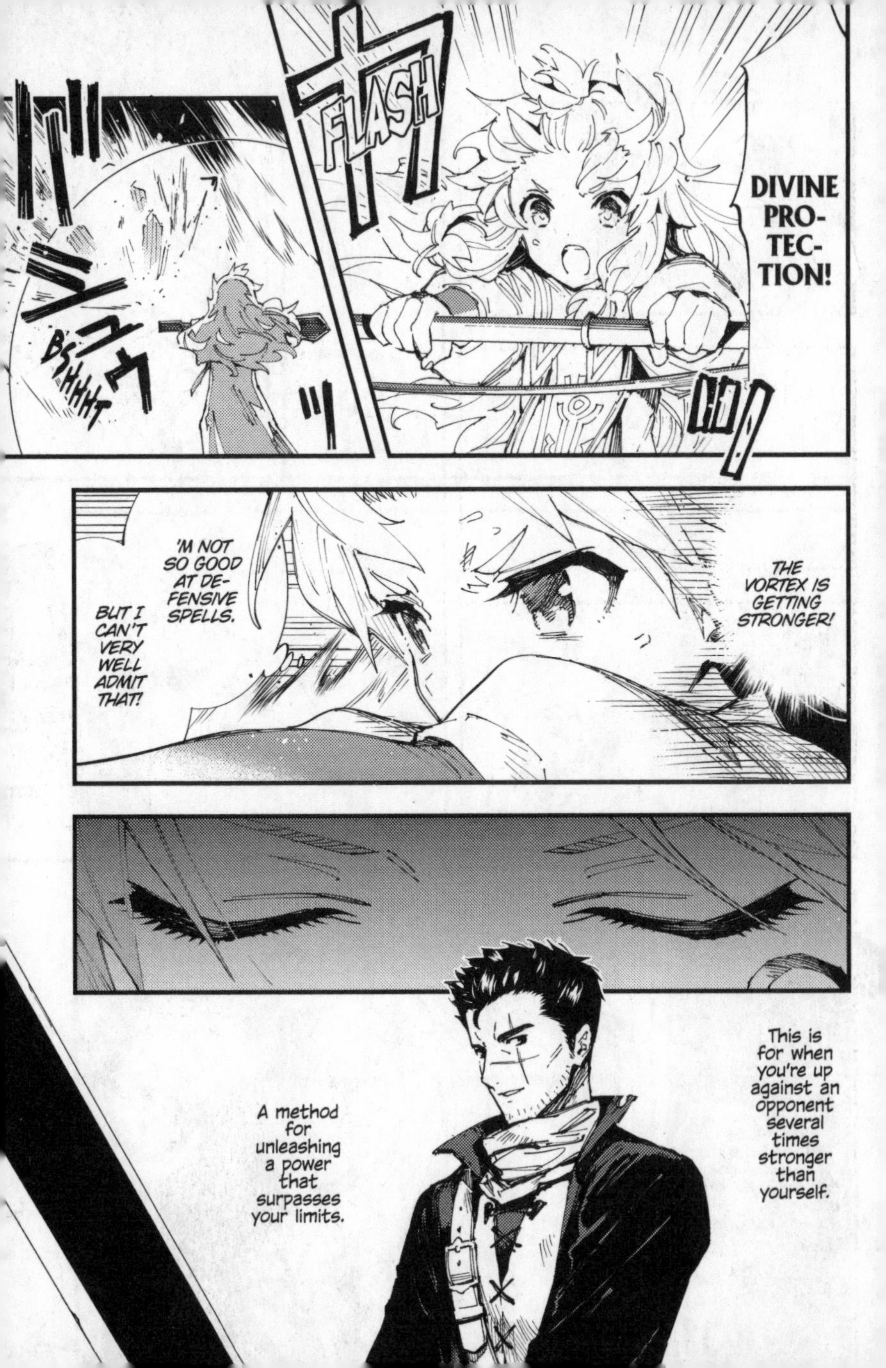
FLASH
DIVINE PRO-TEC-TION!
BSHHHHT
THE VORTEX IS GETTING STRONGER!
'M NOT SO GOOD AT DE-FENSIVE SPELLS.
BUT I CAN'T VERY WELL ADMIT THAT!
This is for when you're up against an opponent several times stronger than yourself.
A method for unleashing a power that surpasses your limits.

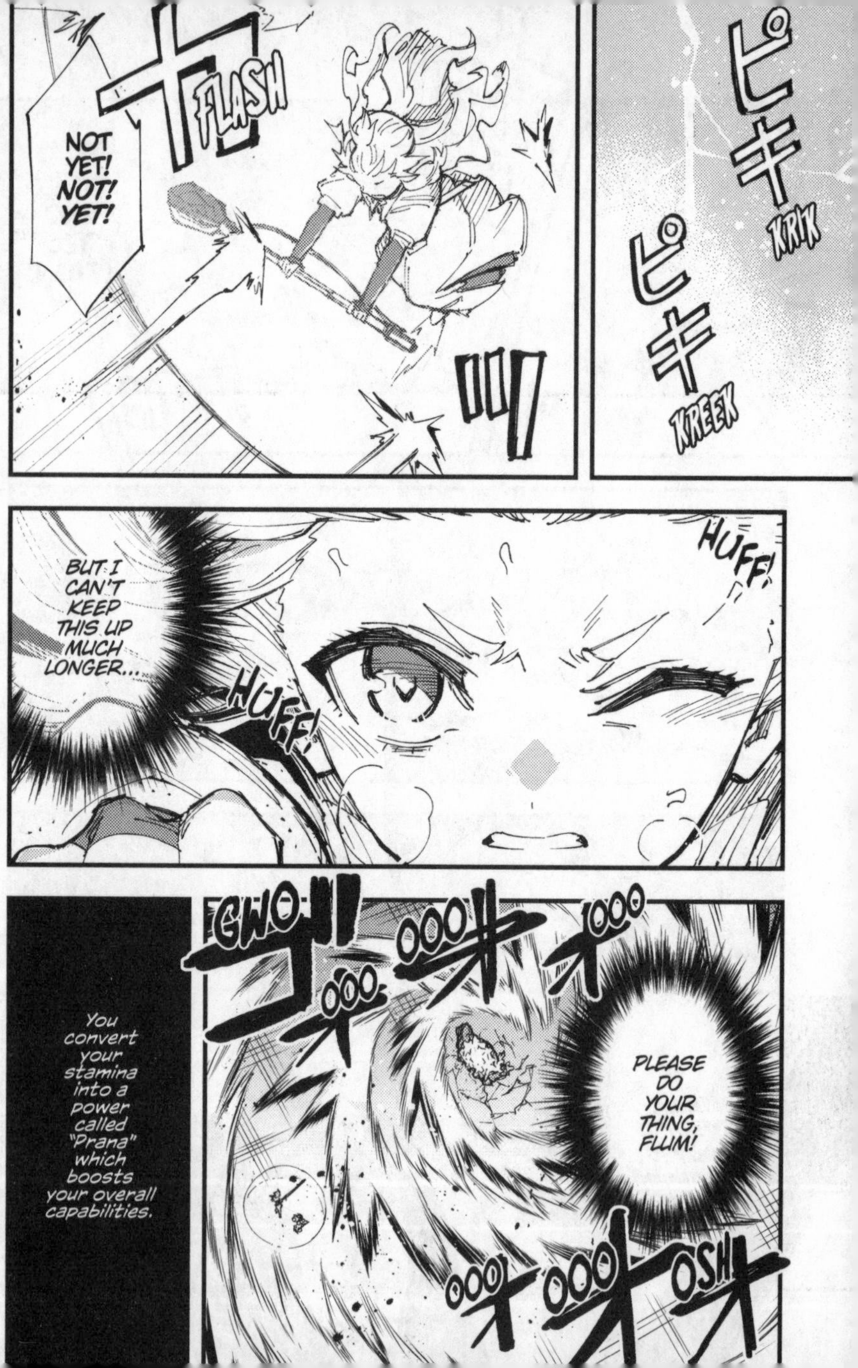
ピキ
KRIK
ピキ
KREEK
FLASH
NOT YET! NOT! YET!
HUFF!
BUT I CAN'T KEEP THIS UP MUCH LONGER...
HUFF!
GWO
OOO
OOO
OOO
PLEASE DO YOUR THING, FLUM!
OOO
OOO
OSH
You convert your stamina into a power called "Prana" which boosts your overall capabilities.

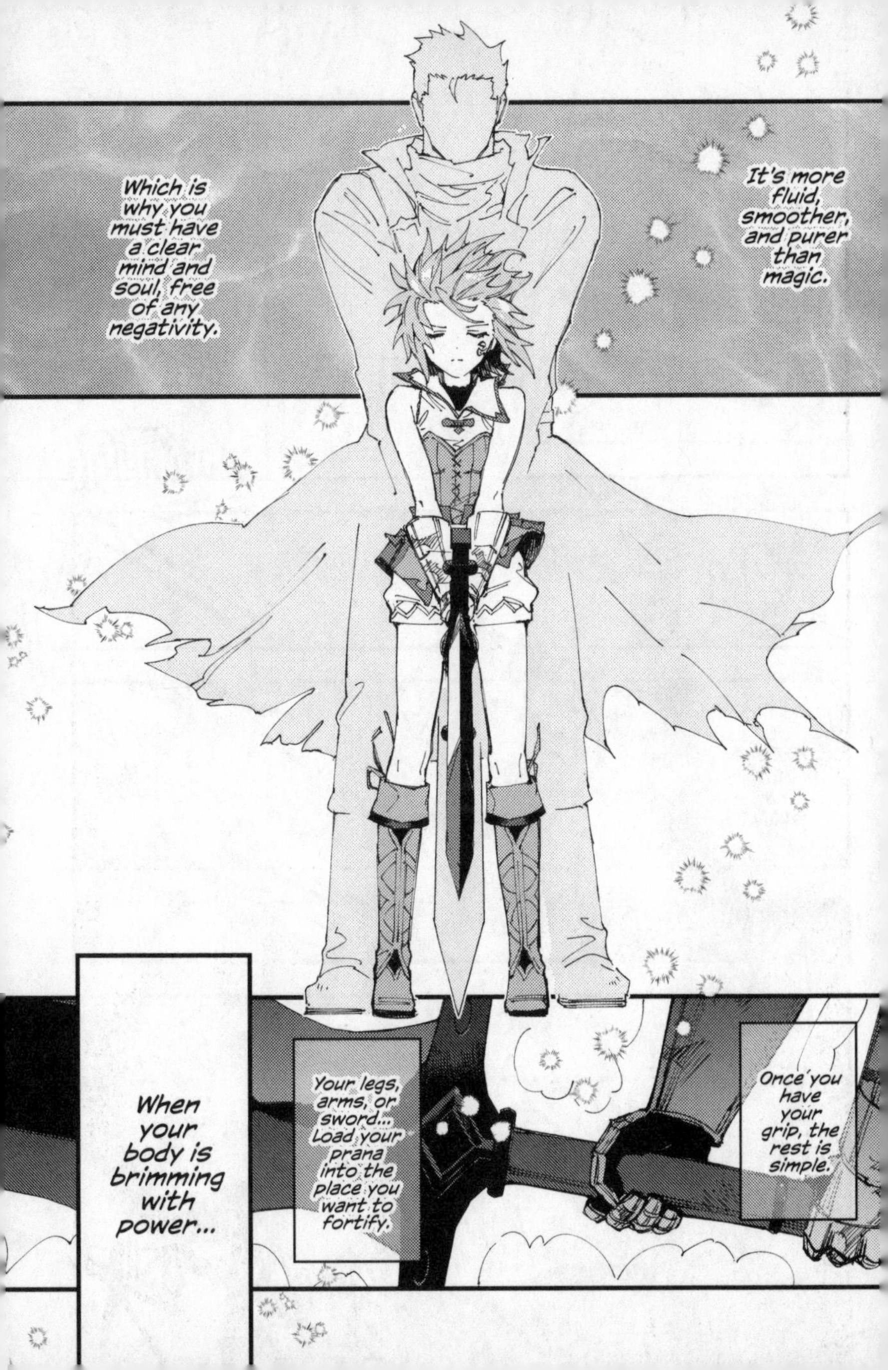
It's more fluid, smoother, and purer than magic.
Which is why you must have a clear mind and soul, free of any negativity.
Once you have your grip, the rest is simple.
Your legs, arms, or sword... Load your prana into the place you want to fortify.
When your body is brimming with power...

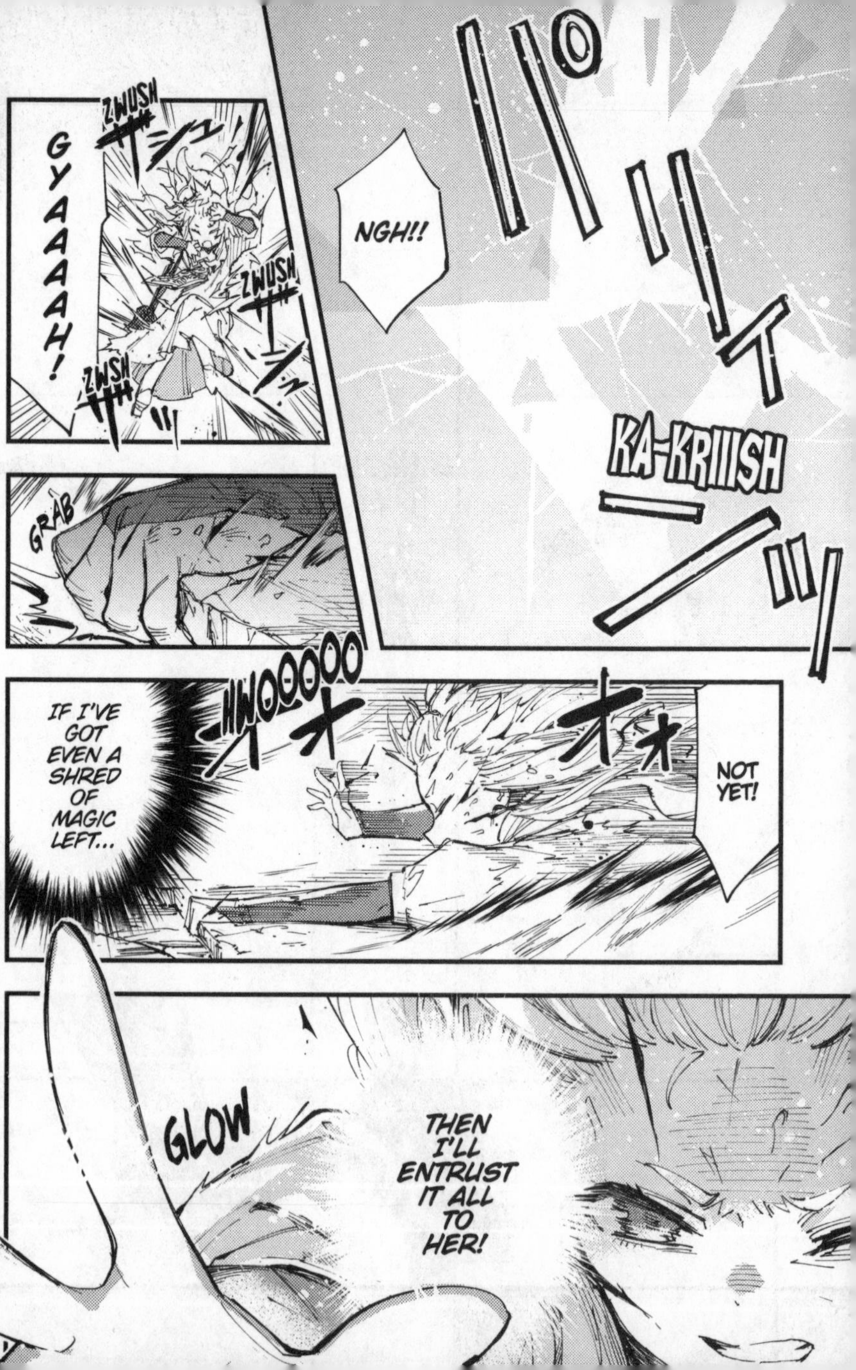
NGH!!
KA-KRIIISH
ZWUSH
GYAAAAAH!
ZWUSH
ZWSH
GRAB
NOT YET!
HWOOOOO
IF I'VE GOT EVEN A SHRED OF MAGIC LEFT...
THEN I'LL ENTRUST IT ALL TO HER!
GLOW

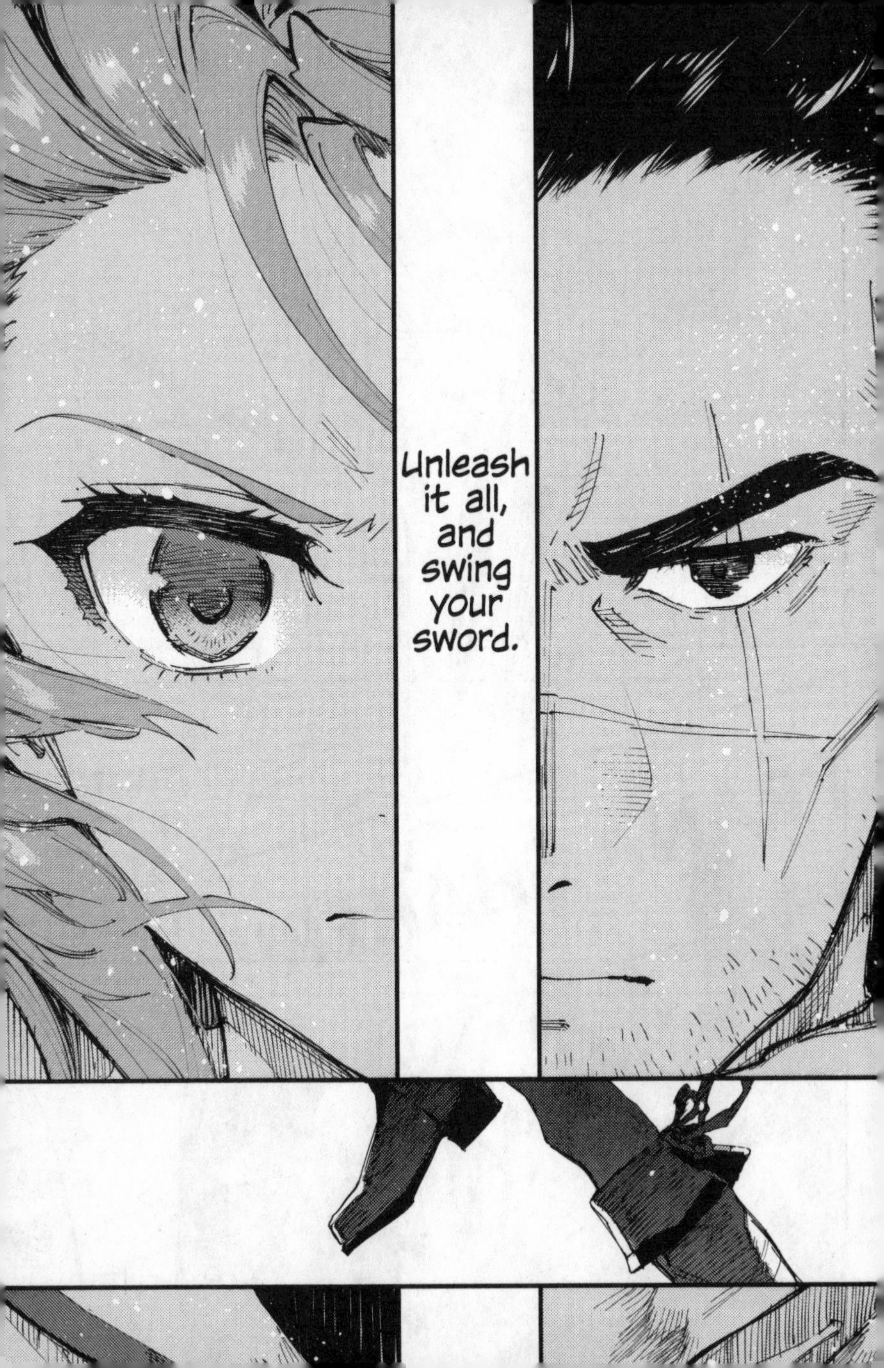
Unleash it all, and swing your sword.

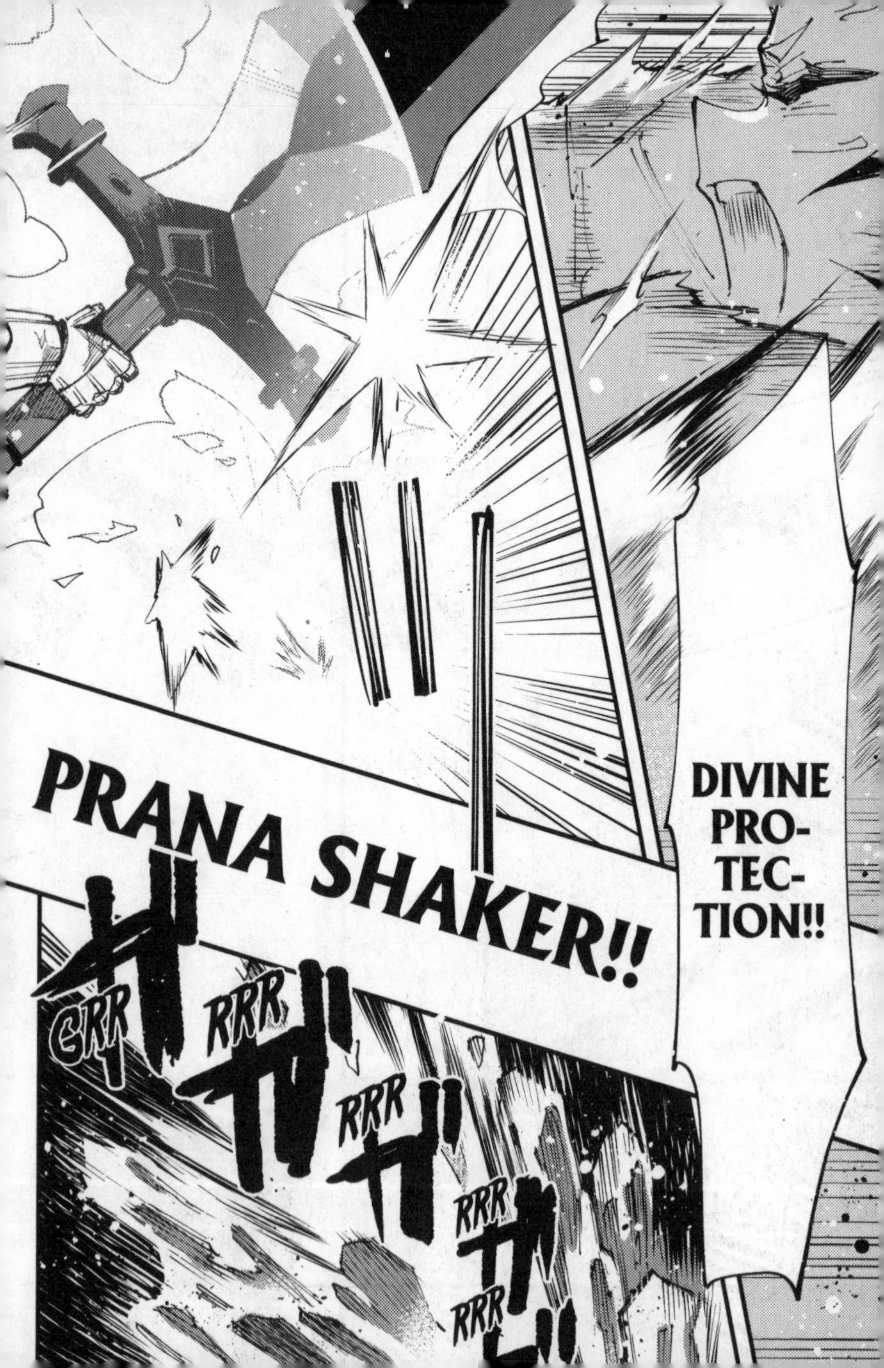
DIVINE PRO-TEC-TION!!
PRANA SHAKER!!
GRR
RRR
RRR
RRR
RRR

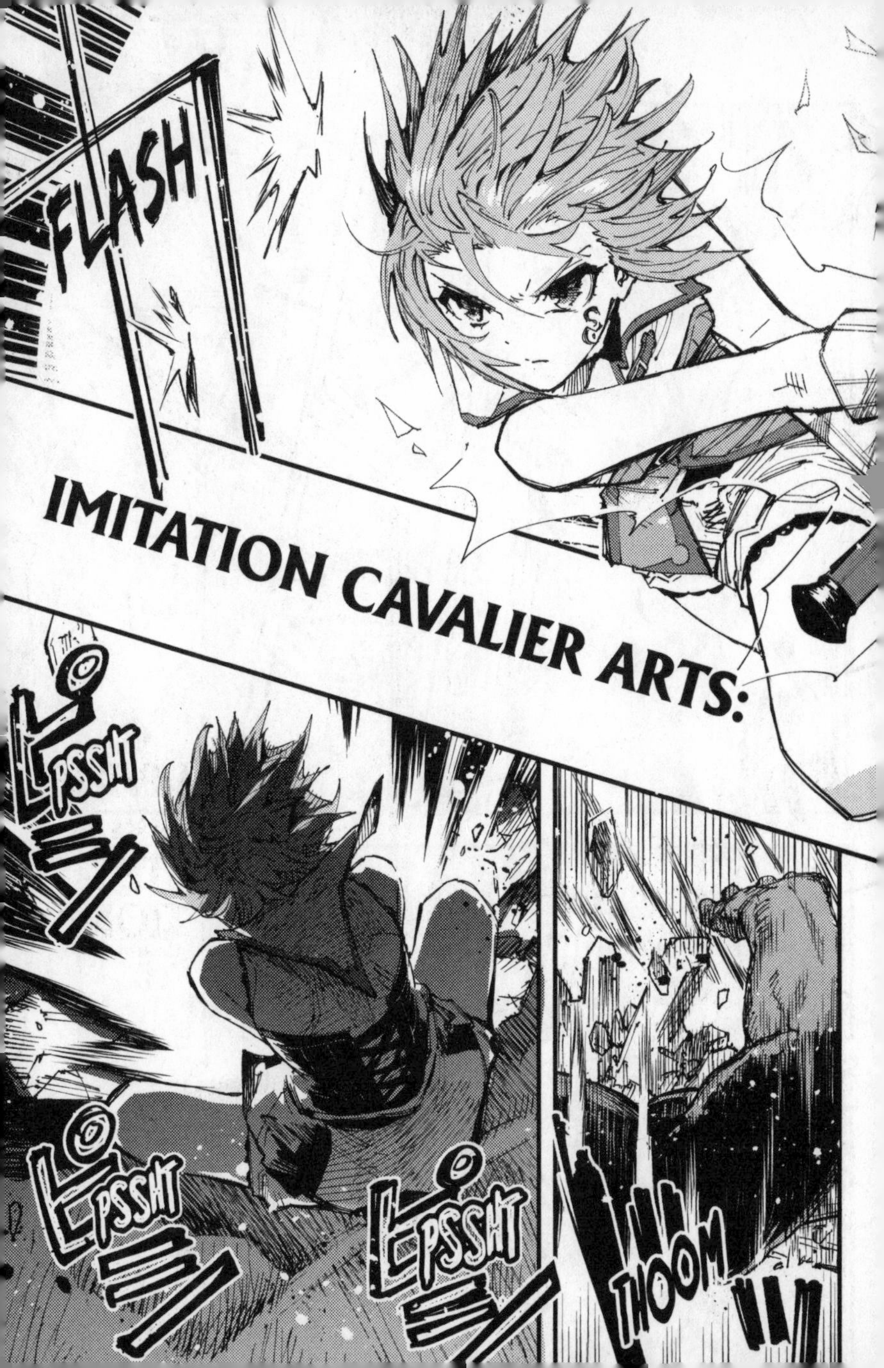
FLASH
IMITATION CAVALIER ARTS:
THOOM
PSSHT
PSSHT
PSSHT
PSSHT

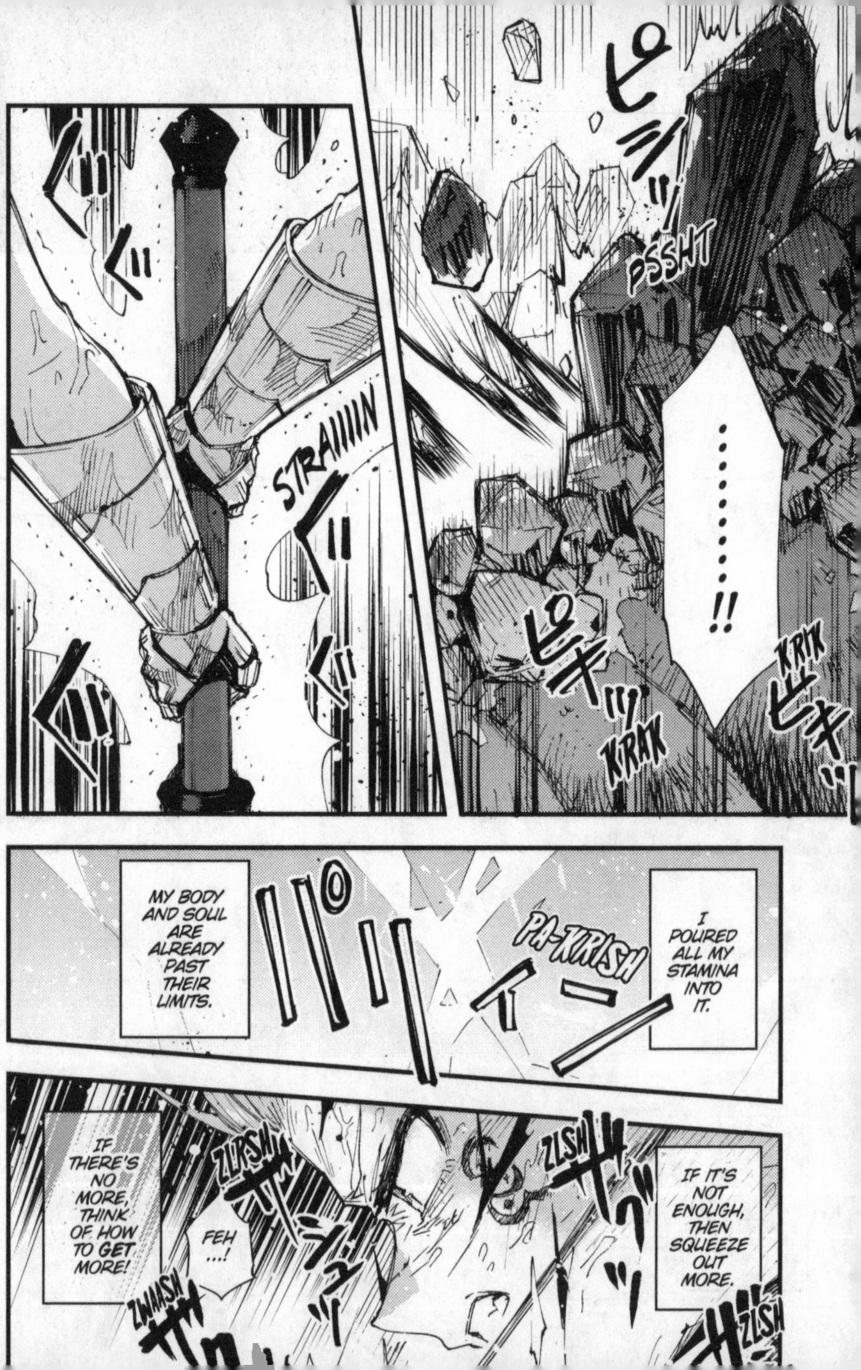
PSSHT
......!!
KRIK
KIRAK
STRAIIIIN
I POURED ALL MY STAMINA INTO IT.
PA-KRISH
MY BODY AND SOUL ARE ALREADY PAST THEIR LIMITS.
IF IT'S NOT ENOUGH, THEN SQUEEZE OUT MORE.
ZLSH
ZLSH
FEH ...!
ZLRSH
IF THERE'S NO MORE, THINK OF HOW TO GET MORE!
ZWAASH

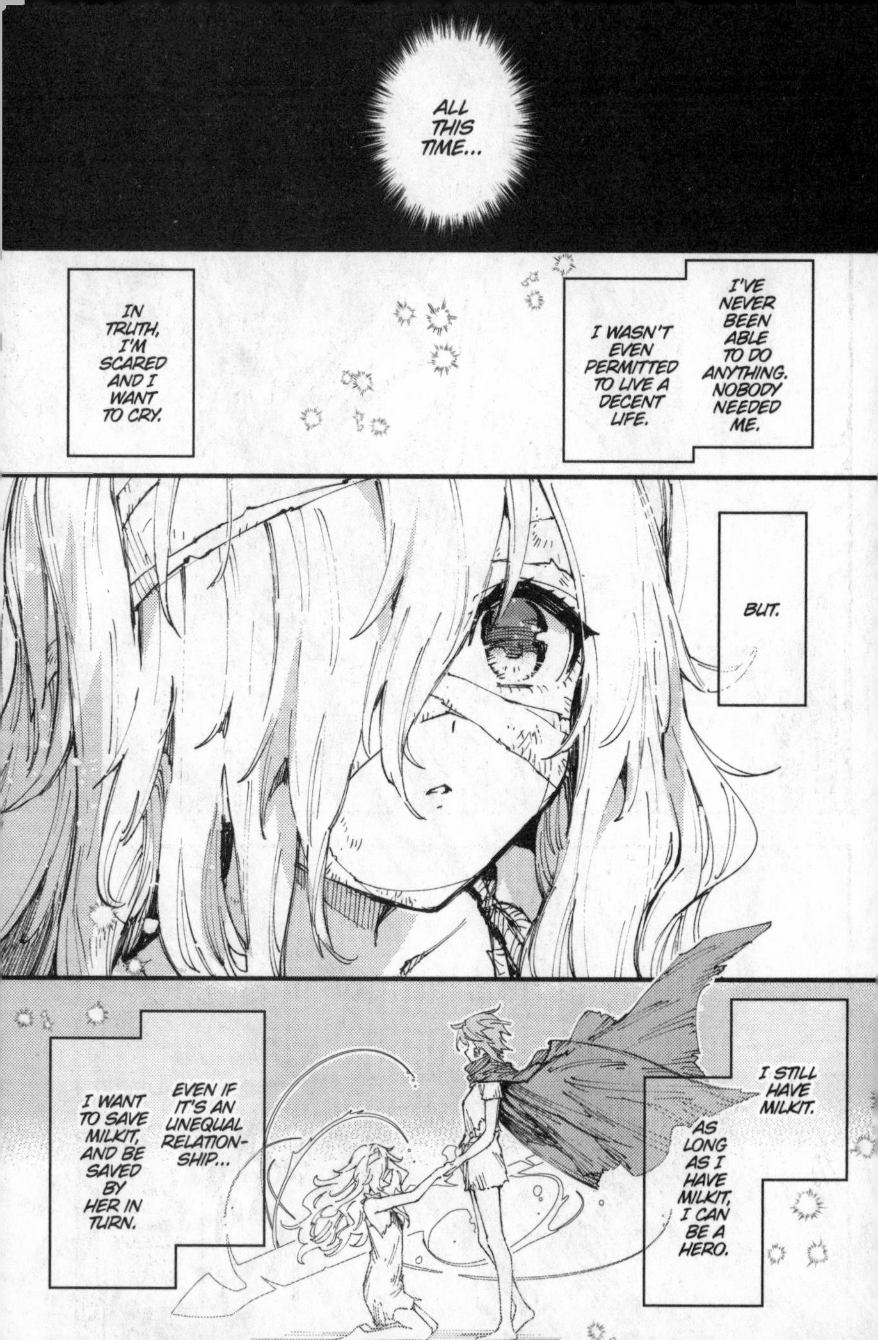
ALL THIS TIME...
I'VE NEVER BEEN ABLE TO DO ANYTHING. NOBODY NEEDED ME.
I WASN'T EVEN PERMITTED TO LIVE A DECENT LIFE.
IN TRUTH, I'M SCARED AND I WANT TO CRY.
BUT.
I STILL HAVE MILKIT.
AS LONG AS I HAVE MILKIT, I CAN BE A HERO.
EVEN IF IT'S AN UNEQUAL RELATION-SHIP...
I WANT TO SAVE MILKIT, AND BE SAVED BY HER IN TURN.

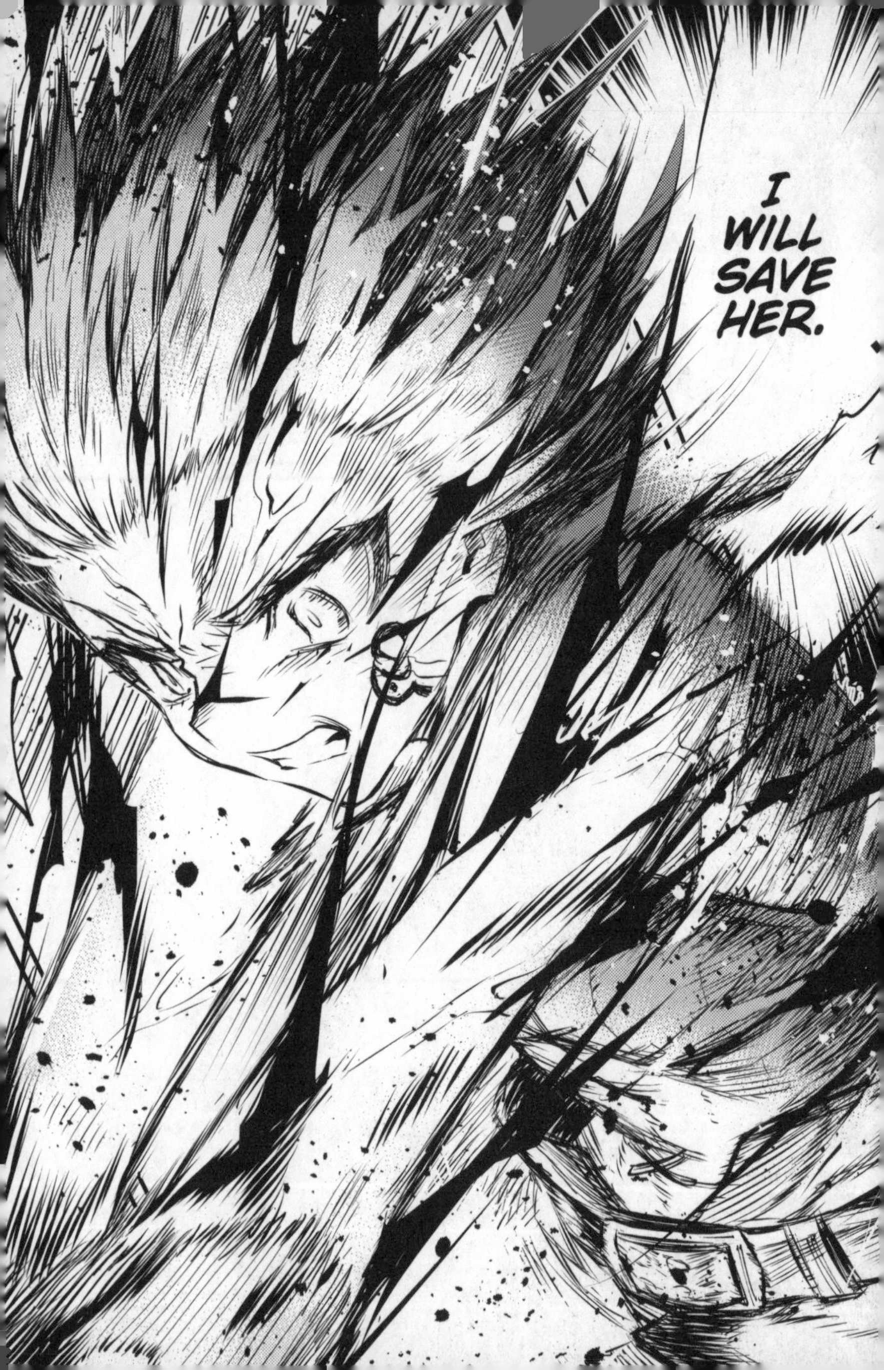
I WILL SAVE HER.

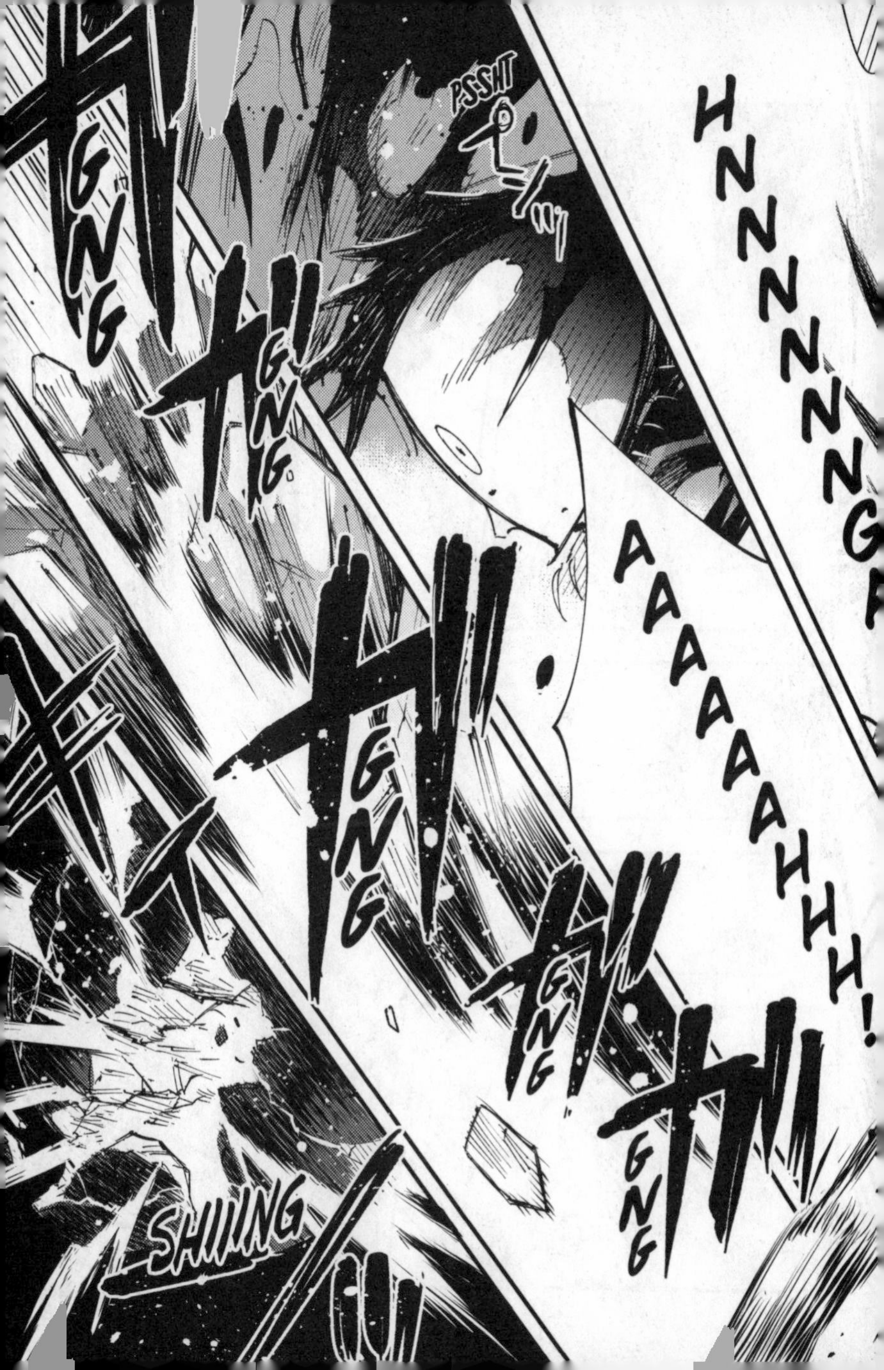
HNNNNNG
AAAAAAHHH!
PSSHT
GNG
GNG
GNG
GNG
GNG
SHIIING

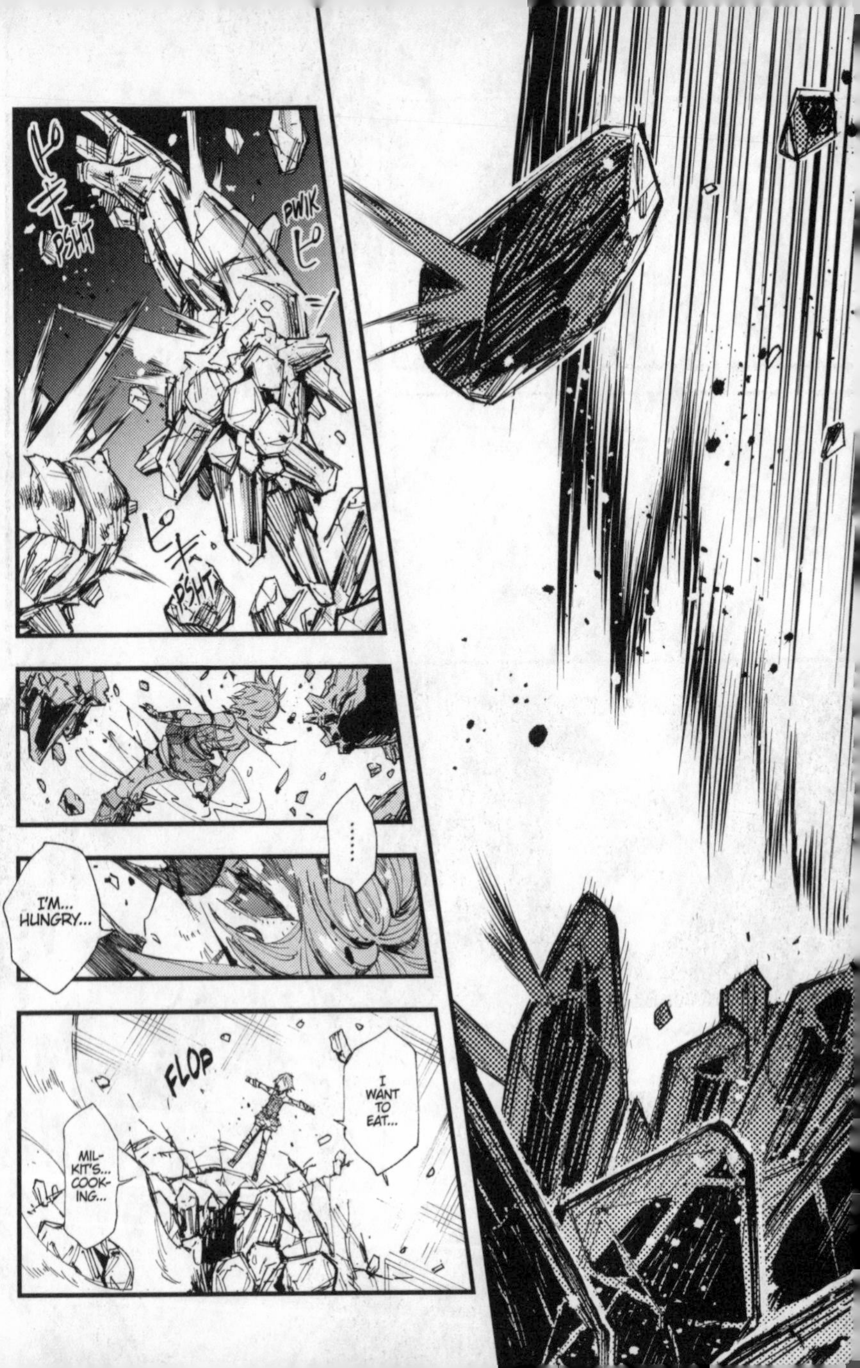
PWIK ピ
ピキ PSHT
ピキ PSHT
......
I'M... HUNGRY...
I WANT TO EAT...
FLOP
MIL-KIT'S... COOK-ING...

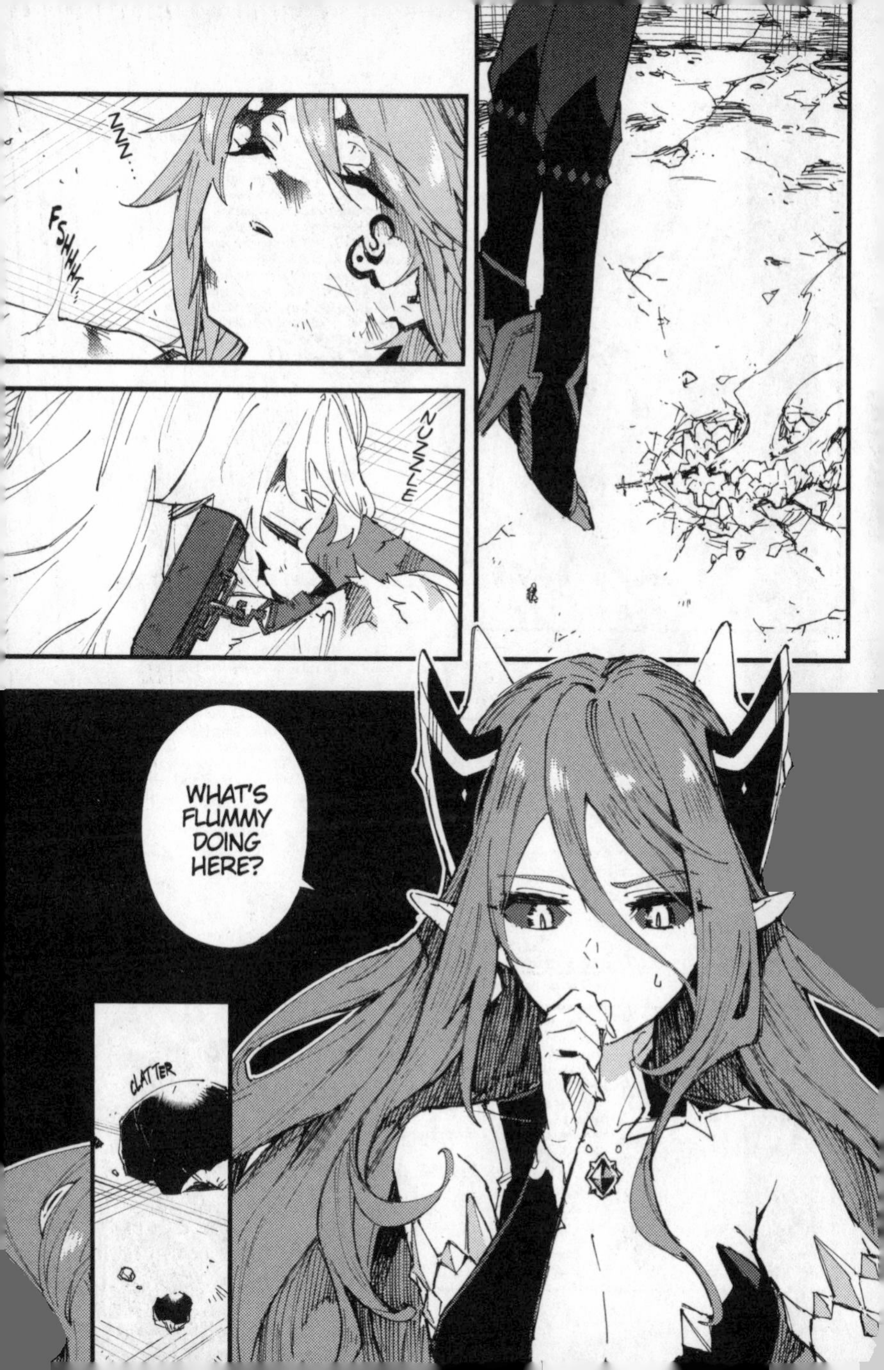

ZZZ...
FSHHH...
NUZZLE
WHAT'S FLUMMY DOING HERE?
CLATTER

MATERIAL

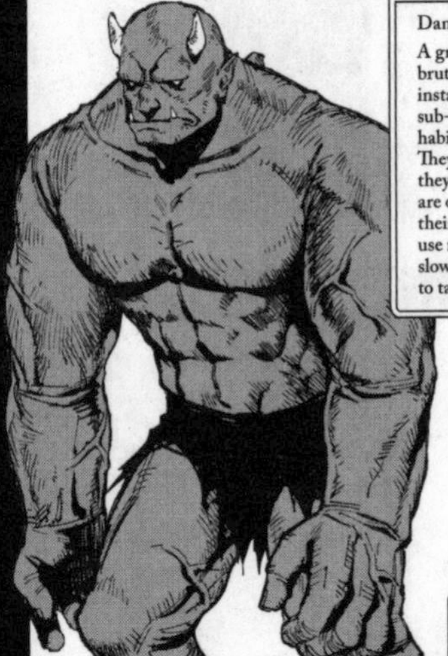

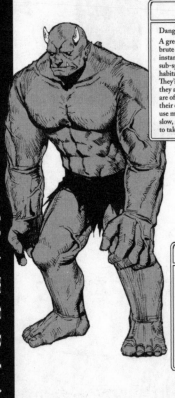

Ogre

Danger Level: ★★★★

A green C-rank humanoid monster with immense brute strength. A direct hit from its fist will mean instant death for the average human. Including the sub-species that have different colored bodies and habitats, they can be found all over the continent. They're carnivores that will eat humans, and since they appear in the vicinity of human villages, there are often quests put out to adventurers' guilds for their extermination. On the other hand, they can't use magic, they don't form packs, and they're pretty slow, so ogres are a popular opponent for adventurers to take on to test their skills.

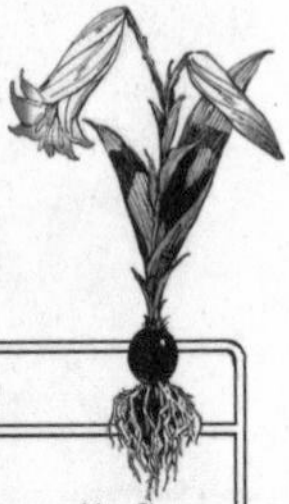

Kialahri

Rareness Level: ★★★★★★

A kind of medicinal herb. It sprouts a blue flower and grows in clusters in the caves near Anichidey. It is highly effective against certain illnesses. Since its applications are limited, there's not much demand for it, but in the past, it could be readily obtained even in the capital.
However, as the church's power grew and the use of medicine became forbidden, now it will only be found on the market through back routes on very rare occasions.

Sandwich

Deliciousness: ★★★★★★★★★★

A homemade meal by Milkit. She learned how to cook back when she was a slave. Even when she cooked, she was never praised, and if the taste was even the littlest bit off, she'd be kicked, struck, and whipped for it.
Thus, she never found much worth in cooking.
But now is different. Probably because she cooks for Flum.

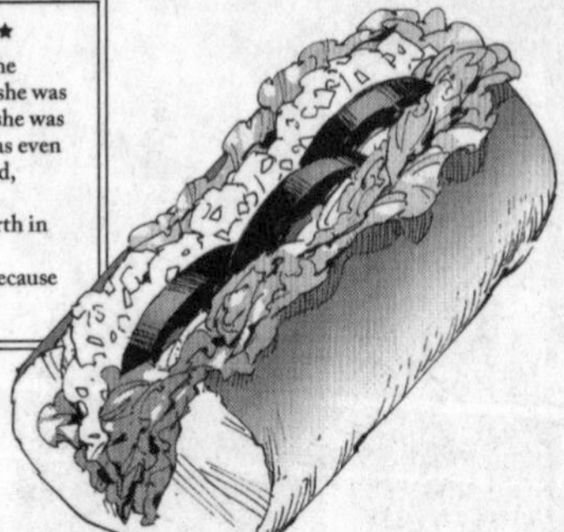

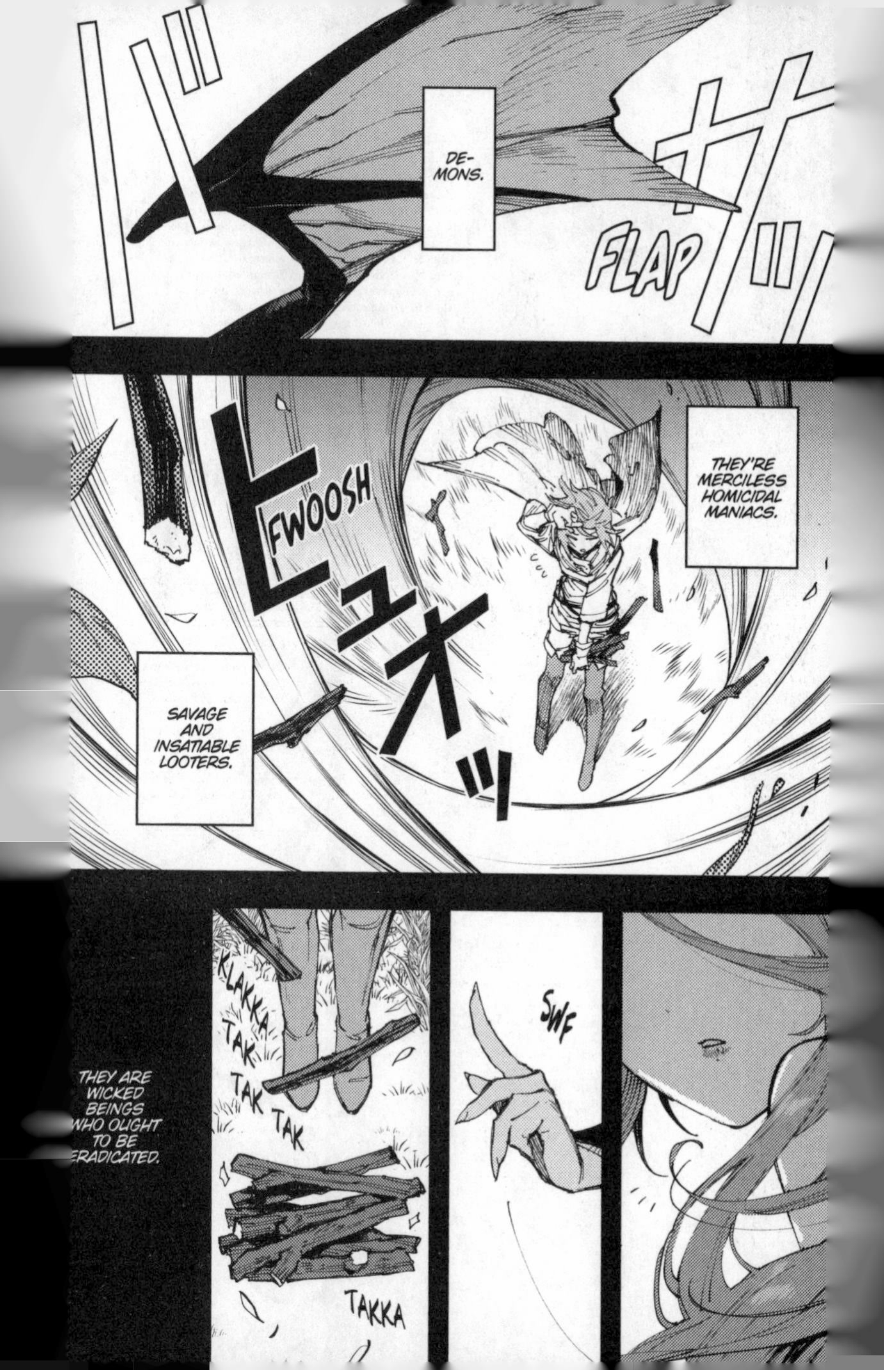

FLAP
DE-
MONS.
THEY'RE MERCILESS HOMICIDAL MANIACS.
FWOOSH
SAVAGE AND INSATIABLE LOOTERS.
SWF
KLAKKA TAK TAK TAK TAK
TAKKA
THEY ARE WICKED BEINGS WHO OUGHT TO BE ERADICATED.

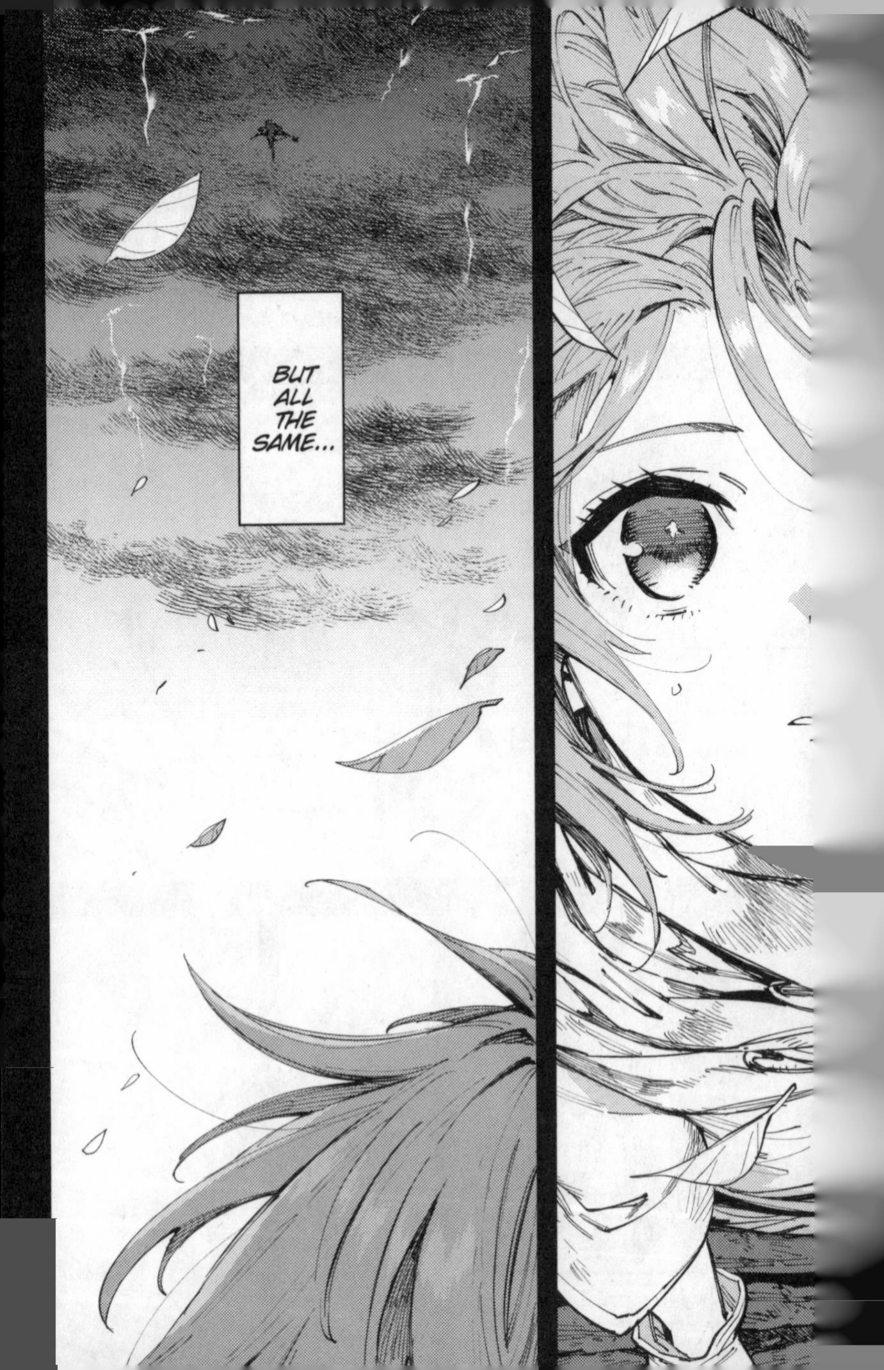
BUT ALL THE SAME...

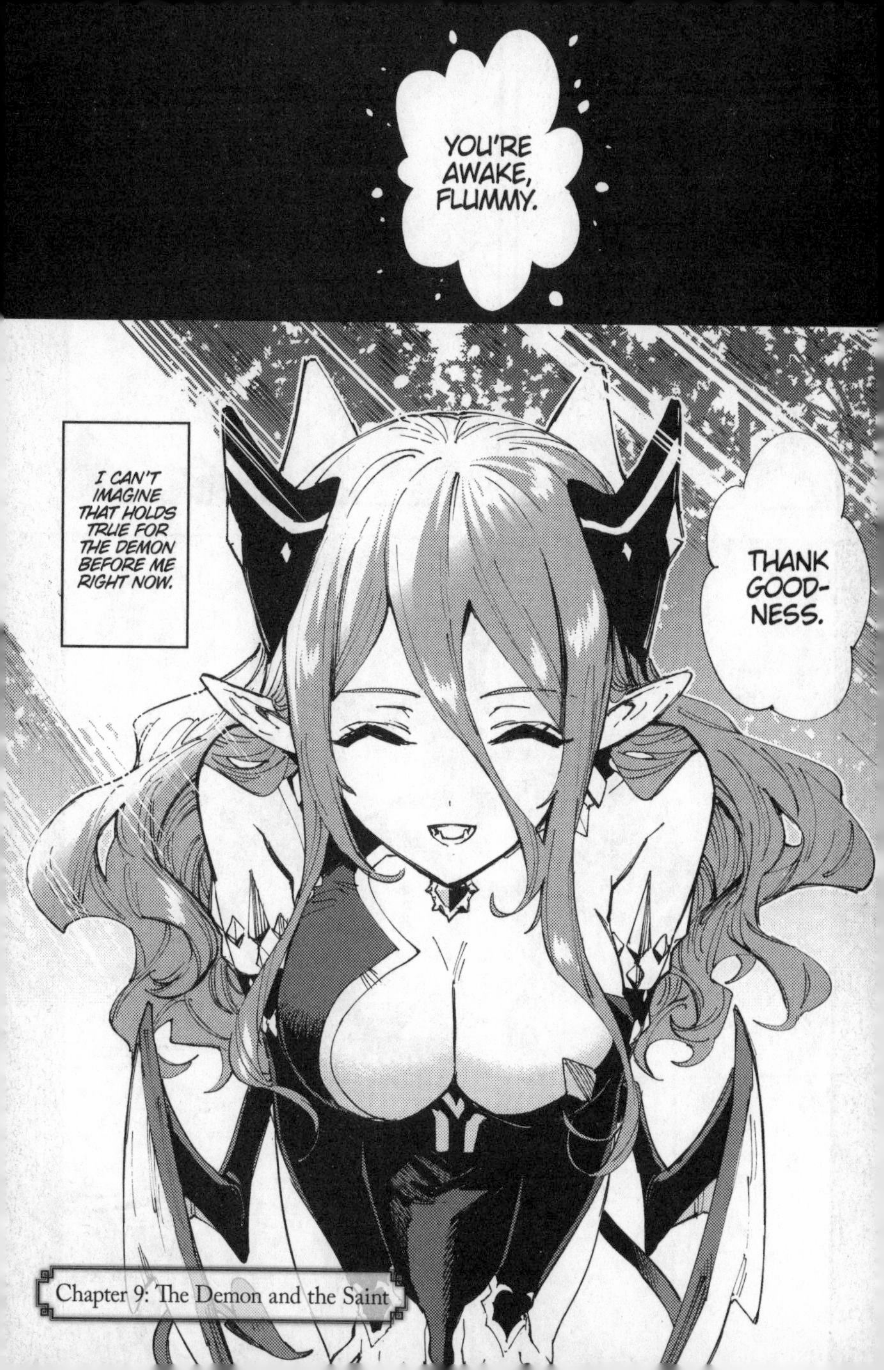
YOU'RE AWAKE, FLUMMY.
THANK GOODNESS.
I CAN'T IMAGINE THAT HOLDS TRUE FOR THE DEMON BEFORE ME RIGHT NOW.
Chapter 9: The Demon and the Saint

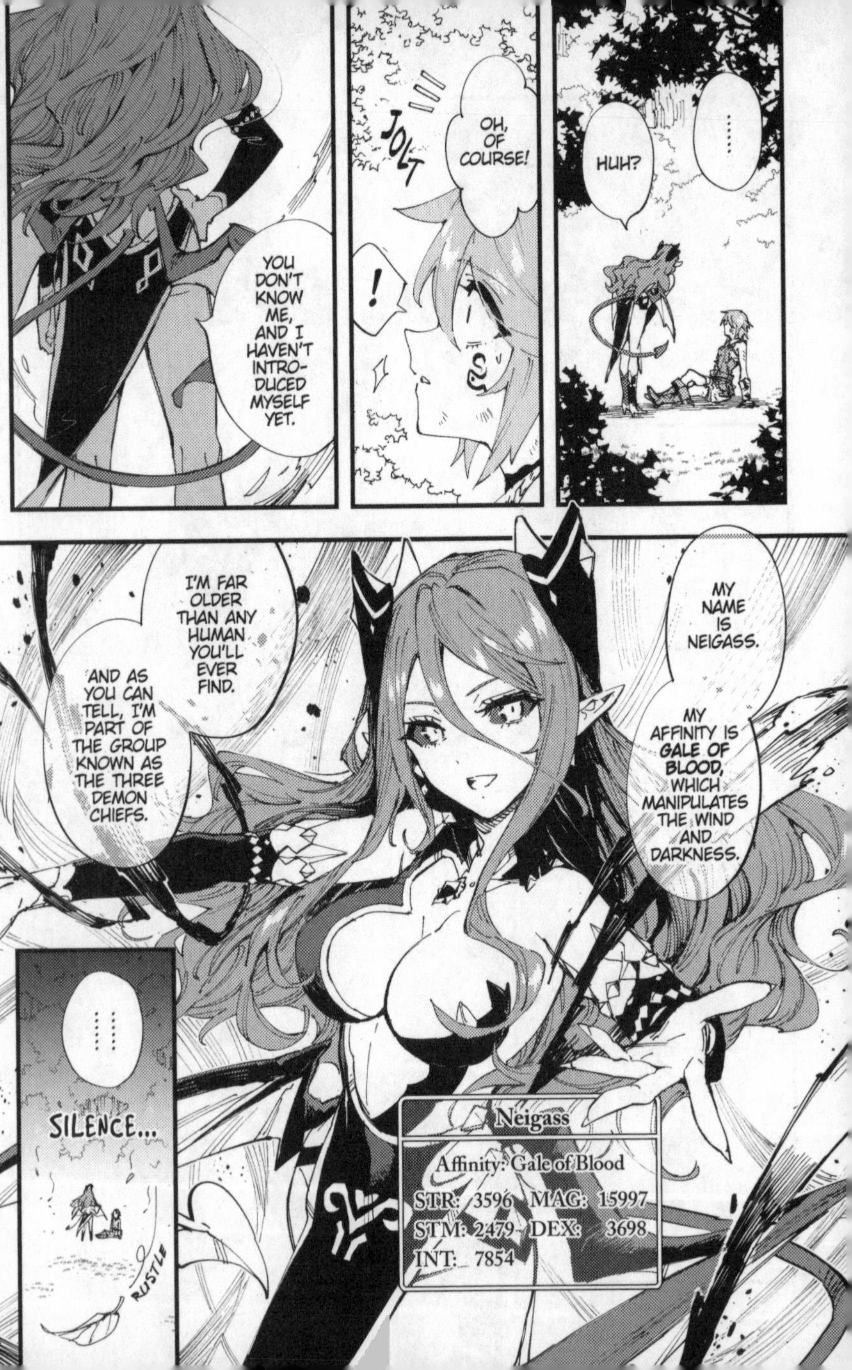

...
HUH?
OH, OF COURSE!
JOLT
!
YOU DON'T KNOW ME, AND I HAVEN'T INTRODUCED MYSELF YET.
MY NAME IS NEIGASS.
MY AFFINITY IS GALE OF BLOOD, WHICH MANIPULATES THE WIND AND DARKNESS.
I'M FAR OLDER THAN ANY HUMAN YOU'LL EVER FIND.
AND AS YOU CAN TELL, I'M PART OF THE GROUP KNOWN AS THE THREE DEMON CHIEFS.
Neigass
Affinity: Gale of Blood
STR: 3596 MAG: 15997
STM: 2479 DEX: 3698
INT: 7854
...
SILENCE...
RUSTLE

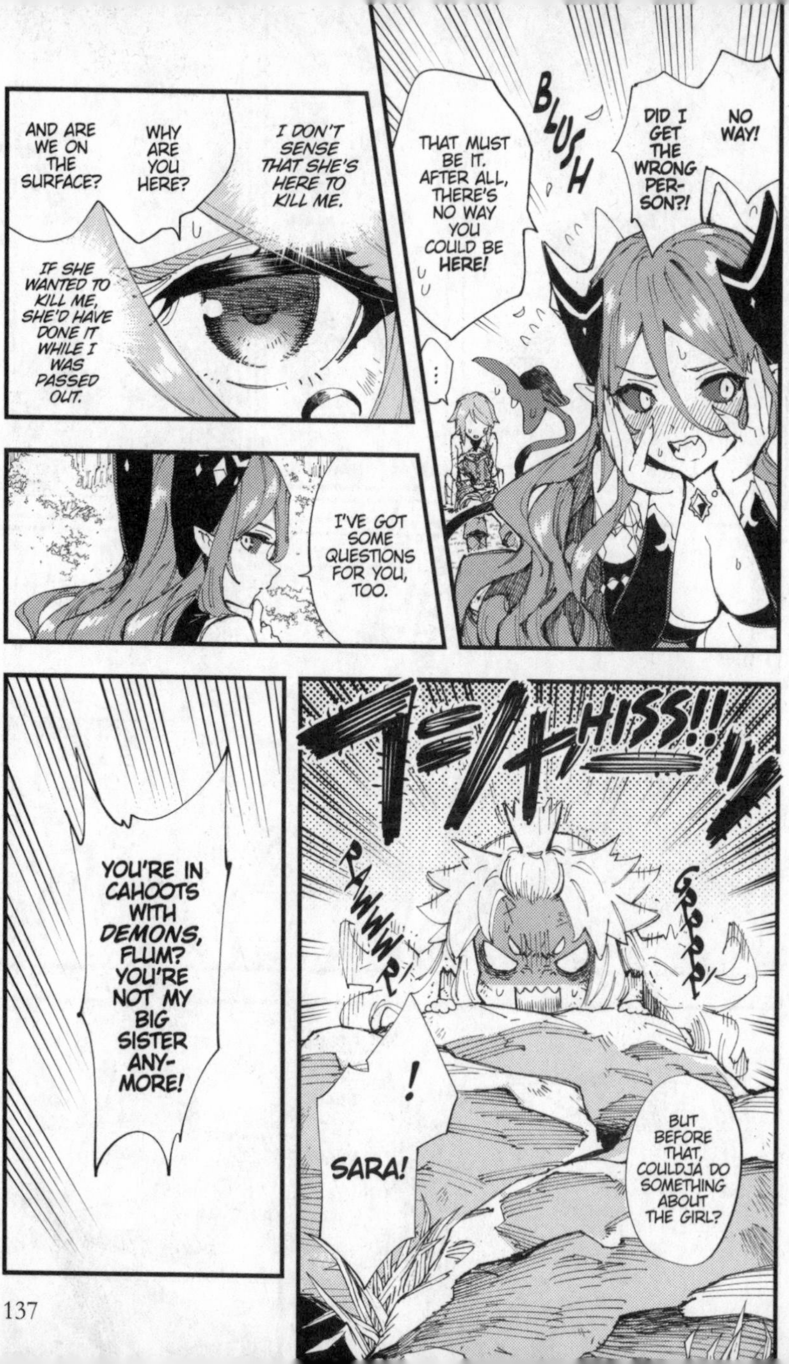
NO WAY!
DID I GET THE WRONG PER-SON?!
BLUSH
THAT MUST BE IT. AFTER ALL, THERE'S NO WAY YOU COULD BE HERE!
...
I DON'T SENSE THAT SHE'S HERE TO KILL ME.
WHY ARE YOU HERE?
AND ARE WE ON THE SURFACE?
IF SHE WANTED TO KILL ME, SHE'D HAVE DONE IT WHILE I WAS PASSED OUT.
I'VE GOT SOME QUESTIONS FOR YOU, TOO.
HISS!!
GRRRR
RAWWWR
BUT BEFORE THAT, COULDJA DO SOMETHING ABOUT THE GIRL?
!
SARA!
YOU'RE IN CAHOOTS WITH DEMONS, FLUM? YOU'RE NOT MY BIG SISTER ANY-MORE!

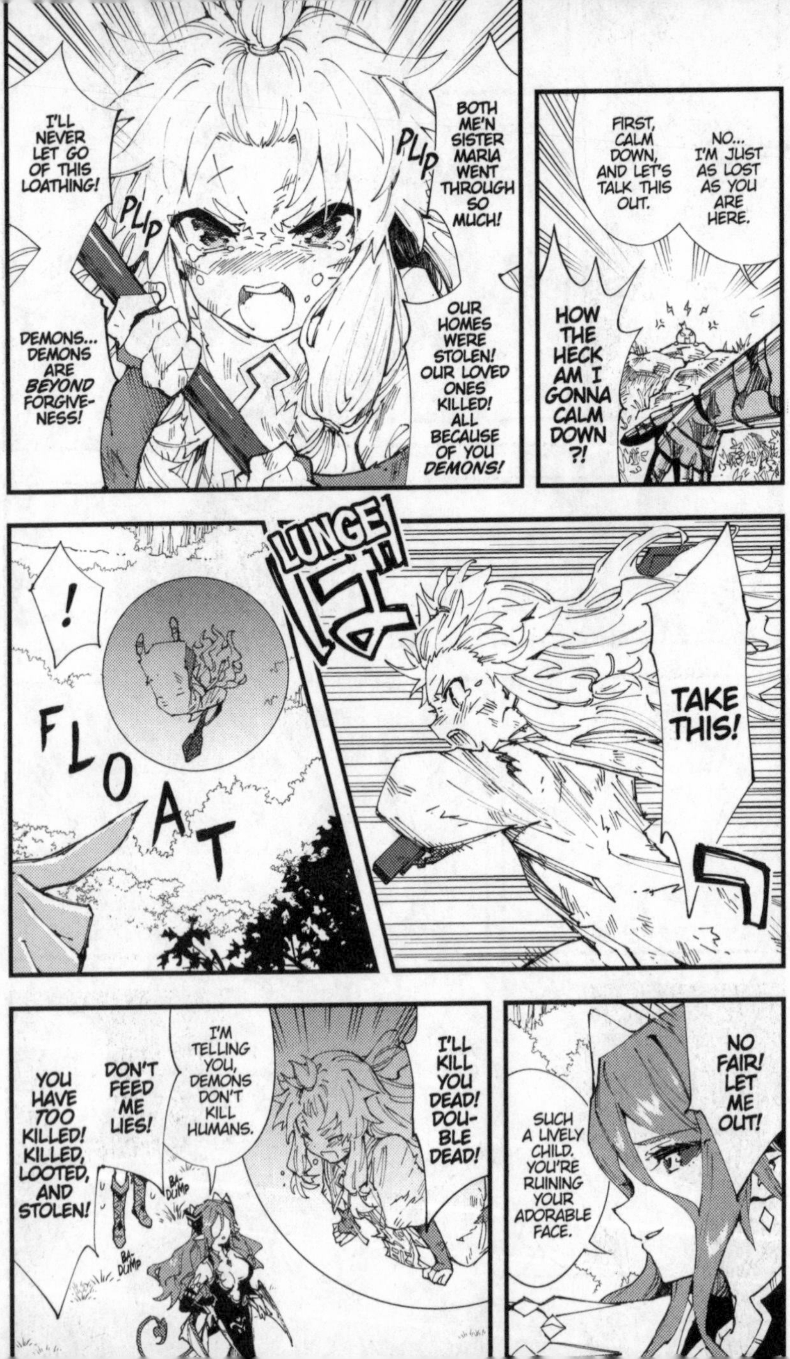
NO... I'M JUST AS LOST AS YOU ARE HERE.
FIRST, CALM DOWN, AND LET'S TALK THIS OUT.
HOW THE HECK AM I GONNA CALM DOWN?!
BOTH ME'N SISTER MARIA WENT THROUGH SO MUCH!
PLIP
OUR HOMES WERE STOLEN! OUR LOVED ONES KILLED! ALL BECAUSE OF YOU *DEMONS!*
I'LL NEVER LET GO OF THIS LOATHING!
PLIP
DEMONS... DEMONS ARE *BEYOND* FORGIVE-NESS!
LUNGE
TAKE THIS!
!
FLOAT
NO FAIR! LET ME OUT!
SUCH A LIVELY CHILD. YOU'RE RUINING YOUR ADORABLE FACE.
I'LL KILL YOU DEAD! DOU-BLE DEAD!
I'M TELLING YOU, DEMONS DON'T KILL HUMANS.
DON'T FEED ME LIES!
YOU HAVE *TOO* KILLED! KILLED, LOOTED, AND STOLEN!
BA-DUMP
BA-DUMP

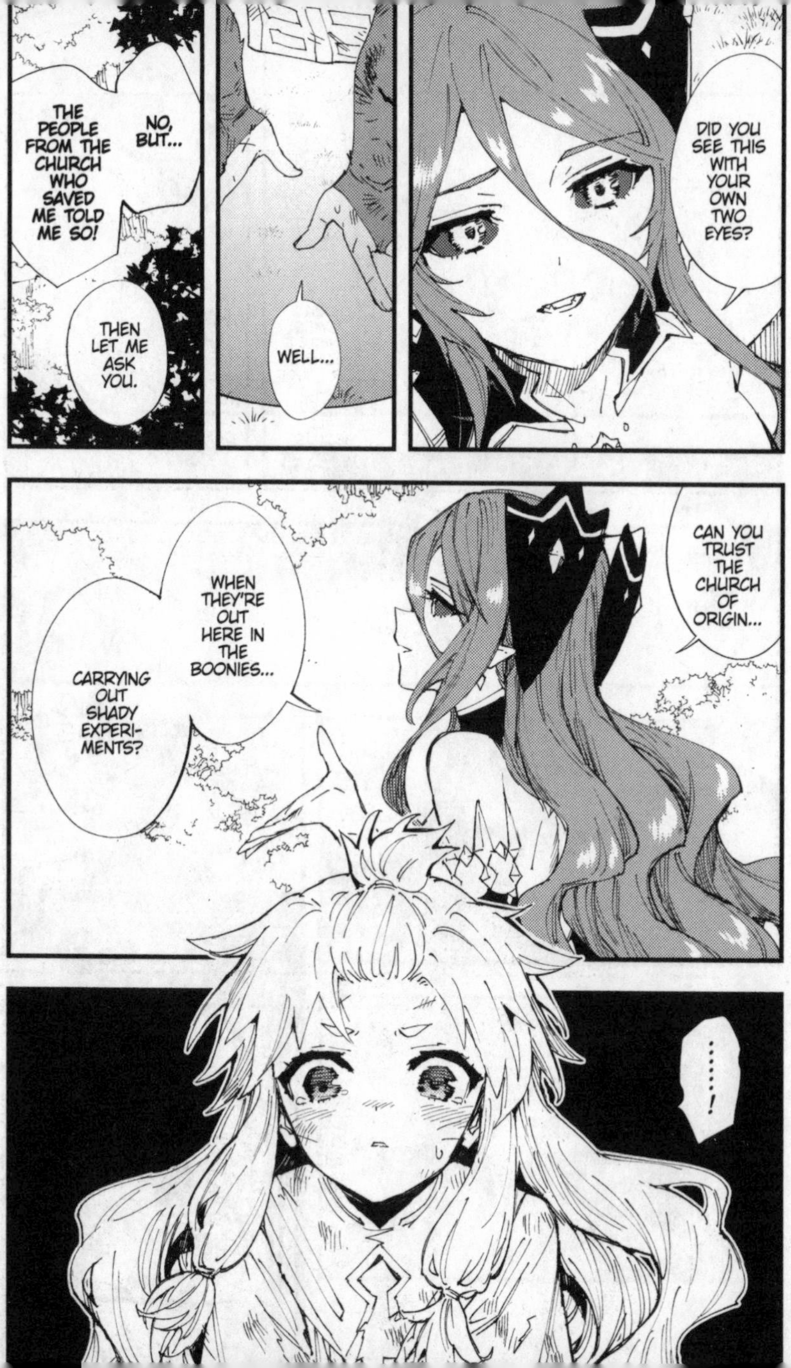
DID YOU SEE THIS WITH YOUR OWN TWO EYES?
WELL...
NO, BUT...
THE PEOPLE FROM THE CHURCH WHO SAVED ME TOLD ME SO!
THEN LET ME ASK YOU.
CAN YOU TRUST THE CHURCH OF ORIGIN...
WHEN THEY'RE OUT HERE IN THE BOONIES...
CARRYING OUT SHADY EXPERIMENTS?
......!

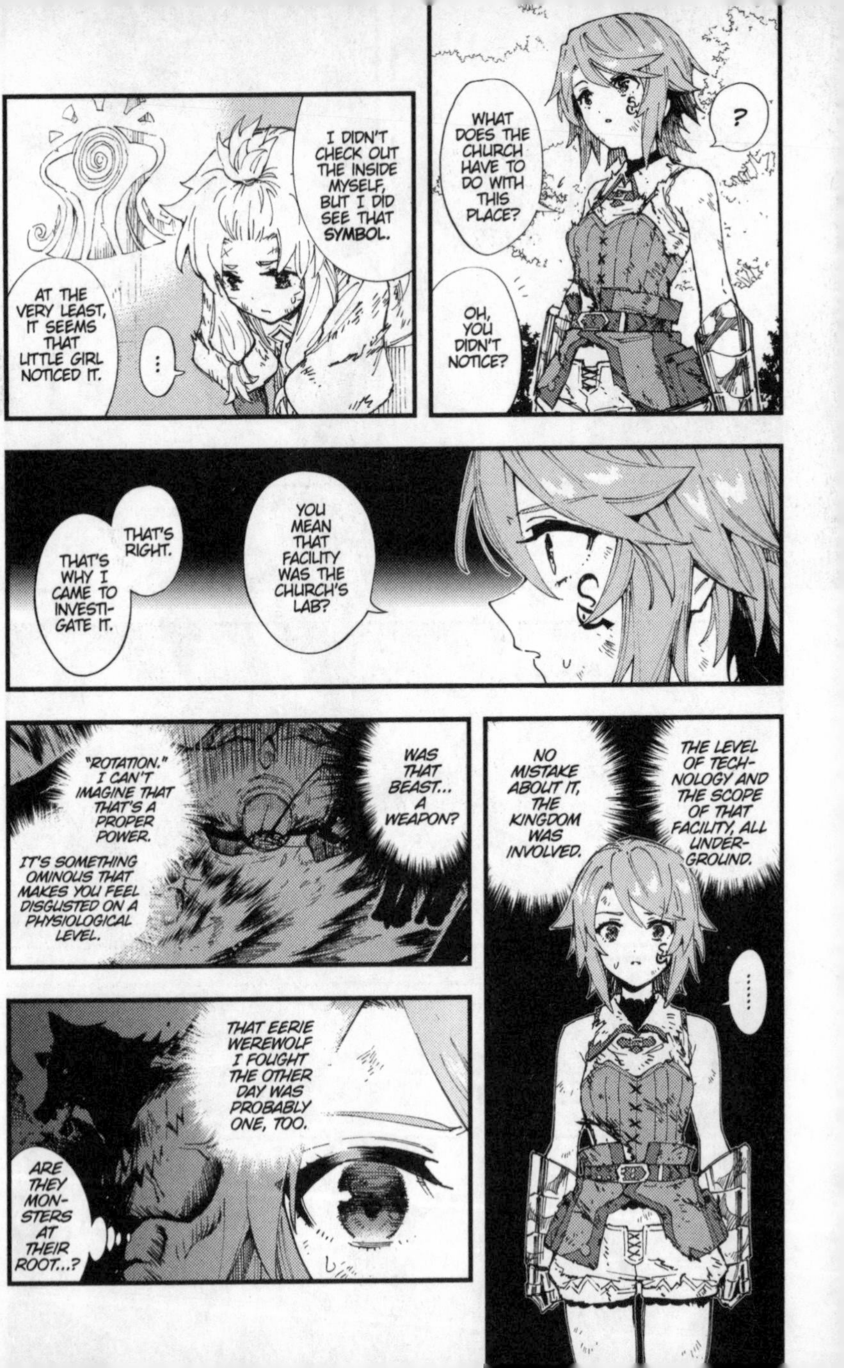
?
WHAT DOES THE CHURCH HAVE TO DO WITH THIS PLACE?
OH, YOU DIDN'T NOTICE?
I DIDN'T CHECK OUT THE INSIDE MYSELF, BUT I DID SEE THAT SYMBOL.
AT THE VERY LEAST, IT SEEMS THAT LITTLE GIRL NOTICED IT.
...
YOU MEAN THAT FACILITY WAS THE CHURCH'S LAB?
THAT'S RIGHT.
THAT'S WHY I CAME TO INVESTIGATE IT.
THE LEVEL OF TECHNOLOGY AND THE SCOPE OF THAT FACILITY, ALL UNDERGROUND.
NO MISTAKE ABOUT IT, THE KINGDOM WAS INVOLVED.
......
WAS THAT BEAST... A WEAPON?
"ROTATION." I CAN'T IMAGINE THAT THAT'S A PROPER POWER.
IT'S SOMETHING OMINOUS THAT MAKES YOU FEEL DISGUSTED ON A PHYSIOLOGICAL LEVEL.
THAT EERIE WEREWOLF I FOUGHT THE OTHER DAY WAS PROBABLY ONE, TOO.
ARE THEY MONSTERS AT THEIR ROOT...?

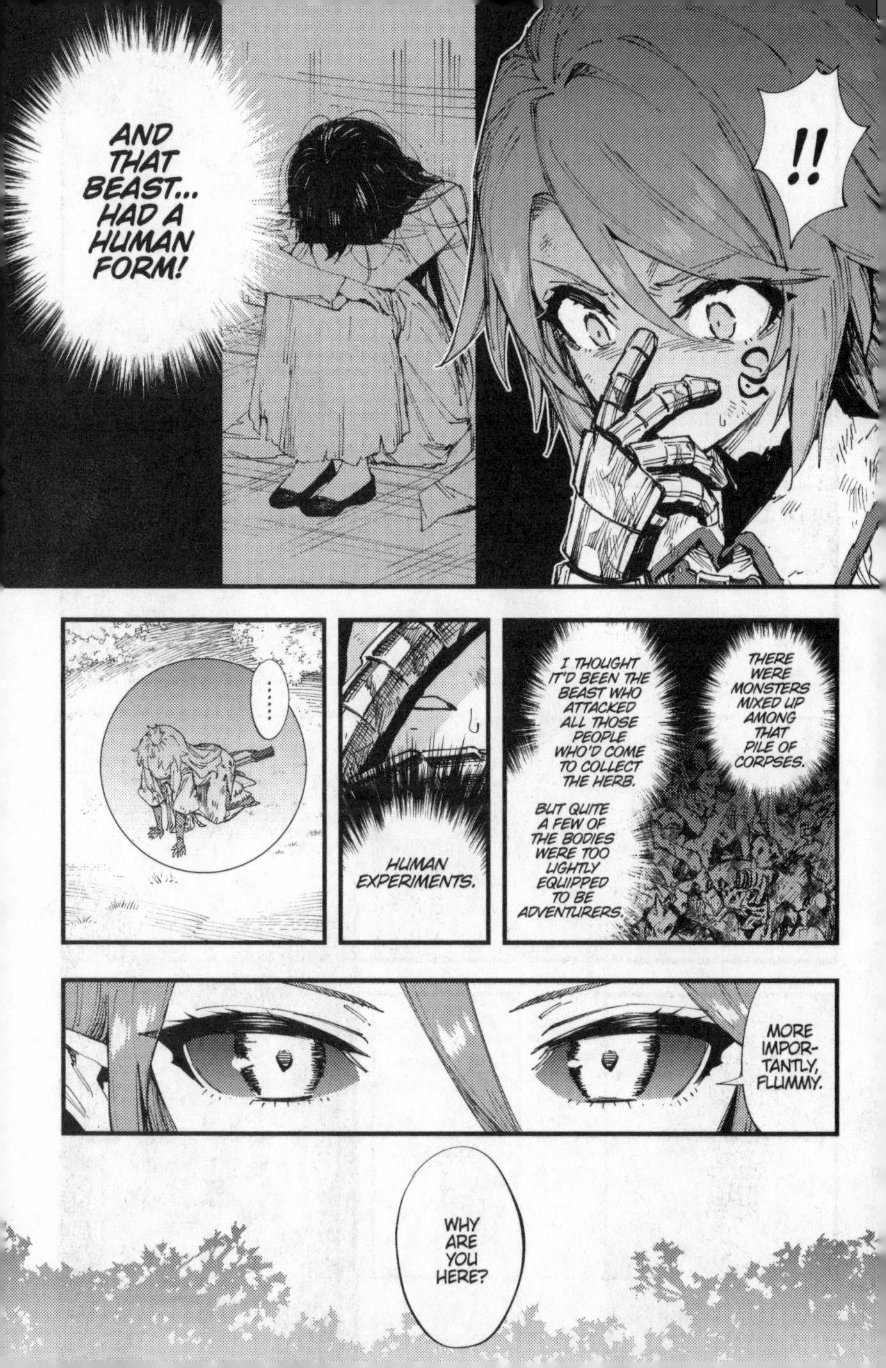
!!
AND THAT BEAST... HAD A HUMAN FORM!
THERE WERE MONSTERS MIXED UP AMONG THAT PILE OF CORPSES.
I THOUGHT IT'D BEEN THE BEAST WHO ATTACKED ALL THOSE PEOPLE WHO'D COME TO COLLECT THE HERB.
BUT QUITE A FEW OF THE BODIES WERE TOO LIGHTLY EQUIPPED TO BE ADVENTURERS.
HUMAN EXPERIMENTS.
......
MORE IMPOR-TANTLY, FLUMMY.
WHY ARE YOU HERE?

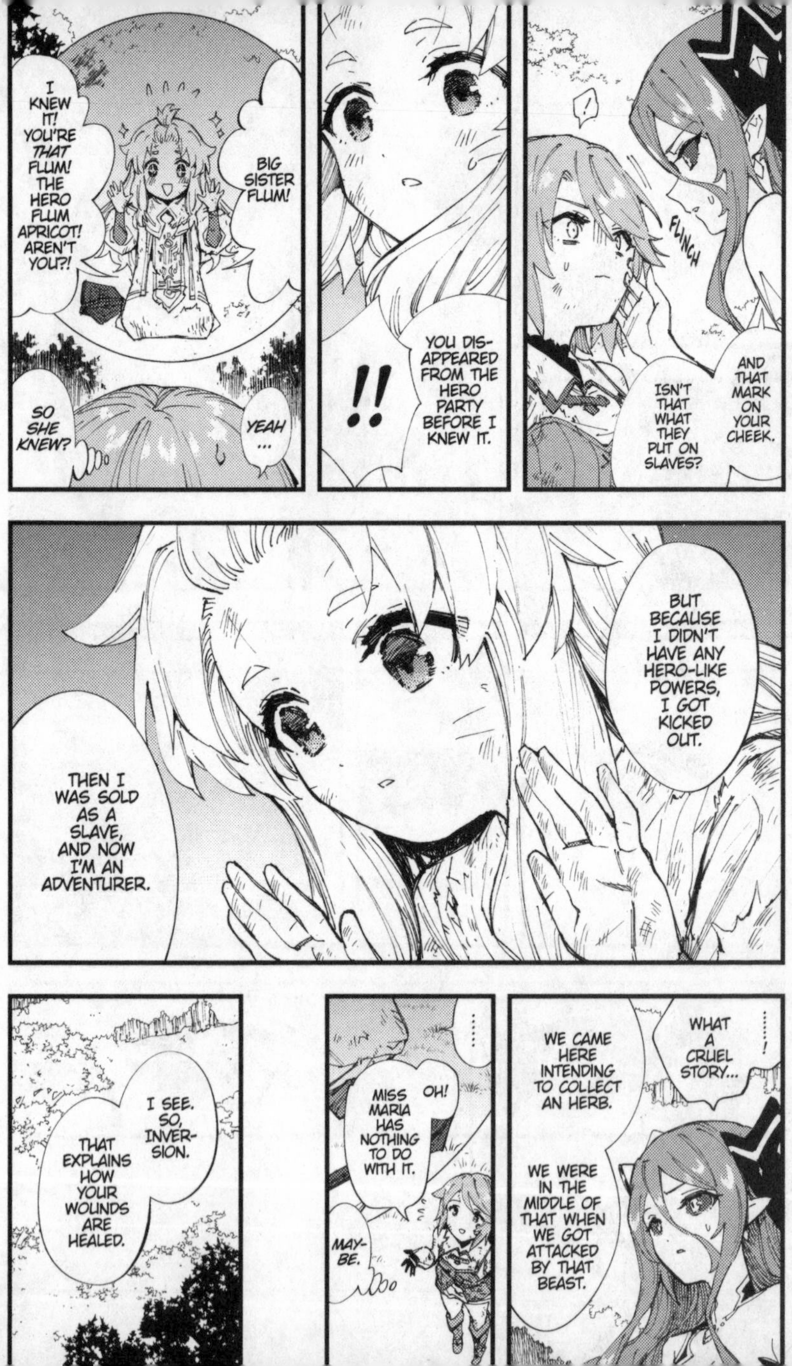
!
FLINCH
AND THAT MARK ON YOUR CHEEK.
ISN'T THAT WHAT THEY PUT ON SLAVES?
YOU DIS-APPEARED FROM THE HERO PARTY BEFORE I KNEW IT.
!!
BIG SISTER FLUM!
I KNEW IT! YOU'RE *THAT* FLUM! THE HERO FLUM APRICOT! AREN'T YOU?!
YEAH ...
SO SHE KNEW?
BUT BECAUSE I DIDN'T HAVE ANY HERO-LIKE POWERS, I GOT KICKED OUT.
THEN I WAS SOLD AS A SLAVE, AND NOW I'M AN ADVENTURER.
......!
WHAT A CRUEL STORY...
WE CAME HERE INTENDING TO COLLECT AN HERB.
WE WERE IN THE MIDDLE OF THAT WHEN WE GOT ATTACKED BY THAT BEAST.
......
OH!
MISS MARIA HAS NOTHING TO DO WITH IT.
MAY-BE.
I SEE. SO, INVERSION.
THAT EXPLAINS HOW YOUR WOUNDS ARE HEALED.

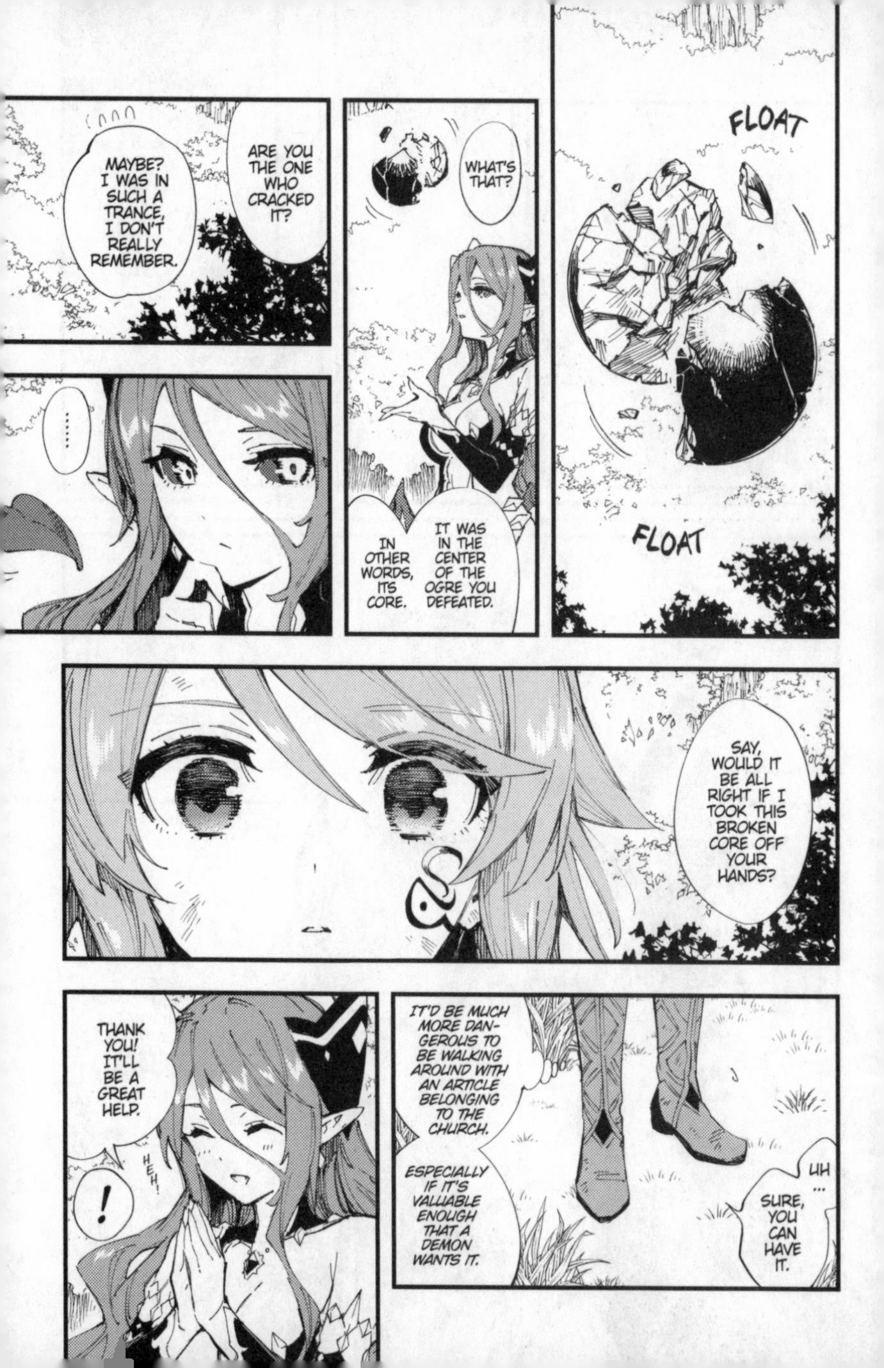
FLOAT
FLOAT
WHAT'S THAT?
IT WAS IN THE CENTER OF THE OGRE YOU DEFEATED.
IN OTHER WORDS, ITS CORE.
ARE YOU THE ONE WHO CRACKED IT?
MAYBE? I WAS IN SUCH A TRANCE, I DON'T REALLY REMEMBER.
......
SAY, WOULD IT BE ALL RIGHT IF I TOOK THIS BROKEN CORE OFF YOUR HANDS?
UH... SURE, YOU CAN HAVE IT.
IT'D BE MUCH MORE DANGEROUS TO BE WALKING AROUND WITH AN ARTICLE BELONGING TO THE CHURCH.
ESPECIALLY IF IT'S VALUABLE ENOUGH THAT A DEMON WANTS IT.
THANK YOU! IT'LL BE A GREAT HELP.
HEH!
!

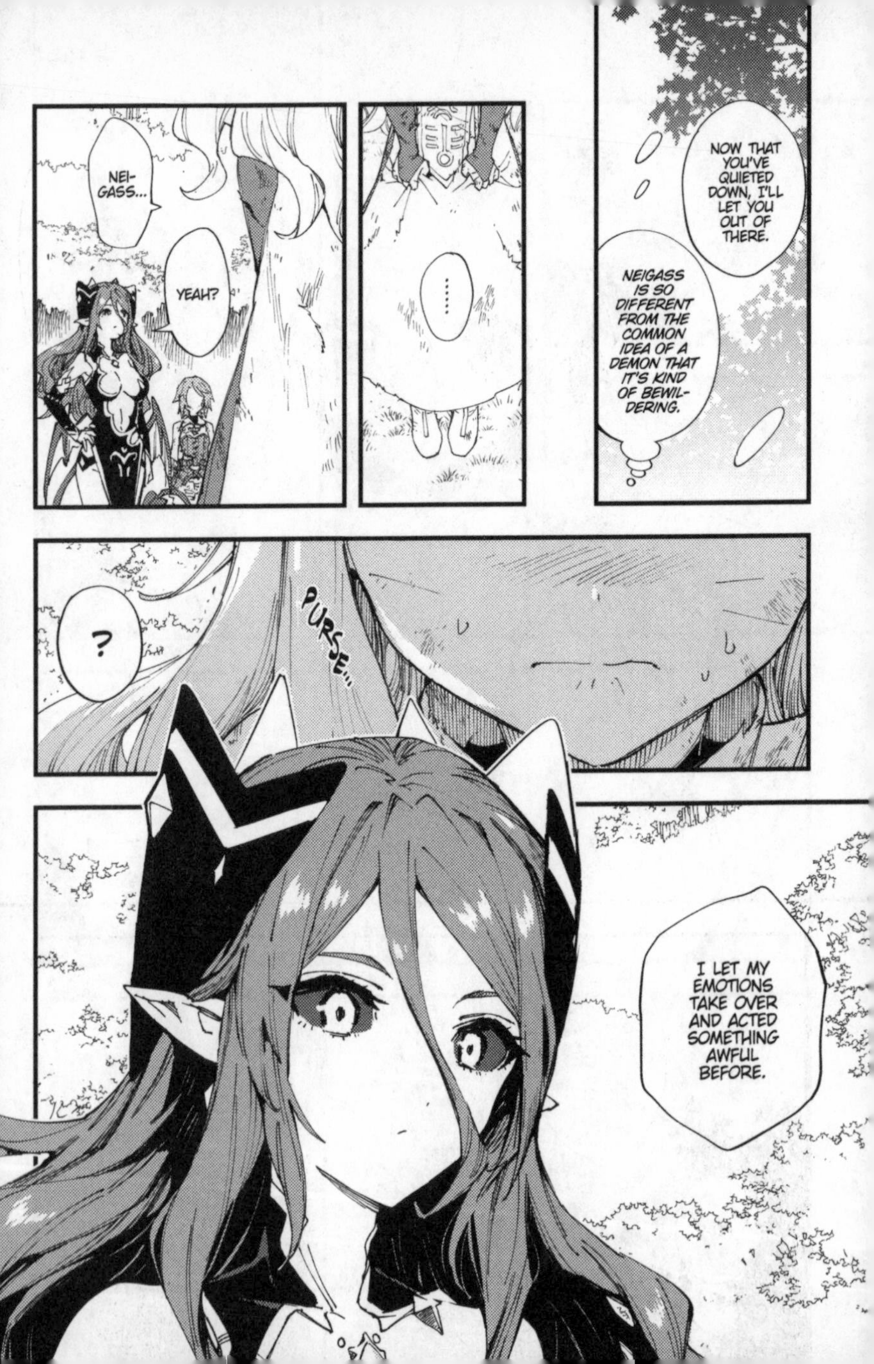
NOW THAT YOU'VE QUIETED DOWN, I'LL LET YOU OUT OF THERE.
NEIGASS IS SO DIFFERENT FROM THE COMMON IDEA OF A DEMON THAT IT'S KIND OF BEWIL-DERING.
......
NEI-GASS...
YEAH?
PURSE...
?
I LET MY EMOTIONS TAKE OVER AND ACTED SOMETHING AWFUL BEFORE.

I'M SORRY.

AND I'M SORRY TO YOU, TOO, BIG SIS.

HUH?

SARA...

I ALWAYS HAD A HUNCH THAT THE PEOPLE HIGHER THAN THE BISHOP WERE HIDING SOMETHING.

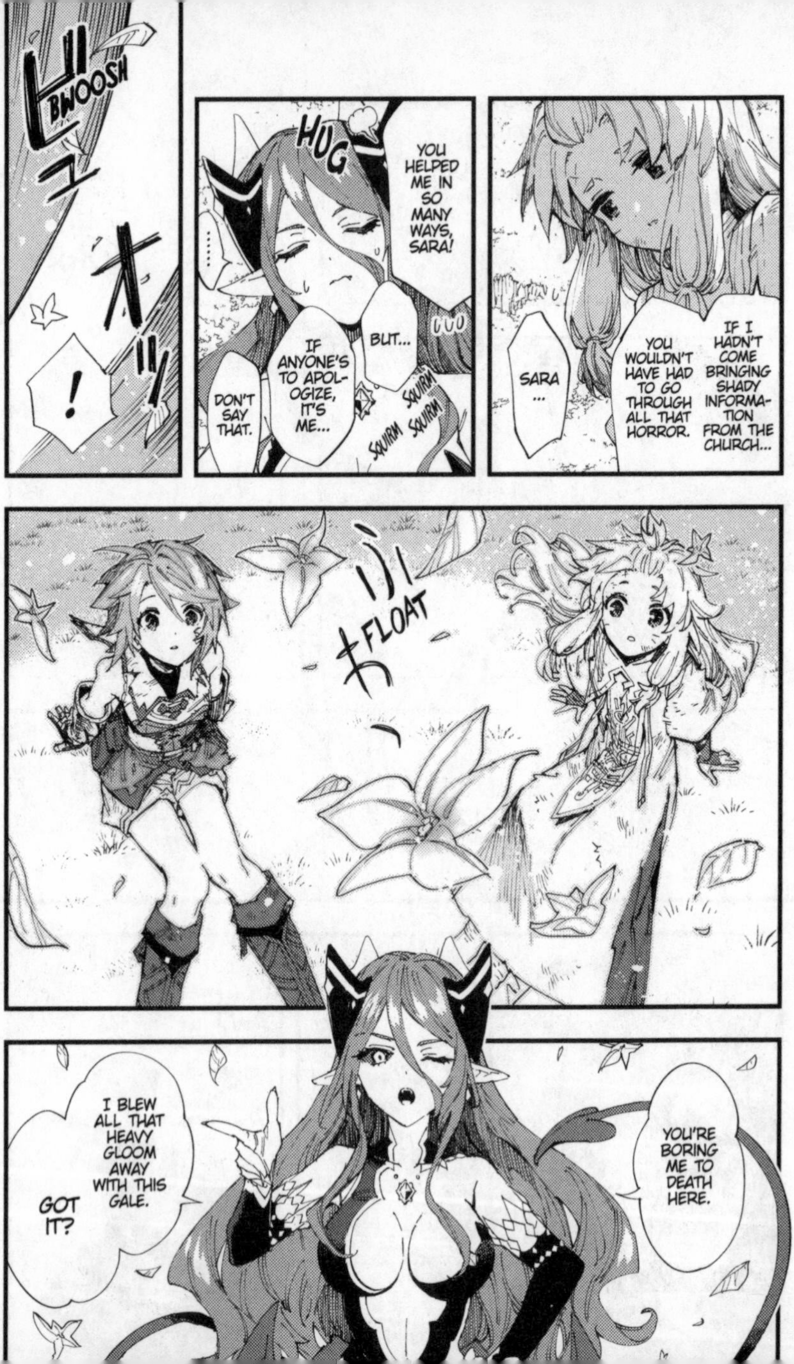
IF I HADN'T COME BRINGING SHADY INFORMATION FROM THE CHURCH...
YOU WOULDN'T HAVE HAD TO GO THROUGH ALL THAT HORROR.
SARA...
HUG
YOU HELPED ME IN SO MANY WAYS, SARA!
......
BUT...
IF ANYONE'S TO APOLOGIZE, IT'S ME...
DON'T SAY THAT.
SQUIRM SQUIRM SQUIRM SQUIRM
BWOOSH
!
FLOAT
YOU'RE BORING ME TO DEATH HERE.
I BLEW ALL THAT HEAVY GLOOM AWAY WITH THIS GALE.
GOT IT?

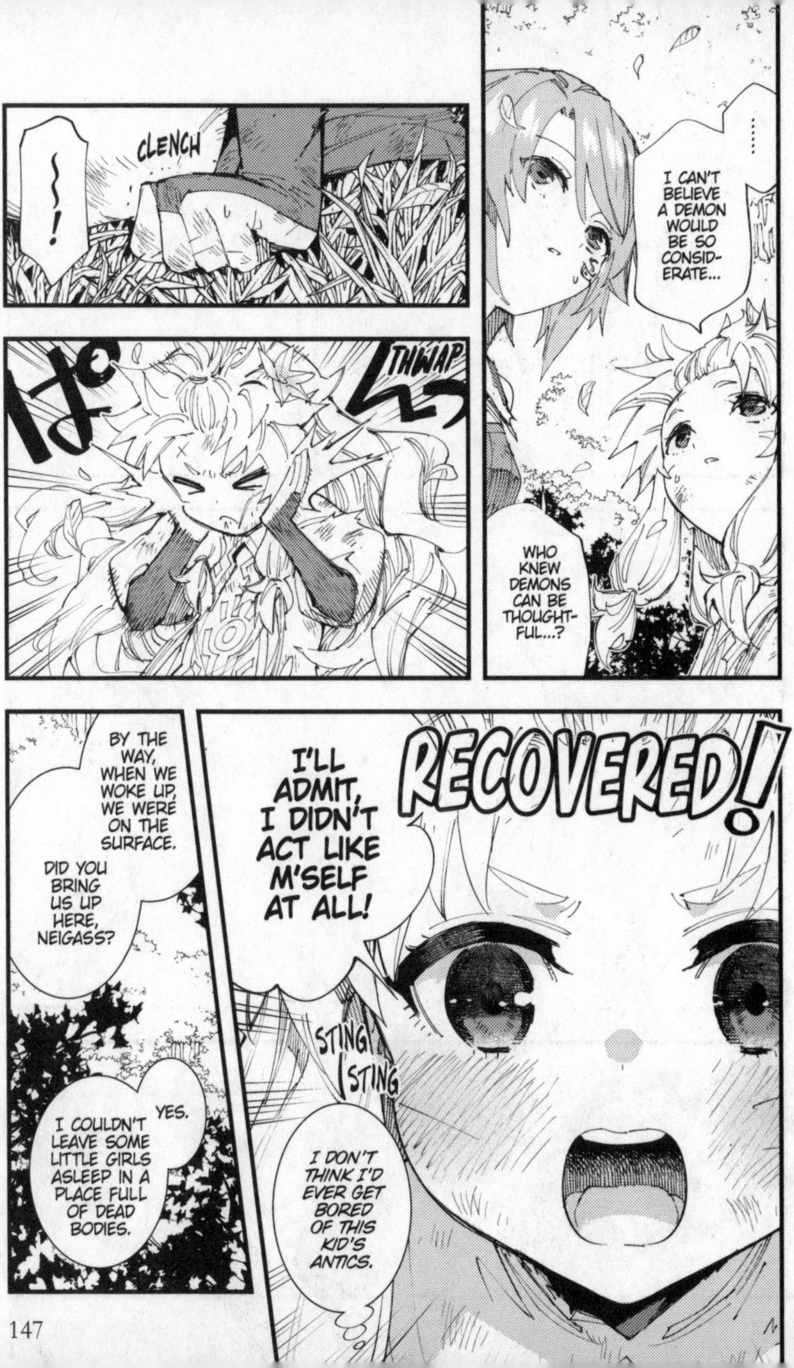
......
I CAN'T BELIEVE A DEMON WOULD BE SO CONSID-ERATE...
WHO KNEW DEMONS CAN BE THOUGHT-FUL...?
--!
CLENCH
THWAP
RECOVERED!
I'LL ADMIT, I DIDN'T ACT LIKE M'SELF AT ALL!
STING
STING
I DON'T THINK I'D EVER GET BORED OF THIS KID'S ANTICS.
BY THE WAY, WHEN WE WOKE UP, WE WERE ON THE SURFACE.
DID YOU BRING US UP HERE, NEIGASS?
YES.
I COULDN'T LEAVE SOME LITTLE GIRLS ASLEEP IN A PLACE FULL OF DEAD BODIES.

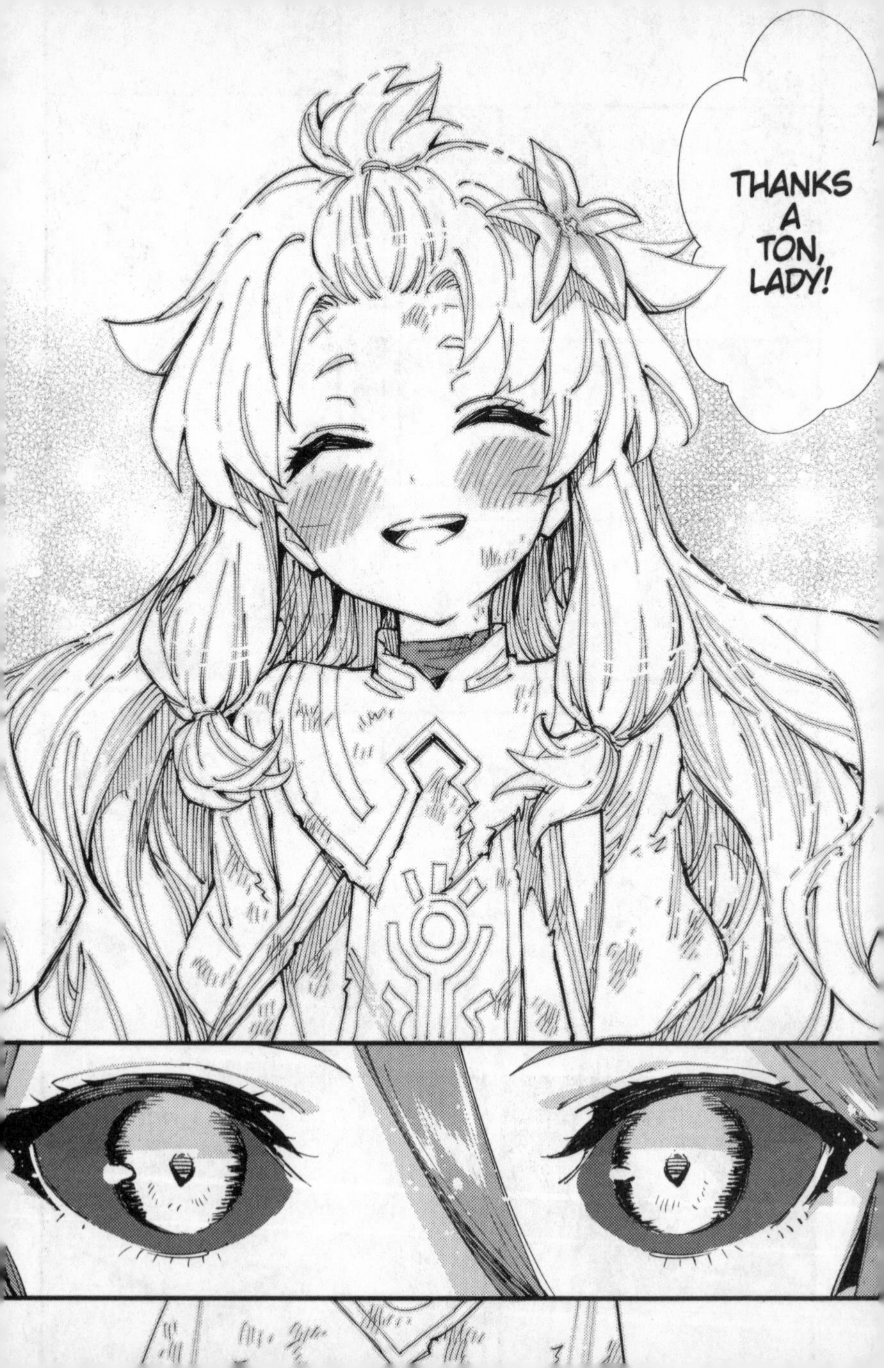
THANKS A TON, LADY!

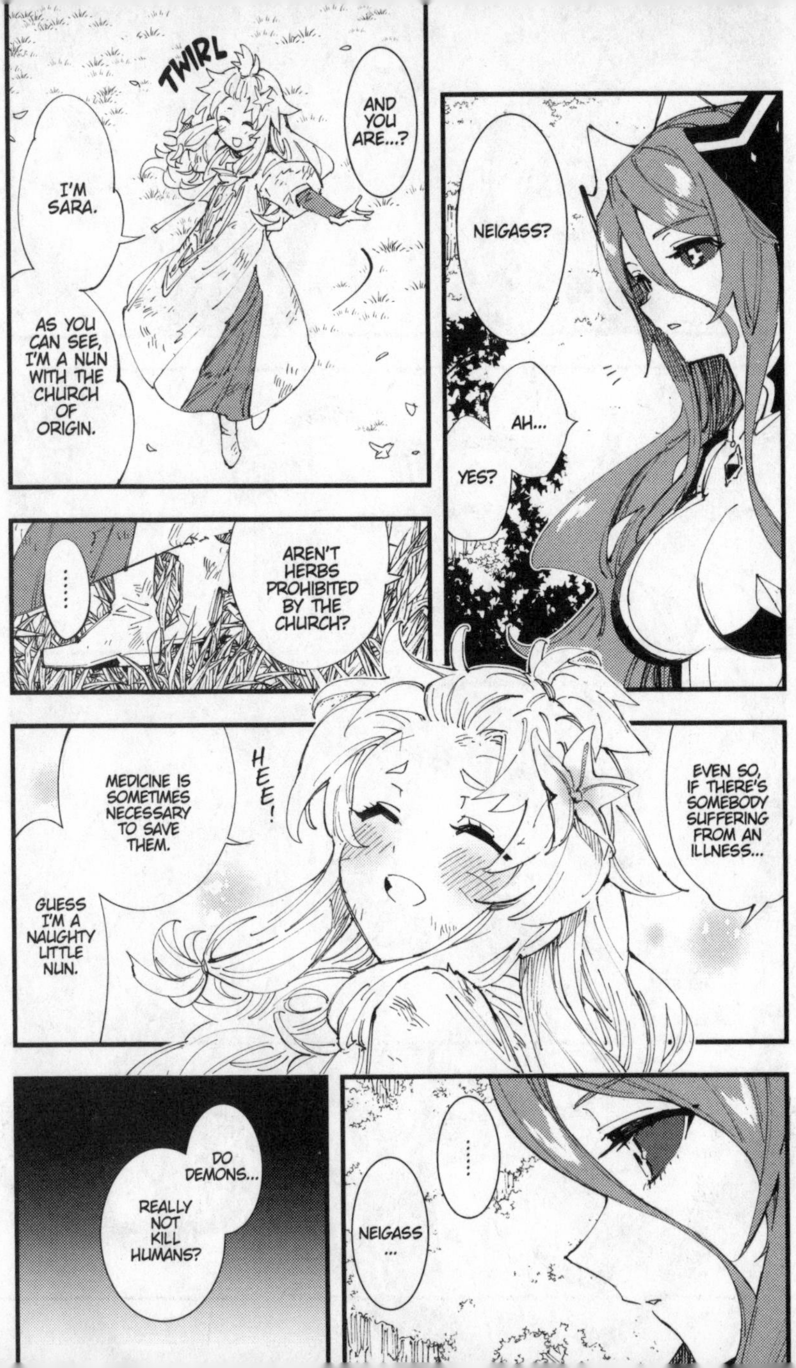
NEIGASS?
AH...
YES?
AND YOU ARE...?
TWIRL
I'M SARA.
AS YOU CAN SEE, I'M A NUN WITH THE CHURCH OF ORIGIN.
AREN'T HERBS PROHIBITED BY THE CHURCH?
......
EVEN SO, IF THERE'S SOMEBODY SUFFERING FROM AN ILLNESS...
HEE!
MEDICINE IS SOMETIMES NECESSARY TO SAVE THEM.
GUESS I'M A NAUGHTY LITTLE NUN.
......
NEIGASS ...
DO DEMONS...
REALLY NOT KILL HUMANS?

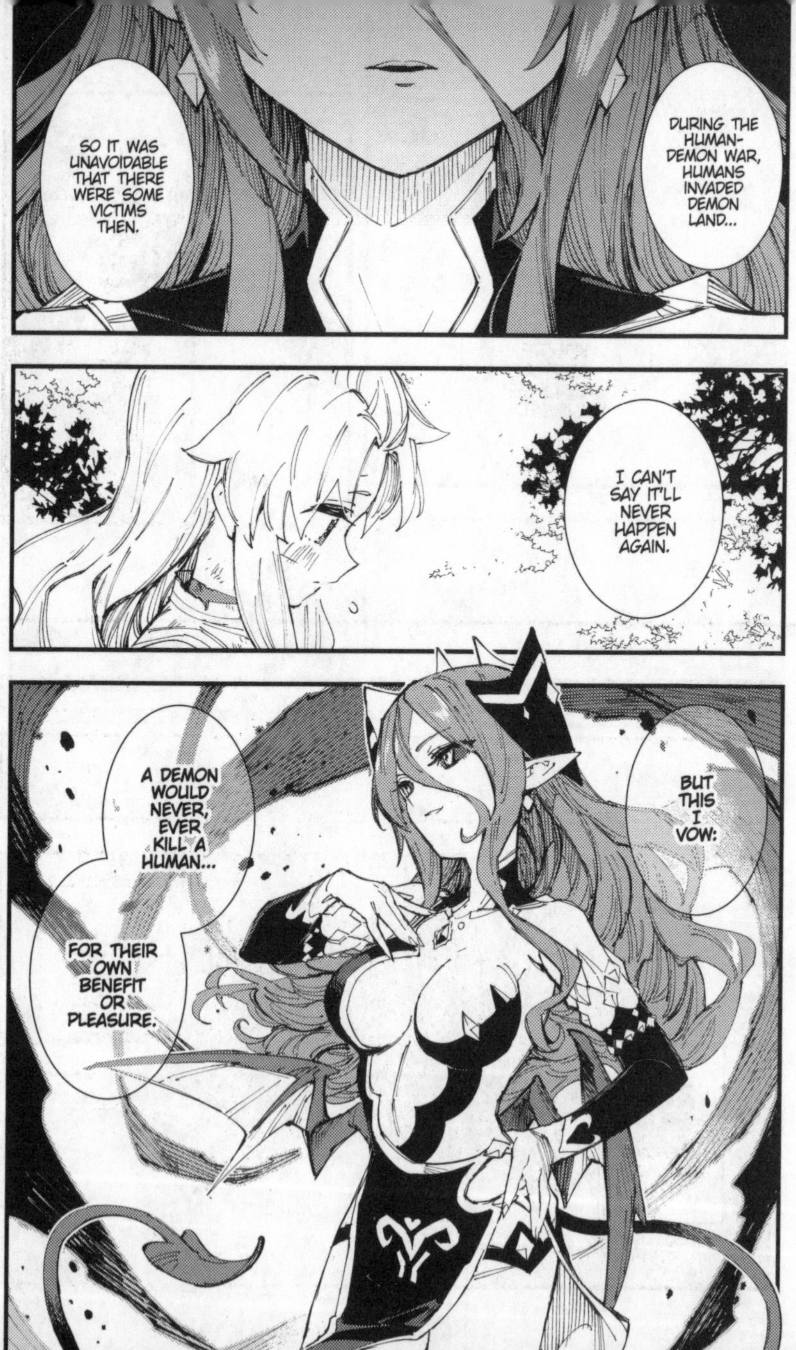
DURING THE HUMAN-DEMON WAR, HUMANS INVADED DEMON LAND...
SO IT WAS UNAVOIDABLE THAT THERE WERE SOME VICTIMS THEN.
I CAN'T SAY IT'LL NEVER HAPPEN AGAIN.
BUT THIS I VOW:
A DEMON WOULD NEVER, EVER KILL A HUMAN...
FOR THEIR OWN BENEFIT OR PLEASURE.

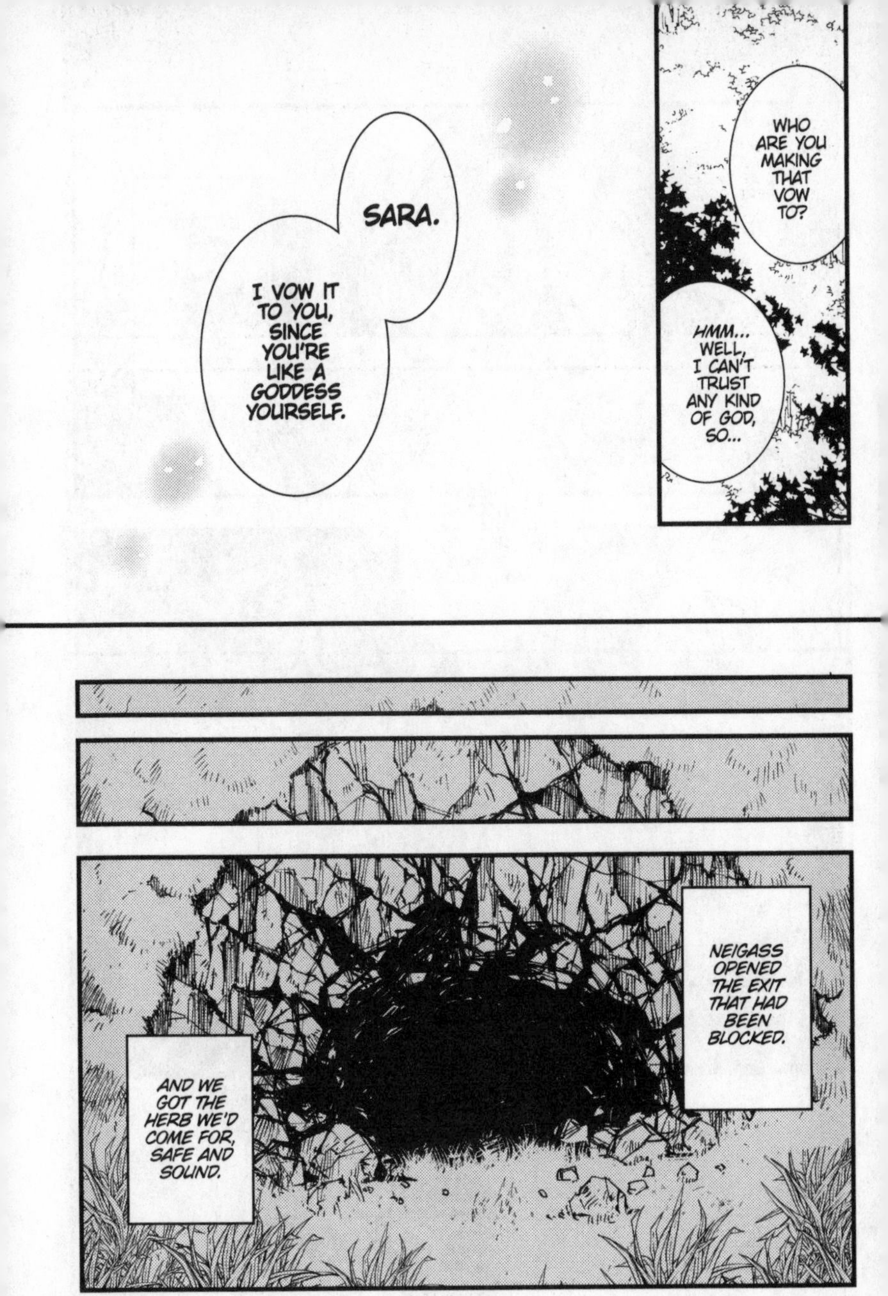
WHO ARE YOU MAKING THAT VOW TO?
HMM... WELL, I CAN'T TRUST ANY KIND OF GOD, SO...
SARA.
I VOW IT TO YOU, SINCE YOU'RE LIKE A GODDESS YOURSELF.
NEIGASS OPENED THE EXIT THAT HAD BEEN BLOCKED.
AND WE GOT THE HERB WE'D COME FOR, SAFE AND SOUND.

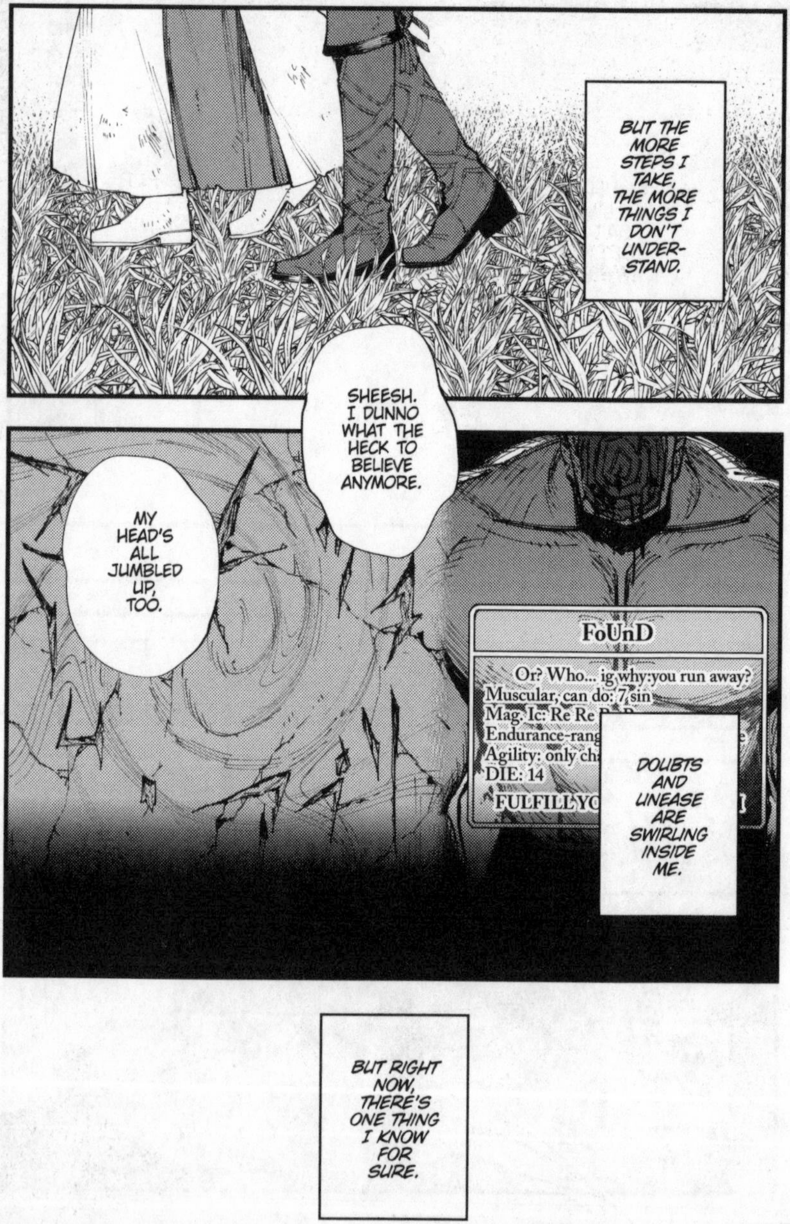
BUT THE MORE STEPS I TAKE, THE MORE THINGS I DON'T UNDER-STAND.
SHEESH. I DUNNO WHAT THE HECK TO BELIEVE ANYMORE.
MY HEAD'S ALL JUMBLED UP, TOO.
FoUnD
Or? Who... ig why:you run away?
Muscular, can do: 7 sin
Mag. Ic: Re Re
Endurance-rang
Agility: only cha
DIE: 14
FULFILL YO
DOUBTS AND UNEASE ARE SWIRLING INSIDE ME.
BUT RIGHT NOW, THERE'S ONE THING I KNOW FOR SURE.

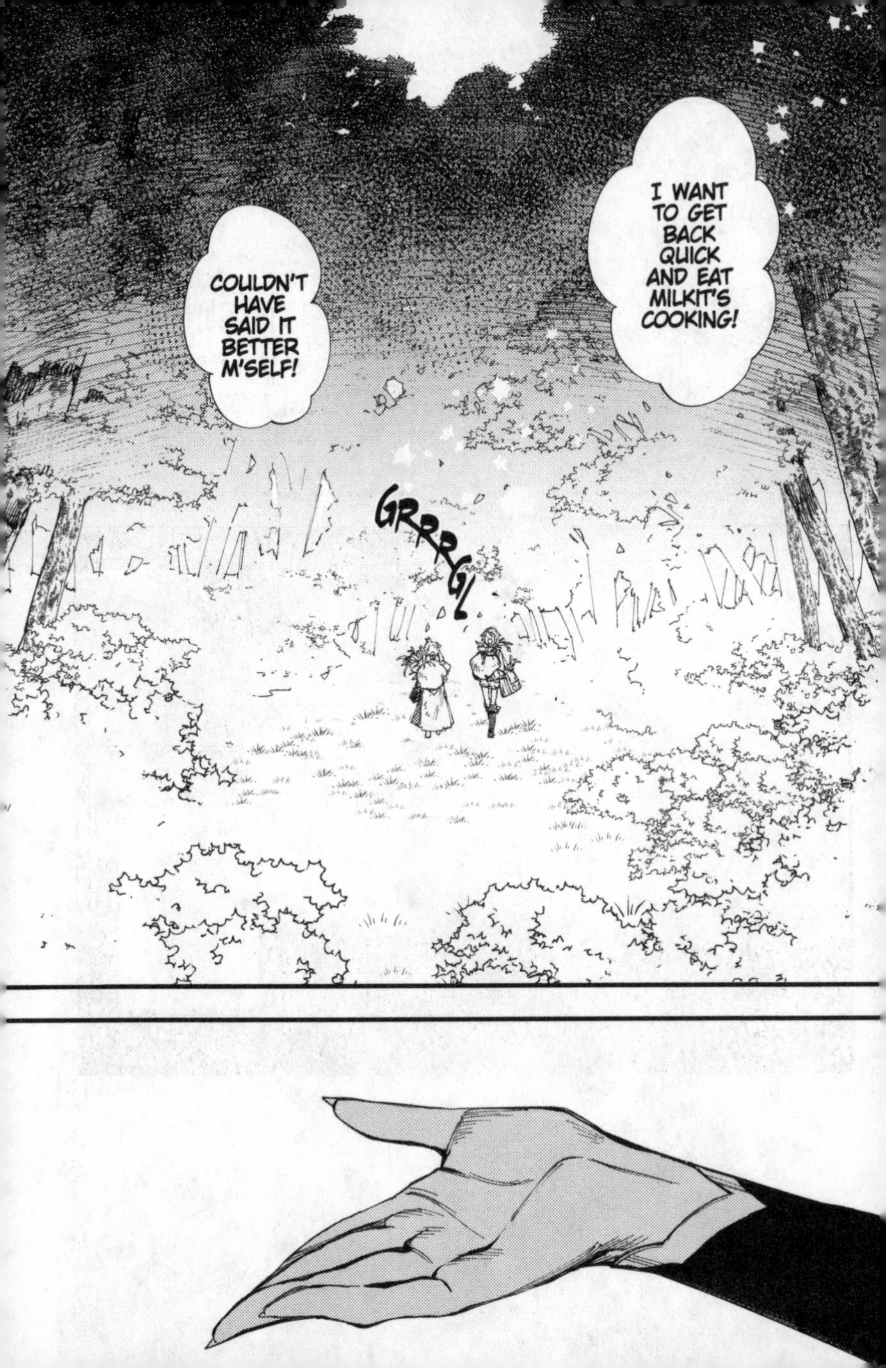
I WANT TO GET BACK QUICK AND EAT MILKIT'S COOKING!
COULDN'T HAVE SAID IT BETTER M'SELF!
GRRRGL

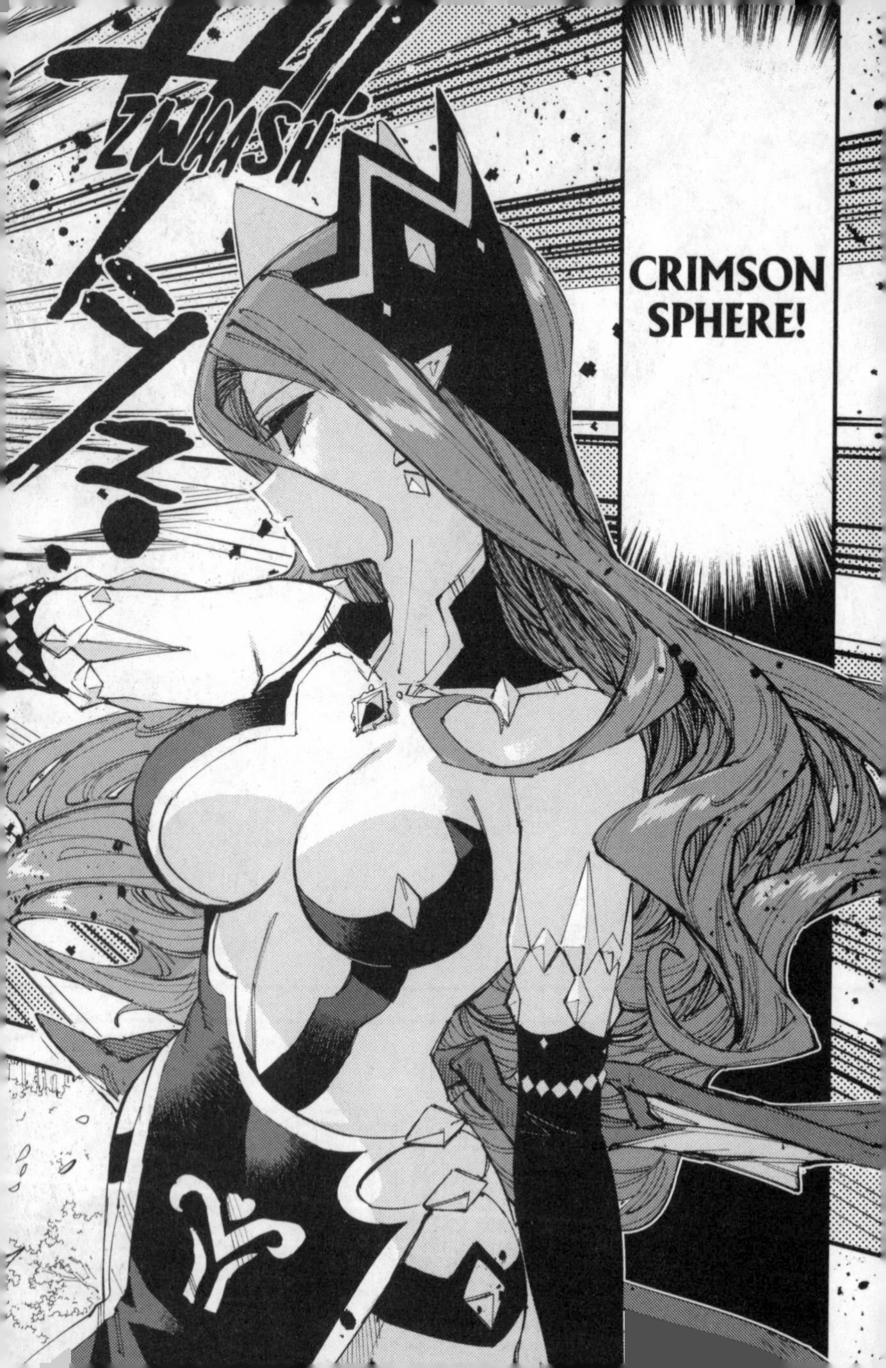
CRIMSON SPHERE!
ZWAASH

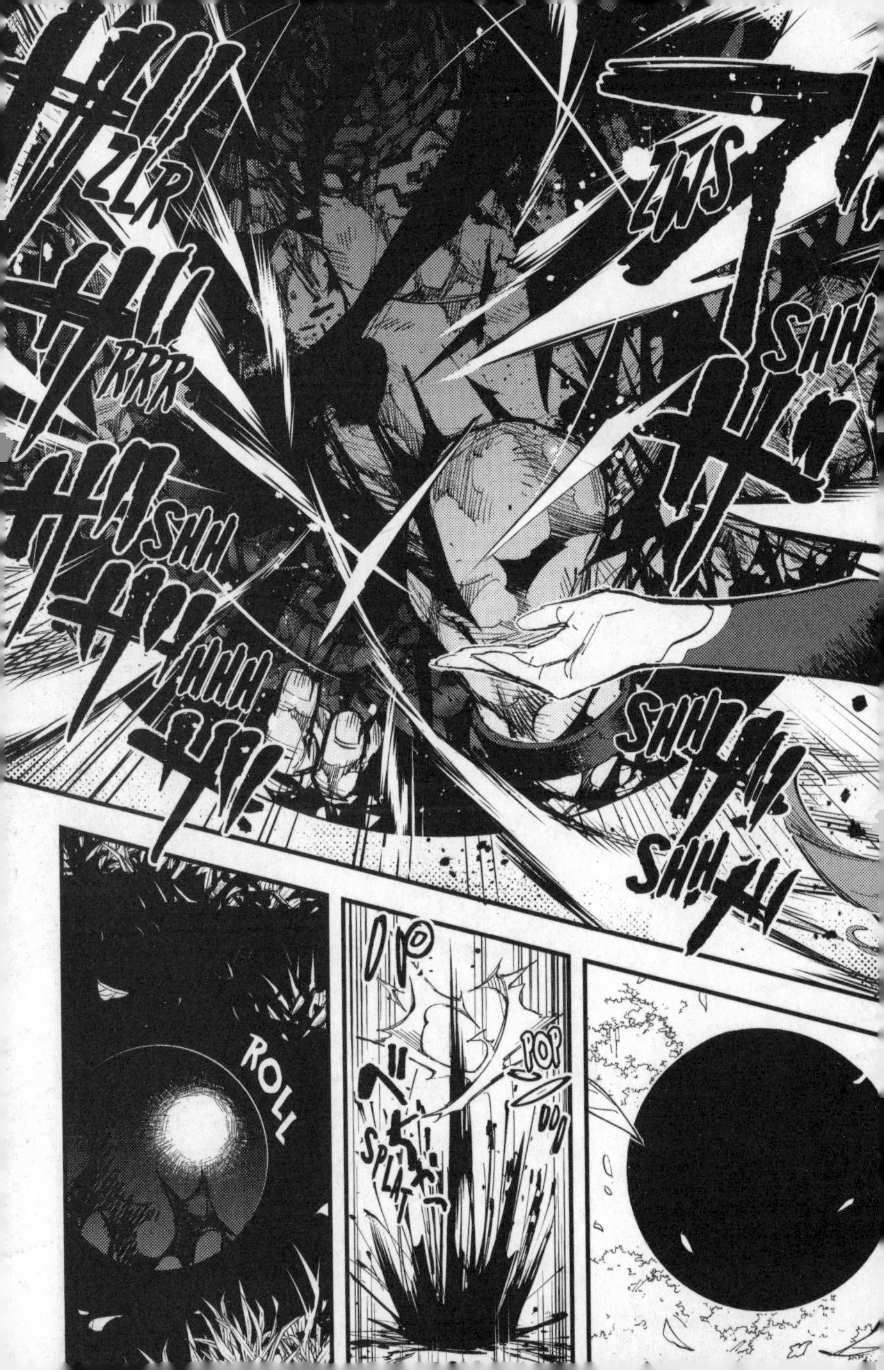

SHH
SHH
SHH
ZZR
RRRR
SHH
POP
SPLAT
ROLL

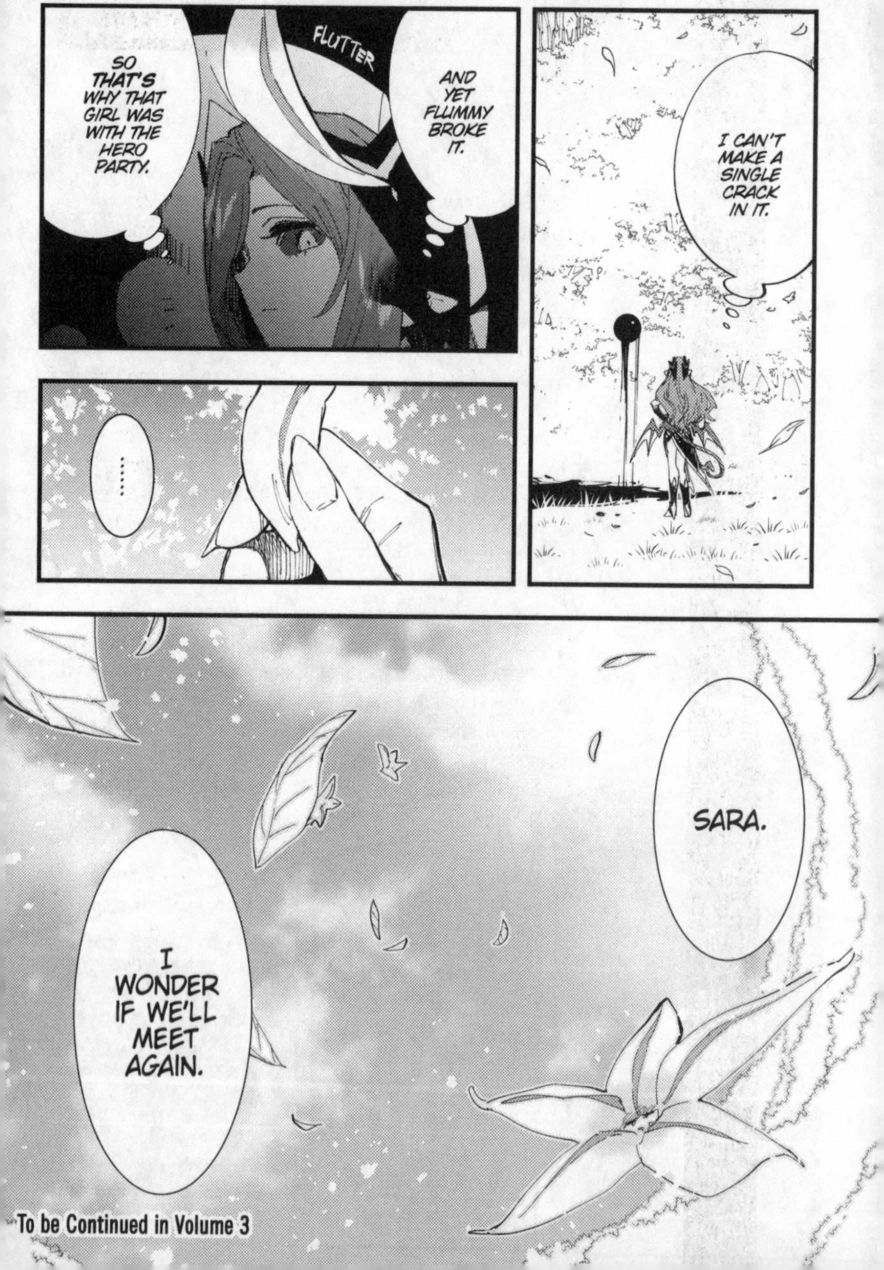
I CAN'T MAKE A SINGLE CRACK IN IT.
FLUTTER
AND YET FLUMMY BROKE IT.
SO THAT'S WHY THAT GIRL WAS WITH THE HERO PARTY.
......
SARA.
I WONDER IF WE'LL MEET AGAIN.
To be Continued in Volume 3

AFTERWORD

A Message from the Author

Thank you very much for purchasing volume 2! This is the author, kiki. How did you like this volume of *Roll Over and Die*? I've been enjoying it!

Sara finally makes her debut in volume 2. She's got a cute way of speaking, wears her heart on her sleeve, and is all energy. Now that they've been put into motion on the manga page, her cuteness and pep have powered up another notch! It was hard writing the script to have such an innocent and good little ten-year-old girl have to fight such a creepy creature. I hope that in the subsequent volumes she's not attacked by any evil demon girls and can live a happy life.

And I don't care what you say, the highlight of this volume was the spiral ogre. Its creepiness level jumped severalfold in manga form! I know how this must sound coming from the person who thought him up, but he was really frightening. Just who is he and what on earth is the mysterious underground facility they encountered him in? And what's up with the Church of Origin that Sara's part of, and how is it connected to Flum...?

As we get closer to the truth, Flum's battles will get rougher. And naturally, the distance between her and Milkit will narrow. Best regards, and please stick around for the subsequent volumes of *Roll Over and Die*—they'll have plenty of highlights to enjoy!

kiki

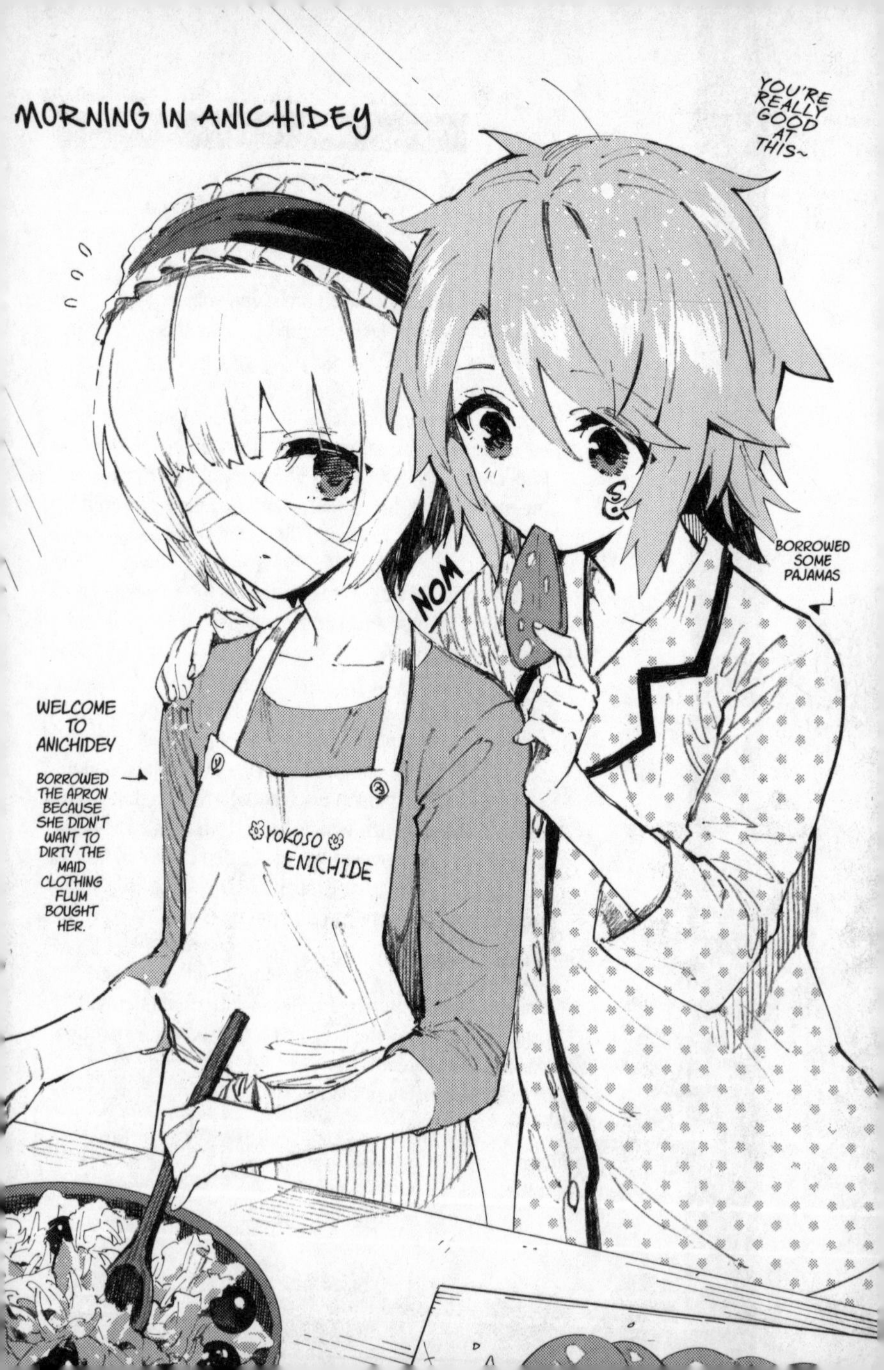
YOU'RE REALLY GOOD AT THIS~
MORNING IN ANICHIDEY
NOM
BORROWED SOME PAJAMAS
WELCOME TO ANICHIDEY
BORROWED THE APRON BECAUSE SHE DIDN'T WANT TO DIRTY THE MAID CLOTHING FLUM BOUGHT HER.
YOKOSO ENICHIDE

SEVEN SEAS ENTERTAINMENT PRESENTS

ROLL OVER AND DIE

I Will Fight for an Ordinary Life with My Love and Cursed Sword!

VOLUME 2

story by KIKI art by SUNAO MINAKATA character design by KINTA

TRANSLATION
Christine Dashiell

LETTERING
Roland Amago
Bambi Eloriaga-Amago

LOGO DESIGN
George Panella

COVER DESIGN
Nicky Lim

PROOFREADER
Leighanna DeRouen

COPY EDITOR
Dawn Davis

EDITOR
Nick Mamatas

PRINT MANAGER
Rhiannon Rasmussen-Silverstein

PRODUCTION ASSOCIATE
Christa Miesner

PRODUCTION MANAGER
Lissa Pattillo

MANAGING EDITOR
Julie Davis

ASSOCIATE PUBLISHER
Adam Arnold

PUBLISHER
Jason DeAngelis

Seven Seas press and purchase enquiries can be sent to Marketing Manager Lianne Sentar at press@gomanga.com. Information regarding the distribution and purchase of digital editions is available from Digital Manager CK Russell at digital@gomanga.com.

ISBN: 978-1-64827-927-0
Printed in Canada
First Printing: December 2021
10 9 8 7 6 5 4 3 2 1

READING DIRECTIONS

This book reads from ***right to left***, Japanese style. If this is your first time reading manga, you start reading from the top right panel on each page and take it from there. If you get lost, just follow the numbered diagram here. It may seem backwards at first, but you'll get the hang of it! Have fun!!

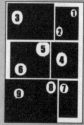

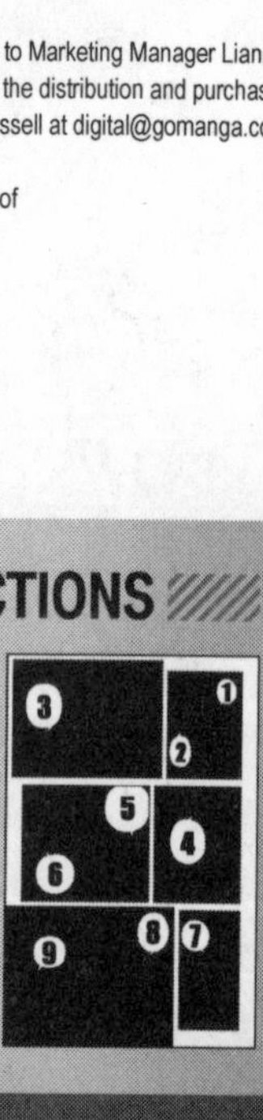

1
2
3
4
5
6
7
8
9